Lima la Moderna

European Migration and
Peruvian Architecture
1937–1969

In memoriam of Professor Giovanni Carbonara

Lima la Moderna
European Migration and Peruvian Architecture 1937–1969

Javier Atoche Intili

Translated by Scott Daniel

The 'La Calcina – John Ruskin' Scrivere di Architettura Prize

Second Edition 2021

Giancarlo Carnevale

Among the many consequences that the COVID-19 pandemic has generated is the suspension, almost a rarefaction, of time: culture and artistic production in general have suffered a kind of slowdown, a loss of energy. The 'La Calcina – John Ruskin,'[1] now in its second edition, despite the critical condition outlined above, has been fortunate to welcome texts of an astonishing level, research of original approach and also, which is not often the case, of high literary quality.

Finally, the jury[2] awarded the work presented by Javier Atoche Intili who, in an impassioned historical reconstruction, using an inductive method, pursued with tenacity and full of insight, reconstructs a little-known but extraordinarily interesting historical event, linked to a hybridisation between indigenous Peruvian culture and European modernist influences.

It is surprising, observing the rich iconographic documentation and comparing the dates and architectural productions collected, how much vitality was unleashed in a short period, following a sudden increase in the economic resources of a country, Peru, kept at the margins of the great flows of rationalist architectural culture.

The book, *Lima la moderna: European migration and twentieth century Peruvian architecture 1937–1969*, is divided into three parts. In the first part, Peru's relations with Europe over time are analysed. In the second part, the author gives prominence to three architects, Paul Linder, Mario Bianco and Theodor Cron (dedicating an entire chapter to each), who not only played a leading role in the technical and cultural formation of several generations of Peruvian architecture, but also turned out to be designers of international standing, culpably ignored by a historically Eurocentric culture, which limits its field of research to a narrow triangulation.

1 The biennial prize was created in 2019 with the intention of giving visibility to architectural writing and research on contemporary issues, with an emphasis on themes of memory and material culture. In the first edition, the winners were divided into two categories: monographs, with the prize awarded to Elisa Pilia with the publication of the text *Urban ruins: Memorial value and contemporary role* by DOM publishers in Berlin, and a short essay category, with three winners according to different judging criteria: Elisabetta Concina, *La Ca' d'oro, da icona monumentale a modello di architettura veneziana tra Ottocento e Novecento* (short essay), Rossella Barozzi, *La Corinthia Macchina: Jacopo Sansovino e la Scuola Grande della Misericordia* (Venice Special Prize), Davide Del Curto, *Il restauro è morto? Viva il restauro!* ('Antico e Nuovo' Special Prize).

2 In the second edition of the prize to which this publication refers, the jury, composed of Giancarlo Carnevale (president), Carmen Andriani, Clemen F. Kusch, Luigi Prestinenza Puglisi, Guido Vittorio Zucconi, was flanked by a technical-scientific committee composed of Marco Agostinelli, Esther Giani, Marina Montuori, Roberta Semeraro and Alberto Soci.

In the third part, the spread of a new architectural category, the multi-storey building, which burst onto the urban scene of the post-war Peruvian capital as a symbol of progress and modernity, is explored. The photographic documentation shows us different and original interpretations of great interest, also highlighting the theme of the conservation of buildings that appear as neglected testimonies of the urban form of a significant historical period.

The book also offers an opportunity for more careful reflection on those phenomena of cultural hybridisation that often remain at the margins of academic research. There is a term in veterinary science, 'hybrid vigour,' which reflects the idea of how much vitalism can be produced by the intersection of different currents – in our case, cultural and philosophical currents.

A final notation concerns the sincere sense of gratitude towards these opportunities for knowledge, which reconcile us with an idea of project, linked to a visionary pragmatism and to a practice of artistic craftsmanship that takes on, with respect to the glittering and phantasmagorical digital world in which we are immersed, the contours, perhaps nostalgic and melancholic, of an irretrievably remote myth.

Preface

Marina Montuori

The 'La Calcina – John Ruskin' Scrivere di Architettura Prize was born in 2018 thanks to a joint initiative of a spontaneous association of architects and architecture lovers, including the director-artist Marco Agostinelli, Corrado Tognon, director of the historical hotel La Calcina and the Venetian Cultural Association RO.SA.M.

La Calcina was, for a long time, the Venetian home of John Ruskin, a scholar and artist whose literary work inspired the competition, which aims to valorise writing to narrate and comment on architecture.

'The prize is aimed at those who have written about the city [...] in its complexity and historical-artistic density, but also in the light of themes posed by the contemporary world, among these: the coexistence between the new and the old, the possibility of making the need to "conserve" coexist with the needs of a modern city and/or with the developments and challenges of the future.'

So says the announcement of the biennial competition, whose first prize is the printed publication of the winning essay[1] by DOM publishers, one of the leading international architecture publishers.

With the inevitable delays caused by the COVID-19 pandemic, the second edition of the prize was finally awarded to Javier Atoche Intili[2] for his research entitled *Lima, la moderna. Migrazioni europee e sviluppo dell'architettura peruviana del XX secolo (1937–1969). Gli edifici multipiano come patrimonio architettonico*, a thesis carried out as part of the PhD programme in Storia, disegno e restauro dell'architettura at the Sapienza Università di Roma in co-tutorship with the Accademia di Architettura at the Università della Svizzera italiana.[3]

The present volume publishes a compendium of this substantial and in-depth work of investigation,[4] which must be acknowledged for its remarkable originality, above all for having re-evaluated events, culpably neglected by European historians,[5] relating to the diffusion in Peru in the 1930s and 1940s of the bearers of the modern movement.

With remarkable skill, Javier Atoche Intili offers multiple points of reflection on the interweaving of events that represent the prodromes of globalisation

1 The first edition of the prize, in 2018, was won by Elisa Pilia with an essay, also PhD-related, entitled *Urban ruins: Memorial value and contemporary role*, to be printed in 2019 to coincide, moreover, with the bicentenary of John Ruskin's birth.

2 A Peruvian architect (Lima, 1977) who graduated in Lima, he moved to Italy in 2004 to further his education in the field of restoration and urban regeneration, obtaining a specialisation at the Scuola di specializzazione in Beni architettonici e del paesaggio (formerly the Scuola di specializzazione in Restauro dei monumenti) of the Sapienza Università di Roma (with a scholarship from the Italian Cultural Institute, Lima), and obtaining a PhD in 2021. Currently, in addition to working as a freelance professional, he collaborates in teaching on the degree course in Building Engineering-Architecture at the Università degli Studi di Brescia.

3 The supervisors of this thesis were Prof. Marzia Marandola (Sapienza Università di Roma) and Roberta Grignolo (Università della Svizzera italiana), with co-supervisor Prof. José Beingolea (Universidad Nacional de Ingeniería).

4 The original text consisted of no less than 610 pages accompanied by a vast and accurate iconographic apparatus.

5 European historiography has shown greater interest in the Brazilian story, in which personalities emerge who produced works of a high qualitative level capable of imprinting profound and radical changes on the face of the city, emphasising above all the influence of Le Corbusier and, in particular, the figures of Oscar Niemeyer and Lúcio Costa (designers of the new capital, Brasília) who responded to the challenges of the period with formal, urban and programmatic innovations, many of which remain relevant today.

and modernisation in Peru between the two wars, highlighted through an in-depth analysis of mostly unpublished bibliographic documents from archives in Italy, Switzerland and Peru,[6] enriched by both past and present iconographic materials, the result of repeated on-site visits by the author.

The interest in the events analysed in this volume has had a sort of karstic development over time, starting as far back as 1955, when the Museum of Modern Art (MoMA) in New York, in its exhibition *Latin American Architecture Since 1945*, offered a broad overview of the work of 56 professional studios from 11 countries, with the intention of demonstrating the modernisation phenomena with images of the Latin American building boom linked to the spread of the development of buildings in height. Henry Russell Hitchcock, author of the exhibition catalogue, presented in a section entitled *Urban Façades* a collection of buildings completed between 1945 and 1955 in the main cities of South America with particular reference to the multi-storey building type.

In 2015, again at the MoMA, the exhibition *Latin America in Construction: Architecture 1955–1980* was staged,[7] an impressive survey of the most significant works built from the second half of the last century until the early 1980s. Works often forgotten in the pages of the history of modern architecture, most of them never exhibited before even in their countries of origin, testifying to a period of self-criticism, exploration and complex political, social and economic changes that involved all Latin American countries. The exhibition investigated some of the key issues of that period, from the role of public administrations in the housing sector to the responses of architecture and town planning, the concepts of development and growth, as well as modernisation and industrialisation policies of both capitalist and communist tendencies.

Departing from these precedents, Javier Atoche Intili's research privileges three types of closely interconnected investigations, corresponding to the three parts in which the monograph is organised: the relationship between America and Western Europe; European designers working in Peru in the twentieth century; and the values of twentieth-century Peruvian architecture. The motivations can be traced back to three phases, the first of which consists of determining the reasons and socio-historical conjunctures that allowed the principles of the modern movement to assert themselves in Peruvian architecture. The external circumstances include the political conditions of Europe, victim of racial persecution and tested by the wartime events of the first half of the last century, which increased the migratory phenomena from the Old to the New World. The role played by those who came from the Old World did not depend, however, so much on the number of migrants – admittedly not very high – as on the fact that they occupied key positions in Peruvian society.

6 The text is accompanied by numerous images, most of which were found in the aforementioned archives. Each chapter is also introduced by a timeline that relates the economic, political and cultural events that occurred in Western countries, the Latin American region and Peru.

7 The exhibition was curated by Barry Bergdoll and Patricio del Real of MoMA's Department of Architecture and Design in collaboration with Carlos Eduardo Comas (Universidade Federal do Rio Grande do Sul) and Jorge Francisco Liernur (Universidad Torcuato Di Tella in Buenos Aires), both as guest curators.

The second phase focuses on the personal, academic and professional histories of some of the designers who moved to Peru in the inter-war period, contextualising them in the local and international debate on architecture and urbanism. The third, finally, includes the selection of some works considered paradigmatic within the vast heritage built in Lima in the twentieth century, emphasising the evolution of the multi-storey architectural type, an index of modernity, an emblem of the acceleration of urban growth and a desire to plan the territory according to new rules. However, favouring development in height – which took place above all in the capital – represents a sort of anomaly with respect to tradition, which generally considered it a gamble due to the constant seismic risk from which it was necessary to defend oneself, just as people had done for millennia by developing ingenious countermeasures.

The research has also made it possible to reconstruct the histories of some of the tall buildings of the Limo landscape, from the genesis of the project to the most recent transformations, demonstrating that the tall building represents the reification of the economic and political plan developed by the government and its foreign advisors for the centre of the Peruvian capital. These artefacts, after a period of vogue and widespread recognition of their architectural qualities, were then guiltily plunged into oblivion, often making them the object of shoddy renovation procedures, or worse still, demolition or abandonment. It is only recently that intellectuals and scholars are reviving the will to consider these buildings as a heritage to be preserved and enhanced.

The uniqueness of these realisations lies, moreover, in the fact that they are the result of a new language or identity that the architects, sensitive to the contexts in which they were working, developed. Their works almost denounce a form of linguistic hybridity: the algid rationalism of the European modern movement is rarely favoured. Rather, in most cases, a lively propensity for chromatism and the mixing of materials in an 'expressionist' style emerges.

The author also particularly emphasised the role played by three key architects – Paul Linder Lob (Lennep, Rhineland 1897 – Haar, Bavaria 1968), Mario Bianco Zanaldo (Varallo Sesia, Vercelli 1903 – Turin 1990) and Hans Theodor Cron Gröber (Basel, 1921 – 1964) – who emigrated to Peru between the two wars and were considered fundamental for the turning point they were able to impart to the capital's urban development, especially by favouring the construction of a considerable number of multi-storey buildings.

For Paul Linder and Mario Bianco, to whom two chapters of the volume are dedicated, in addition to their fundamental contributions in the construction of the city, their cultural contribution in the sphere of teaching and the consequent didactic turnaround imparted to Lima's university structures was essential.

The two architects introduced real innovations at the didactic level in the field of architecture, resulting in a break with the late-nineteenth century academic education firmly anchored in the traditions of the past. In this period, studies and training in the discipline were encouraged and given greater autonomy. This was also possible as a consequence of the Reforma Universitaria implemented in 1946, which provided for the reorganisation of the curriculum and the introduction of new subjects related to housing and land planning policies.

To conclude, a further element of interest of this research should be emphasised, which lies in having analysed the role played by trade publications, not only as an instrument for the dissemination of architectural culture, but also as an element of coagulation, cohesion and interaction between the realm of professionals and the academic world.

In essence, this volume is an important building block for understanding the present with an eye to the past, but without ever forgetting one's roots.

Introduction

This book presents the conclusions of doctoral research on European migrations and their repercussions for Peruvian architecture in the twentieth century, carried out between 2015 and 2021 in Peru, Italy and Switzerland.[1]

The study focuses on the transfer of European architects and engineers to Latin America between the 1930s and the end of the 1960s, a period that research has shown to be particularly significant for several reasons. In the period affected by the Second World War, there was a simultaneous increase in the number of migrants from the Old to the New World and the consequent reception, diffusion and affirmation of the precepts of the modern movement in the urban-architectural debate and practices of the host countries.

Modern society is characterised by three things: the conflictual relationship between capitalism and industrialisation, on the one hand, which aim at the universalisation of the market and production systems; and civil society, on the other, which aims at its own democratisation.[2] The American political scientist Marshall Berman states that in the West, the modernisation of civil society, identified with the overcoming of oligarchy and religion by the bourgeoisie and politics, had its cultural expression in modernism.[3] The Hispano-Peruvian philosopher José Ignacio López Soria explains that Peru only experienced full modernity in the twentieth century and that the formation of the nation-state in this country sees modernisation and modernism as parallel processes and not, as was the case in the West, one springing from the other.[4]

Peru, the cradle of civilisations thousands of years old and an important administrative centre on the continental level in the viceregal era, can provide valuable insights into the mixture of tradition-modernity and the coexistence of modernisation-modernism, conditions that are widespread in non-Western countries. Despite this, research on the history of twentieth century Peruvian architecture is fragmentary and lacking in depth. The late recognition of the historical and artistic importance of Peru's architectural heritage is reflected in an incipient process of 'heritagisation,' which makes works from this period susceptible to transformations that may distort their characteristics. The study of the historical relations between Europe and Peru, which began in the sixteenth century and continued throughout the last century, can help to overcome the Eurocentric vision, established during the viceroyalty of Peru (1542–1821), contributing to the consolidation of a collective identity in the Latin American country.

1 The doctoral thesis is entitled *Lima, la moderna: Migrazioni europee e sviluppo dell'architettura peruviana del XX secolo (1937–1969). Gli edifici multipiano come patrimonio architettonico*, supervised by Prof. Marzia Marandola (Sapienza Università di Roma) and Roberta Grignolo (Università della Svizzera italiana), with co-supervisor Prof. José Beingolea (Universidad Nacional de Ingeniería).

2 Heller, Ágnes, *Teoria della storia* (Rome, 1982), p. 289.

3 Berman, Marshall, *Tutto ciò che è solido svanisce nell'aria: l'esperienza della modernità* (Bologna, 2012), p. 133.

4 See López Soria, José Ignacio, *Filosofía, arquitectura y ciudad* (Lima, 2017).

Research objectives

Cusco

Javier Atoche Intili (2018)

This monograph details the decisive circumstances for the establishment of modern culture in Peruvian architecture through the work of the European designers who moved there.

What were the factors that facilitated the inclusion of professionals of European origin in Peruvian lands? As the Peruvian sociologist Aníbal Quijano points out, the relationship established between Europe and America led those from the Old World to see themselves as the final stage in the process of evolution from a primitive state of the human condition to a civilised one.[5] For Quijano, the Europeans not only saw themselves as the exclusive bearers of modernity, but also managed to impose this historical perspective in the conquered territories, establishing a cultural, as well as political and economic, hegemony that was still present in the last century.

The first aim of this research is to illustrate the external and internal circumstances that allowed European modernism to establish itself in Peruvian architecture. The external circumstances include the political and economic conditions in the United States of America (which aimed to establish alliances with the countries of the Latin American region during the Second World War) and Europe (tested by the wartime events of the first half of the last century), which significantly increased migration from the Old to the New World.

The second aim of the research is to trace and recompose the personal, academic, and professional histories of some of the designers who moved to Peru during the period affected by the Second World War, contextualising them within both local and international debates on architecture and town planning.

As a third aim, the research identifies the paradigmatic works of architecture built in twentieth century Lima, revealing the archetypes, repetitions and exceptions to the norm, and tracing their history, in a period marked by accelerated urban growth and a desire to organise this expansion through urban planning.

5 Quijano, Aníbal, *Cuestiones y horizontes: de la dependencia histórico-estructural a la colonialidad/descolonialidad del poder* (Buenos Aires, 2014), p. 790.

Arequipa
Javier Atoche Intili (2018)

Investigation paths

The research is organised around three closely connected cognitive paths, which correspond to the three parts into which the monograph is organised:

—the historical relationship between America and Western Europe.
—European designers working in Peru in the twentieth century.
—the identification of the values of twentieth-century Peruvian architecture.

The first path is proposed as a contribution to the identification of the main elements (people, actions, situations) that characterised the migratory flows from Europe to Peru, especially in the period between 1937 and 1955. As Aníbal Quijano reminds us, since the beginning of the Modern Age, the history of the American continent, and especially that of Peru (the first administrative centre for the whole of South America during Spanish rule), has been characterised by the existence of close cultural ties with the West, first created during the conquest and maintained after the independence of these territories. This condition favoured in twentieth-century Peru the continuation of privileged relations with certain countries: Peru's predominant cultural dependence on Europe (in the first third of the century) was followed by a growing North American presence (in the years when totalitarian regimes came to power in the Old World), up to a nascent desire for autonomy (in the second half of the last century).

The second track deals with the topic of the migration of Europeans and the introduction of their modern culture in Peru. The research identifies those Peruvian political and cultural figures, as well as institutions, that favoured the dissemination of certain architectural theories and forms. Likewise, the study gives ample space to the Peruvian experiences of the three European designers who present, in comparison to their foreign colleagues, the largest corpus of works realised in the Andean country: Paul Linder Lob (1897–1968), Mario Bianco Zanaldo (1903–1990) and Hans Theodor Cron Gröber (1921–1964). The study of their biographies made it possible to identify the motives (political, professional, cultural) that conditioned their relocation, and the repercussions in the Peruvian cultural sphere: through Linder, Bianco and Cron, some of the most up-to-date European theses on university education, urban planning and the post-war debate concerning the relations between abstract universalism and local specificities in architecture made their way to Peru.

The two paths of investigation presented so far aim to provide more articulate, circumspect and pertinent keys to understanding the adoption of modernism in Peru, contributing to a deeper understanding of twentieth century

Peruvian architecture and thus, also, to its heritagisation. Retracing these paths and identifying their points of concurrence makes it possible to reconstruct the stories that made the realisation of these works possible and to address the question of the recognition of their artistic and historical values. It also ensures the transmission of Peruvian architectural heritage of the twentieth century to future generations.

This work identifies those European designers active in Peru in the mid-twentieth century who facilitated the spread of new architectural types. A considerable number of realisations were multi-storey buildings constructed in Lima between the 1940s and 1960s, resulting from the rejection of the fundamental principles of the so-called 'Functional City' set out in the *Charte d'Athènes*. These works were decisive in the urban evolution of the Peruvian capital, in defining the twentieth century transformations of its historical core, as well as in strengthening its administrative-directional vocation.

Illustrated monographs of the time, such as *Wohnhochhäuser* by Paulhans Peters, consecrated the multi-storey building as an architectural type.[6] According to Peters' definition, the vertical apartment block is a special type of multi-storey building.[7] The intention of this course of research is not the mere cataloguing of examples of multi-storey buildings in the city of Lima, but rather an analysis of the political, cultural and technical motivations behind the adoption of this vertical construction.

Research method and documentary sources

The approach of this investigation follows the *modus operandi* of the Roman School of Restoration, combining archival research with an analysis of textual, iconographic and oral sources alongside a direct study of the buildings, as well as the construction techniques and materials used. The co-tutorship project signed between Sapienza Università di Roma (Dipartimento di Storia, disegno e restauro dell'architettura) and the Università della Svizzera italiana (Accademia di Architettura) was fundamental in framing the research within the Italian and Swiss historiographical framework.

Consultation of bibliographic sources made it possible to identify the most interesting archives for research purposes, located in Basel, Bellinzona, Berlin, Lima, Madrid, Milan, New York, Rome, Turin, Venice and Zurich. At the same time, between 2016 and 2018, the heirs and scholars of the European designers herein studied were interviewed. The research into documentary sources and interviews with the protagonists of the period were substantiated

6 Peters, Paulhans, *Wohnhochhäuser: Punkthäuser* (Munich, 1958), p. 38.

7 The Architectural Dictionary defines a skyscraper as a building of many storeys, of exceptional height achieved using steel structure, with representative functions. It can therefore be said that the multi-storey type includes tower buildings, skyscrapers and, in general, buildings that depart from the classical tripartition of basement, main floor and penthouse. Pevsner, Nikolaus et al. Dizionario di architettura (Turin, 1994), p. 294.

GFC

by special visits to Peru, which made it possible to view the actual state of a large group of multi-storey buildings constructed in Lima. These buildings, chosen for the construction technologies and contemporary materials used, as well as their urban scale that departs from that of the viceregal tradition, became the subject of in-depth study in the monograph. Inspections carried out in the Peruvian capital have made it possible to document the loss of some of these works, through demolition or distortion of their characteristic elements, or due to the precarious state of conservation of the great majority, including buildings by Linder, Bianco and Cron. The study of these works and their authors, therefore, also contributes to the valorisation and preservation of Peru's twentieth century architectural heritage.

State of the art

In his 2015 review of the exhibition *Latin America in Construction: Architecture 1955–1980* at the Museum of Modern Art in New York, the British architecture critic Rowan Moore asks: 'Just what is it that makes South American architecture so appealing?' He suggests that the interest is probably due to the tension between modernity and local traditions; thus, the peculiar rejection of modernism in architecture is more evident in this region.[8] In recent years, the attention of historians has turned to the presence of modern European culture in the architecture of non-Western countries, leading to the appearance of several publications on modern culture and Latin America, on the relationship between modernity, modernisation, modernism and, on the heritagisation of twentieth century Peruvian architecture.

By reviewing the state of the art, it emerges that studies on the factors that determined the establishment of modern culture in Peru, from the perspective of migratory phenomena between Europe and America in the twentieth century, remain largely unpublished.

These contributions, although fundamental for the understanding of Latin American architecture in the last century and the heritagisation of related works, nevertheless give a fragmented picture of the relationship between the Old and New Worlds in the second half of the twentieth century, not to mention the cultural repercussions in the Peruvian context. The present work provides a transversal reading that traces local events within a broader, and not only national, cultural history.

8 See Moore, Rowan, 'Latin America was a place where Modernist dreams came true' (2 January 2023).

Text structure

The monograph consists of six chapters, each preceded by a chronological timeline, organised into three parts concerning: the historical relationship between America and Western Europe, European designers working in Peru in the twentieth century and the 'heritagisation' of Peruvian architecture in the last century.

The first chapter reviews the main factors that contributed to the political, professional and cultural migratory phenomena of the period under study. The second chapter is dedicated to the German architect Paul Linder, one of the most influential lecturers in the Department of Architecture of the Escuela Nacional de Ingenieros. The third chapter deals with the figure of Mario Bianco, whose studies in the field of urban planning and whose design activity in Italy allowed him to participate in the preliminary studies for the drafting of Lima's Regulatory Plan, developed by the Oficina Nacional de Planeamiento y Urbanismo, as well as to take part in other local and foreign forays in that discipline. The fourth chapter is dedicated to the Swiss designer Theodor Cron, the first of a large group of architects trained at the Eidgenössische Technische Hochschule in Zurich to move to Peru after the Second World War. The fifth chapter provides a more complete picture of the reception of the multi-storey typology in Peru. In the sixth and final chapter, the research addresses questions of the protection, conservation and valorisation of built heritage in twentieth-century Peru.

If the first chapters provide the tools to grasp the peculiarities of modern architecture in Lima and gradually construct relevant reading criteria, the monograph represents – to use the terms employed by the French sociologist Nathalie Heinich – a contribution to the construction of twentieth century heritage in Peru.[9]

9 See Heinich, Nathalie, *La fabrique du patrimoine: de la cathédrale à la petite cuillère* (Paris, 2009).

PART I

On the historical relationship between America and Western Europe

EUROPEAN MIGRATION AND URBAN DEVELOPMENT IN LIMA (1937–1955)

EUROPEAN POLITICAL, PROFESSIONAL, CULTURAL MIGRATIONS TO THE AMERICAN CONTINENT

1932
Modern architecture: international exhibition (MoMA, New York)

1933
Charte d'Athènes (CIAM, Athens)

1936
Spanish Civil War

1937

ITALY *Piano Regolatore della Valle d'Aosta* (BBPR et al., 1936–1937)

GERMANY Walter Gropius and Mies van der Rohe move to the USA

FRANCE *Plan de Paris* (Le Corbusier, Paris, 1937)

1938

USA Tennessee Valley Authority (1933–1938)

ARGENTINA *Plan Director de Buenos Aires* (Le Corbusier, in collaboration with Ferrari-Hardoy and Kurchan, 1937–1938)

1939

End of the Spanish Civil War

Beginning of Second World War

ARGENTINA *Hacia un Arquitectura* (Le Corbusier, Benos Aires)

1940

Benito Mussolini declares war on the Allies

SWITZERLAND *Die Neue Architektur: Dargestellt an 20 Beispielen – 1930–1940* (Alfred Roth)

1941

USA *Space, Time and Architecture: The Growth of a New Tradition* (Sigfried Giedion, Cambridge-Massachusetts)

1942

USA *Can our cities survive?* (Josep Lluís Sert, Cambridge-London)

BRAZIL Josep Lluís Sert and Paul Lester Wiener (Town Planning Associates) hold a lecture series

1930s

FERNANDO BELAÚNDE TERRY, AGRUPACIÓN ESPACIO, THE EUROPEANS IN PERU

1937

El Arquitecto Peruano's first issue

Sociedad de Arquitectos del Perú

1938

Consejo Nacional de Urbanismo

1939

Architect Paul Linder moves to Peru

1940

Earthquake and tsunami in Lima and Callao

National Census

1942

Corporación Peruana del Amazonas

1943

FRANCE Urbanisme des CIAM / La charte d'Athènes (Le Group CIAM-France, Paris)

BRAZIL Ministerio da Educação e Saúde Pública (Affonso Reidy et al., consultant Le Corbusier, Rio de Janeiro, 1937–1943)

1943

USA Brazil Builds (MoMA, New York)

1944

USA *Built in USA* (MoMA, New York)

1945

End of the Second World War

ITALY *Verso un'architettura organica* (Bruno Zevi)

Piano Regolatore Milanese (Architetti Riuniti, 1944–1945)

USA Good Neighbour Policy (1933–1945)

1946

BRAZIL *Cidade dos Motores* (Town Planning Associates, Rio de Janeiro, 1943–1946)

ITALY *Piano Regionale Piemontese* (ABRR, Astengo, Bianco, Renacco, Rizzotti, 1944–1946)

Pietro Maria Bardi and Lina Bo move to Brazil

1943

Corporación Peruana del Santa

Corporación Peruana de Aviación Comercial

1944

Establishment of the Instituto de Urbanismo del Perú

City Hall in Lima (Emilio Harth-Terré, José Álvarez Calderón, Lima, 1939–1944)

Paul Lester Wiener in Peru

1945

Espacio en el Tiempo: La arquitectura como fenómeno cultural (Luis Miró Quesada, Lima)

Richard Neutra in Peru

1946

Reforma Universitaria

Letter from Adolfo Cordova, Carlos William, José Polar and Julio Ferrand to the newspaper *El Sol* in Cusco

Peruvian urban planning regulations: Ley de propiedad horizontal, Oficina Nacional de Planeamiento y Urbanismo, Corporación Nacional de Vivienda, Centros Climáticos de Esparcimiento

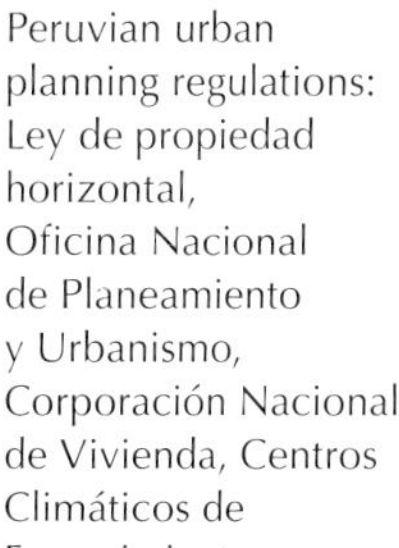

1947

Club de Tiro (Adolfo Córdova, José Polar, Carlos William, Arequipa, 1946–1947)

Expresión de Principios de la Agrupación Espacio

Josep Lluís Sert in Peru

EUROPEAN MIGRATION AND URBAN DEVELOPMENT IN LIMA (1937–1955)

1947

BRAZIL Treaty of Rio

UK CIAM VI (Bridgewater)

USA *Two cities: planning in North and South America* (MoMA, New York)

1948

ITALY Luigi Piccinato, Ernesto Nathan Rogers and Enrico Tedeschi move to Argentina

Publication of *I piani urbanistici* (Giovanni Astengo)

Publication of *Saper vedere l'architettura* (Bruno Zevi)

1949

COLOMBIA *Plan Piloto de Tumaco* (Town Planning Associates, 1948–1949)

1950

ARGENTINA *Plan Regulador de Buenos Aires* (EPBA, 1948–1950)

BRAZIL I Bienal do Museu de Arte Moderna de Sao Paulo (1951)

1940s

Designer Mario Bianco moves to Peru

VI Congreso Panamericano de Arquitectos

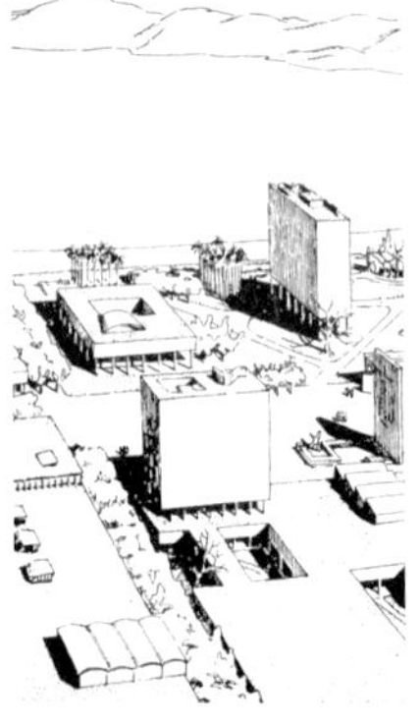

1948

Plan Piloto de Chimbote (Town Planning Associates, 1948–1949)

Architect Theodor Cron moves to Peru

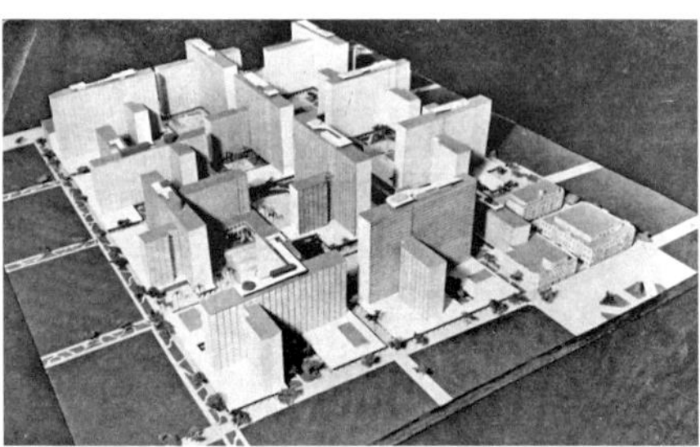

1949

Plan Piloto de Lima (ONPU, advised by di Ernesto Nathan Rogers, Josep Lluís Sert, 1947–1949)

Unidad Vecinal no. 3 (Corporación Nacional de Vivienda, Lima, 1945–1949)

1950s

Nota a Vallejo

¡Cuando las catedrales eran blancas!

ESPACIO

1950

Espacio's first issue

1951

SWITZERLAND *A decade of new architecture* (Sigfried Giedion, Zurigo)

ARGENTINA *Introducción a la Historia de la Arquitectura* (Enrico Tedeschi, Tucumán)

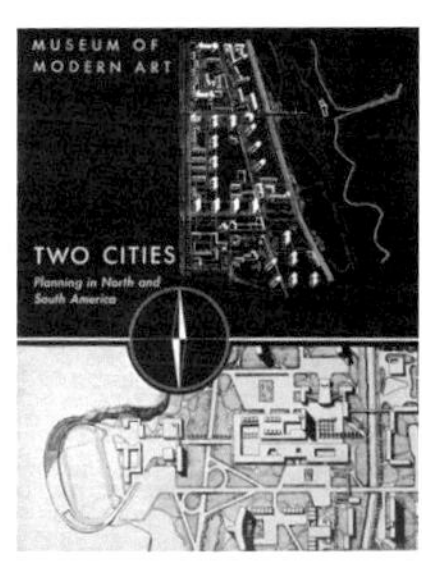

1952

USA *The Heart of the city* (ed. by Josep Lluís Sert et al., New York / London & Bradford)

ITALY *I piani regionali* (Ministero dei lavori pubblici)

1953

COLOMBIA *Plan Piloto de Bogotá* (Town Planning Associates, Le Corbusier et al., 1949–1953)

1954

BRAZIL II Bienal do Museu de Arte Moderna de Sao Paulo (1953–1954)

ARGENTINA Casa Curutchet (Le Corbusier, La Plata, 1948–1954)

Carta de Atenas (Le Corbusier, Buenos Aires)

USA *Ancient arts of the Andes* (MoMA, New York)

1955

USA Latin America since 1945 (MoMA, New York)

1951

Proposal for the Department of Architecture building at the Escuela Nacional de Ingenieros

1952

Chavín Prize awarded to Edificio Guzmán Blanco (Manuel Villarán, Lima, 1952)

1953

Department of Architecture at the Escuela Nacional de Ingenieros (Mario Bianco et al., Lima, 1951–1953)

Josef Albers in Peru

Walter Gropius and Josep Lluís Sert in Peru

1954

Walter Gropius in Peru

Henry-Russell Hitchcock in Peru

Chavín Prize awarded to Edificio Radio El Sol (Luis Miro Quesada, 1953–1954)

1955

Centro Climático de Huampaní (Corporación Nacional de Vivienda, Lima, 1947–1955)

Dissolution of Agrupación Espacio

Chavín Prize awarded to Edificio Radio El Sol (Luis Miro Quesada, 1953–1954)

Chapter I
European migration and urban development in Lima

I.1. European participation in Lima planning

A brief history of migration between the European and American continents should mention the discovery of new territories at the end of the fifteenth century and the consequences that came about as a result: on the one hand, it entailed the beginning of the phenomenon known today as globalisation; on the other hand, it meant the establishment of the first modern geo-cultural entities, America and Western Europe, and their historical relations. As the Peruvian sociologist Aníbal Quijano points out, this relationship led those from the Old World to see themselves as the final stage in the evolutionary process of humanity from a primitive state to a civilised one. According to Quijano, Europeans not only saw themselves as the exclusive bearers of modernity, but also managed to impose this historical perspective on the territories they controlled, establishing a cultural hegemony that lasted well into the twentieth century.[1]

I.1.1. The foundation of the 'City of Kings' (1535–1821)

The political and economic domination exercised by the Spanish Crown for almost three centuries conditioned the characteristics of the ethno-cultural groups that moved to the American territories.[2] If the landing of Christopher Columbus on the island of Guanahani, on 24 October 1492, marked the arrival of Europeans on the American continent, then the landing of Francisco Pizarro in Tumbes, in April 1532, marked the Spanish presence in today's Peruvian territory. It was from that point on that the inexorable decline of the Tahuantinsuyo[3] began, culminating on 15 November 1532 with the imprisonment of Atahualpa in Cajamarca, marking the end of the Pre-Hispanic Period.[4]

The vast Inca Empire, which had already assimilated other cultures developed along the Andean mountains,[5] was subjugated forthwith. From the Andes, which had long served as the backbone of Incan civilisation, there began a shift towards the Pacific coast, with its better connections to Europe. For this reason, Pizarro chose a wide, flat valley for the foundation of the region's main administrative centre. With its mild climate, Lima was irrigated by the Rímac River, whose hydraulic works had been built by previous populations. It was also home to a natural pier called Callao. The connection between Lima and Callao was consolidated during the foundational phase of the viceroyalty.

As the capital of all Spanish possessions on the American continent, Lima was founded by Pizarro on 18 January 1535. The Ciudad de los Reyes, or 'City of Kings,' would go on to become the centre of political,

1 Quijano, Aníbal, *Cuestiones y horizontes: de la dependencia histórico-estructural a la colonialidad/descolonialidad del poder* (Buenos Aires, 2014), p. 790.

2 Padilla, Abraham, 'Inmigración española, alemana e irlandesa', *Boletín de Lima* (1998), p. 19.

3 Original name, in the ancient *Quechua* language, identifying the unitary set of territories under Inca rule, which referred to the territorial division into four regions or *suyo: Chinchaysuyo and Antisuyo* to the north of Cusco, the capital, and *Contisuyo and Collesuyo* to the south.

4 See Scaletti, Adriana, *La casa cajamarquina: arquitectura, minería y morada* (Lima, 2013).

5 Residing mainly in the region currently occupied by Peru (whose founding core was in the present-day city of Cusco), Colombia, Ecuador, Bolivia, Chile, and Argentina.

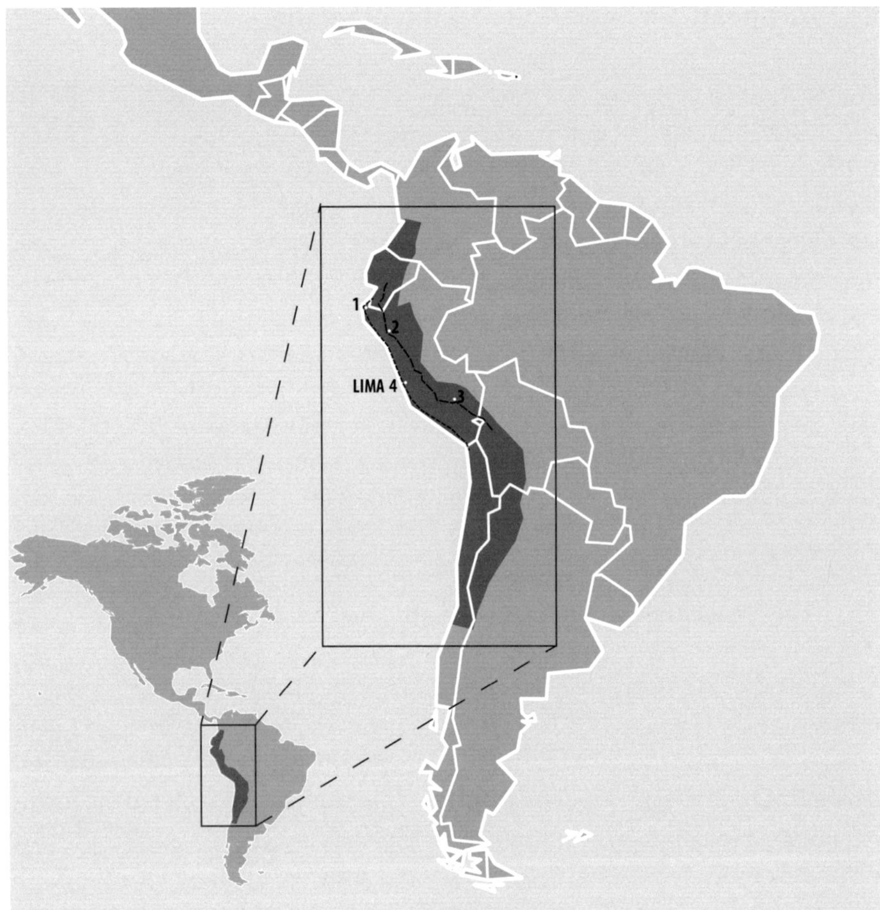

Tahuantinsuyo
Overlapping of the territories dominated by the Incas and today's Latin American geopolitical boundaries, with the identification of the pre-Hispanic Andean axis and the colonial coastal axis:
1. Tumbes
2. Cajamarca
3. Cusco
4. Lima

Javier Atoche Intili (2021)

Reconstruction of the Foundation Layout – 1535
Evolución urbana de Lima
1944

José Barbagelata, Juan Bromley in *El Arquitecto Peruano* (August 1945)

cultural and religious power for the entire region during the viceregal period. It would also come to be recognised as one of the first examples of modern Latin American urbanism.

The viceroy's authority in Lima was supported by a Spanish and Creole ruling class. This led to the manifestation in Peru of the continental independence movement in the early nineteenth century. It culminated in the formation of new Latin American republics; in Peru, it led to the declaration of independence on 28 July 1821 and, consequently, a transition to the republican period.[6]

Following the Spanish-American wars of independence, not to mention a consolidated Ligurian presence, there were innumerable English and French officers who, after having served in the Latin American liberation armies, settled

6 See Basadre, Jorge, *Historia de la República del Perú* (Lima, 1968).

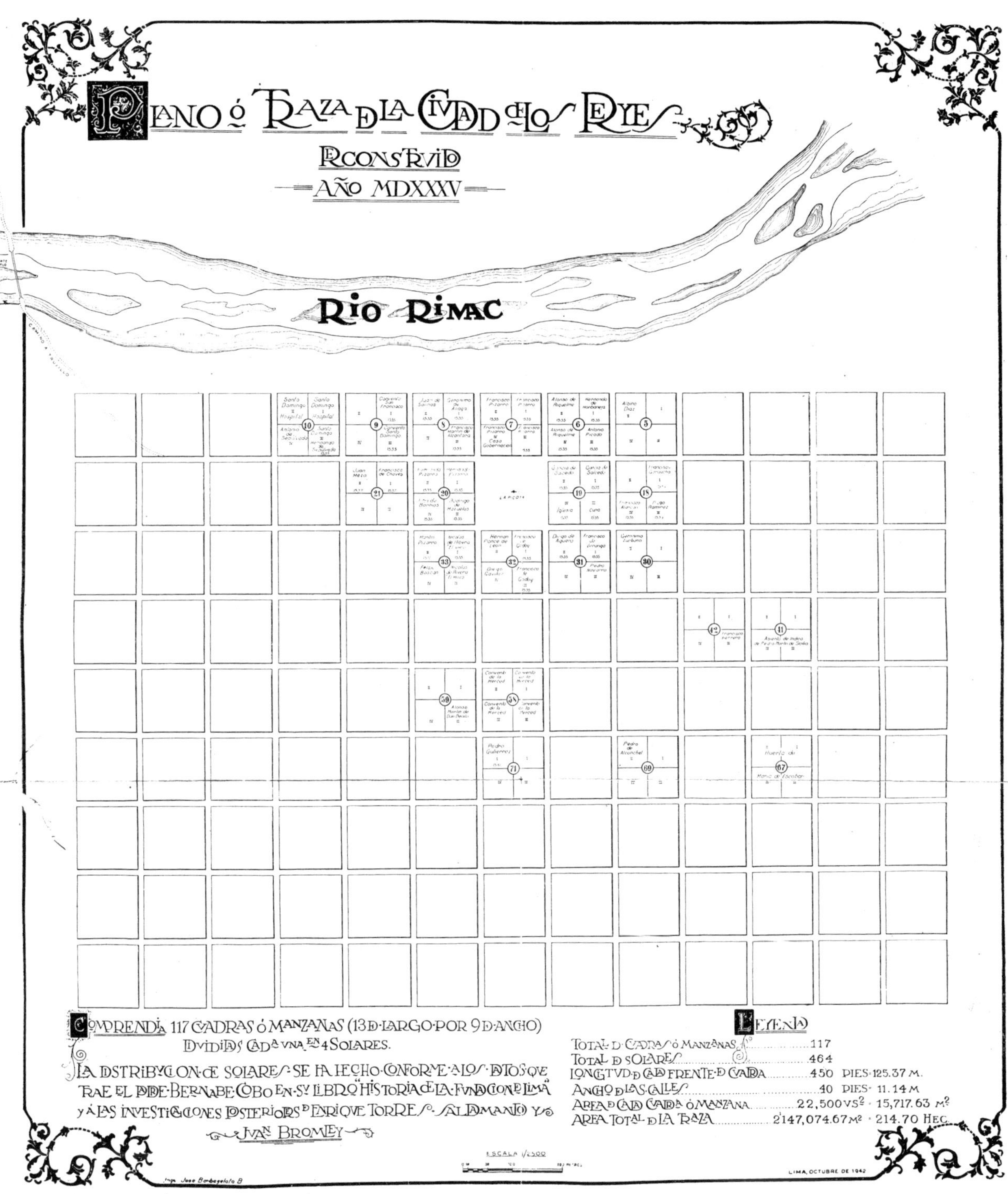

Plano ó Traza de la Ciudad de los Reyes
Reconstruido
Año MDXXXV
Rio Rimac
Comprendía 117 cuadras ó manzanas (13 de largo por 9 de ancho) divididas cada una en 4 solares.
La distribución de solares se ha hecho conforme a los datos que trae el Padre Bernabe Cobo en su libro "Historia de la Fundación de Lima" y a las investigaciones posteriores de Enrique Torres Saldamando y Juan Bromley
Leyenda
Total de cuadras ó manzanas 117
Total de solares 464
Longitud de cada frente de cuadra 450 pies 125.37 m.
Ancho de las calles 40 pies 11.14 m
Area de cada cuadra ó manzana 22,500 vs² 15,717.63 m²
Area total de la traza 2'147,074.67 m² 214.70 Hec.
Escala 1/2500
Lima, Octubre de 1942

Historic centre of Lima – 1944
Overlay of Spanish foundation grid on historical photo
1. Lima's main square
2. Government Palace
3. Rímac River
4. Cathedral
5. Private buildings
6. City Hall
Javier Atoche Intili (2021)

in Peruvian territory.[7] These three groups – Ligurian, English and French – would have constituted the founding nucleus of the most important European colonies established in Peru in the nineteenth century, in terms of commercial operations and number of members. They would also have continued the Andean country's relationship of economic dependence with the West in the republican era.

I.1.2. **The modernisation of the Peruvian capital (1821–1880)**

In Peru, the Spanish-era social structure remained relatively unchanged after its independence from the Crown, representing a clear example of an independent state coexisting with colonial society at the same time.[8] The Hispano-Peruvian philosopher José Ignacio López Soria suggests that the economic model of exporting raw materials, consolidated during Spanish rule, remained unchanged in the republican era, replacing mining with the commercialisation of guano and nitratine. The reality of economic dependence on Western countries, present after the viceregal period, reinforced ties to the Old World.[9]

7 Harriman, Brenda, 'Inmigración inglesa', *Boletín de Lima* (1998), pp. 25–26; Riviale, Pascal, 'Los franceses en el Perú del siglo XIX: retrato de una emigración discreta', *Bulletin de L'Institut Francais d'Etudes Andines* (2007), p. 112.

8 Quijano, Aníbal, *Cuestiones y horizontes: de la dependencia histórico-estructural a la colonialidad/descolonialidad del poder* (Buenos Aires, 2014), pp. 818–823.

9 See Bonfiglio, Giovanni, 'Introducción al estudio de la inmigración europea en el Perú', *Boletín de Lima* (1986), pp. 93–127; Harriman, Brenda, 'Inmigración inglesa', *Boletín de Lima* (1998), pp. 25–30; Riviale, Pascal, 'Los franceses en el Perú del siglo XIX: retrato de una emigración discreta', *Bulletin de L'Institut Francais d'Etudes Andines* (2007), p. 109–121.

A sketch of the Plaza Mayor of Lima, mid-nineteenth century
Evolución urbana de Lima
1944

José Barbagelata, Juan Bromley in *El Arquitecto Peruano* (August 1945)

Unlike what happened in other countries in the region, the fall of the Iberian trade monopoly did not lead to the massive arrival of Europeans in Peru. The small number of these migrants was due to cyclical and structural factors related to the host country. In the first years of republican life, political instability and internal wars discouraged the choice of Peru as a destination for expatriation. Once this phase was over, the colonial imprint remained in the local economy, which favoured the employment of entrepreneurs or self-employed workers at the expense of unskilled labourers. Finally, its geographical position so near to the Andes made it difficult to reach those same mountainous areas, as well as the eastern Peruvian territories, so rich in raw materials.

Unlike other Spanish-speaking countries, such as Argentina or Uruguay, certain characteristics of the Peruvian economy prevented the creation of large-scale employment, inhibiting massive European migration. Indeed, jobs in the country's nascent industrial sector were limited, while agricultural employment was subject to forms of exploitation, inherited from the viceregal past, which imposed a slavery-like regime on workers. These limitations were documented by the meagre effects of the migration legislation enacted by the Peruvian state for the colonisation of its territories, particularly in the Eastern region.[10]

10 The Law of 21 November 1832 provided for the handing over of cultivation lands to foreigners who colonised territories in the Peruvian Amazon region. See Ravines, Rogger, 'Migración y colonización en el Perú: Preámbulo necesario', *Boletín de Lima* (1998), p. 11.

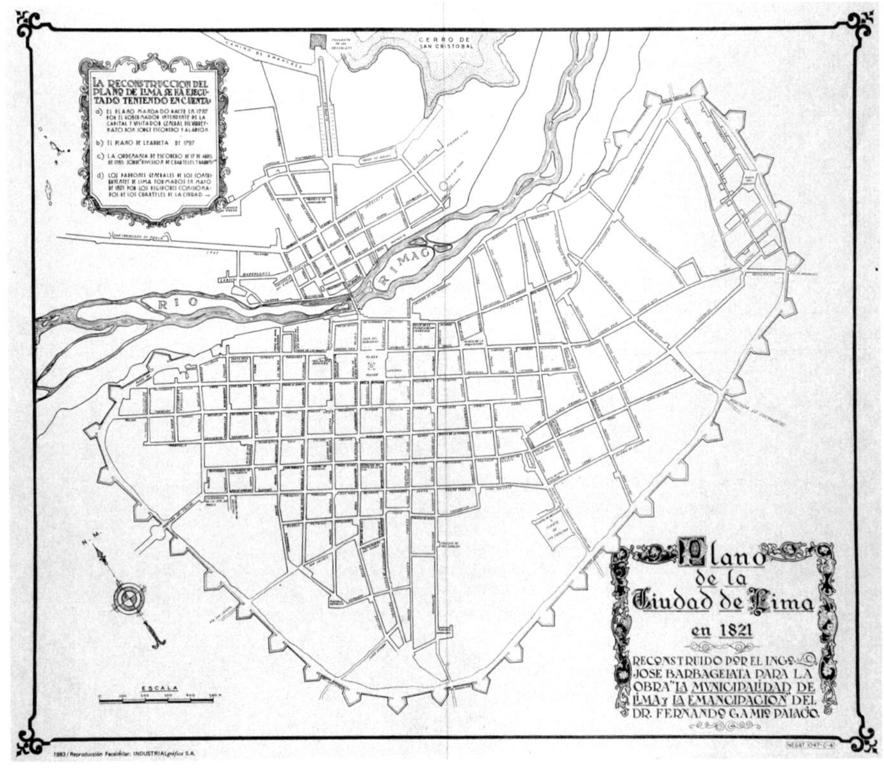

Plan at the time of independence (reconstruction)
Evolución urbana de Lima
1944

José Barbagelata, Juan Bromley in *Planos de Lima, 1613–1683* (1983)

The Peruvian situation in the first half of the nineteenth century highlighted the need to recreate an entrepreneurial class, weakened through the process of gaining independence from Spain. This vacuum was filled by European economies – such as the Kingdom of Sardinia, as well as the United Kingdom of Great Britain and Ireland, and France – that boasted groups of navigators and merchants seeking business opportunities. They formed the most numerous European colonies in Peru which, although they did not represent a high percentage of the total population, established important trade routes with their countries of origin.[11] Thus, the contribution of those who came from the Old World did not depend as much on the number of migrants, admittedly not very high, as on the fact that they occupied key positions in Peruvian society.[12]

To coincide with the celebrations to mark the fiftieth anniversary of Peru's declaration of independence, which took place on 28 July 1871 during the government of José Balta y Montero (1868–1872), the American engineer Henry Meiggs[13] and the Italian agronomist Luigi Sadà di Carlo[14] were commissioned

11 Bonfiglio, Giovanni, *Introducción al estudio de la inmigración europea en el Perú* (Lima, 1986), p. 114.

12 Basadre, Jorge, *Historia de la República del Perú* (Lima, 1968), p. 235.

13 Boston, Massachusetts, 1811 – Lima, 1877.

Palacio de la Exposición
Lima
Antonio Leonardi
1871–1872
Museo de Arte de Lima

in 1872 by the state: the former to carry out the demolition of Lima's viceregal walls and the latter to prepare the city's new urban facilities on the freed land.[15] The works were largely completed by the second half of the 1870s, laying the foundations for the first major expansion of the Peruvian capital in the republican era.

With the demolition of the viceregal defensive walls, the Exposición Nacional was set up in the south of the city, an exhibition complex of several pavilions, the Palacio de la Exposición (Antonio Leonardi, 1871–1872) being the main one, inaugurated by Balta ahead of the independence celebrations. Meiggs himself was commissioned to build the Ferrocarril Central, during the government of Manuel Pardo y Lavalle (1872–1876), while the English Great Eastern Ship Company was responsible for the telegraph connection between Peruvian ports and those of Bolivia and Chile.[16]

The construction of communication and transport infrastructure, as well as the urban expansion of Lima, came to a halt in the late 1870s, due to the deteriorating economic situation. The accumulated public debt held by British and French creditors, a direct result of the policies which demanded cash advance in exchange for the commercialisation of guano, became unsustainable after the fall in price of this commodity on the international market. The end of the guano boom was followed by the Pacific War, between Peru, Bolivia and Chile, for

14 1821–1889.
15 Günther, Juan, *Planos de Lima, 1613–1983* (Lima, 1983), p. 11.
16 Harriman, Brenda, 'Inmigración inglesa', *Boletín de Lima* (1998), p. 28.

domination of those territories rich in nitratine, a potential replacement as mineral fertiliser. The defeat of the Peruvian-Bolivian allies led to a further contraction of the local economy, with a consequent reduction in trade.

The coexistence of an independent state alongside colonial society, the result of its historical relations with Spain, meant that Peru was delayed in the start of its modernisation process. In contrast to western countries, Peruvian industrial development and civil society participation in the *res publica* did not occur in consistent form until the first half of the twentieth century. This period saw both the diversification into commercial activities of the Europeans, as well as an expansion of Peru's major cities.

I.1.3. **The growth of Lima in the first half of the twentieth century (1897–1939)**

The contradictions presented by the modern condition, those tensions between capitalism, industrialisation and the democratisation of society identified by Agnes Heller,[17] become more articulated in Latin American post-colonial realities. As such, Peru, a country where the formation of the nation-state began later than in the United States of America and Western Europe, experienced full modernity only in the last century.[18] This condition brought about, in the European colonies, the transition from commercial to industrial and banking activities. It also determined their participation in Lima's urban expansion process.

The urban development of Lima in the first quarter of the twentieth century, which was based on proposals drawn up by Georges-Eugène Haussmann for Paris, included, in addition to the partial demolition of the Peruvian capital's ancient viceregal layout, its replacement with wide radial avenues connecting the founding nucleus with the peripheral ones located towards the sea (Callao and Magdalena, to the west; Ancón, to the north; Miraflores, Barranco and Chorrillos, to the south). If the demolition of the urban defensive system had laid the foundations for the expansion of the Peruvian capital, the economic conditions in the early twentieth century were ripe for a strong speculative market in construction, mostly on behalf of Europeans. One factor that boosted the Peruvian economy, for example, was the opening of the Panama Canal in 1914, which meant a faster connection to Europe and a consequent increase in trade between both shores.

In 1925, during the second government of Peruvian President Augusto B. Leguía (1919–1930), the *Plan de la Gran Lima* was drafted. It represented the first example of planning by way of rationalising territory in the republican era,

17 Heller, Ágnes, *Teoria della storia* (Rome, 1982), p. 289.

18 See López Soria, José Ignacio, *Filosofía, arquitectura y ciudad* (Lima, 2017).

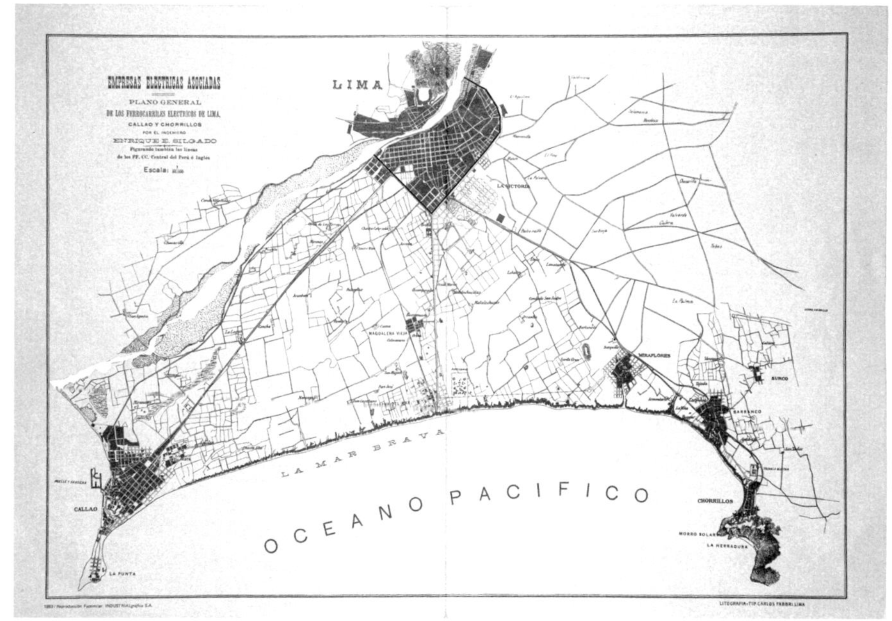

General plan of Lima, Callao and seaside towns by the engineer Enrique E. Silgado, 1908
Evolución urbana de Lima
1944

Enrique E. Silgado in *Planos de Lima, 1613–1683* (1983)

translated into the enactment of an urban regulatory framework.[19] The design of public facilities and the capital's hydraulic-sanitary network was entrusted in 1926 to the German engineer Werner Benno Lange.[20]

Under Leguía's auspices, work began on the construction of the Plaza San Martín (1926–1940) by the Spaniard Manuel Piqueras Cotolí[21] in collaboration with the Peruvian architect Rafael Marquina.[22] In addition, the Parque de la Exposición was redeveloped, as well as other urban facilities in the capital, including the Paseo 9 de Diciembre and the Parque Universitario. Finally, the different communities of foreigners established in Peru donated celebratory monuments, such as the Museo de Arte Italiano (1921–1923) and the Fuente de la Colonia China (1921), both works by Gaetano Moretti, gracing the Parque de la Exposición.

With the arrival of the new century, migratory connections were established with southern Italy, in contrast to what had happened before with those from north-western Italy. The economic activities of this expatriate colony showed significant dynamism, strong growth and great diversification. Such was the case with Pietro D'Onofrio,[23] an Italian entrepreneur in the food sector who, after settling with his family in Lima in 1897, grew a successful business at the national level in little more than thirty years.[24] The same family later appeared

19 Ludeña, Wiley, *Tres buenos tigres. Piqueras – Belaúnde – La Agrupación Espacio. Vanguardia y urbanismo en el Perú en el siglo XX* (Huancayo, 2004), p. 154.
20 Union of American Republics, *Bulletin of the Pan American Union* (Washington, DC, 1926), p. 413.
21 Manuel Piqueras Cotolí (Lucena, Córdoba, 1885 – Lima, 1937). Sculptor and architect, student of Miguel Blay. Settled in Peru, he was one of the main promoters of neo-Peruano, an eclectic style that combined elements of pre-Columbian cultures with those of the viceregal period. See Gutierrez, Ramón, *Dizionario enciclopedico*, in Dieste, Eladio et al. (eds.), *Architettura e società: l'America Latina nel XX secolo* (Milano, 1996), pp. 391–392.
22 José Rafael Marquina y Bueno (Lima, 1884 – 1964).
23 Sessa Aurunca, 1859 – Lima, 1937.
24 Bonfiglio, Giovanni, *Dizionario storico-biografico degli Italiani in Peru* (Bologna, 1998), pp. 133–134.

Plaza San Martín and old Lima's penitentiary in background
Lima
1943–1944
Servicio Aerofotografico Nacional

among the clients of European designers, such as the Italian Mario Bianco (see III.3.), for the construction of their residences and company headquarters in the Peruvian capital.

The economic affairs involving the Italian colony in Peru changed considerably over time, from the retail food sector to wholesale industrial production, and from the cultivation of agricultural products to investment in banking, accommodation and construction. At that time, of the total 31,456 hectares of agricultural land located close to the consolidated centre of Lima, around 40 per cent was owned by families of Italian origin.[25] During the first decades of the twentieth century, these families actively participated in the urban growth of the Peruvian capital, initiating an unprecedented process of expansion. The European settlers themselves were early protagonists of the migratory processes from the provinces to Lima that began in the 1930s, characterised by strong demographic growth and dizzying urban expansion.

As such, the increase in population and urban development favoured the prosperity of construction-related industrial activities. One example is the Sociedad Maderera Ciurlizza Maurer, a company specialised in the extraction, processing and commercialisation of wood. It was founded in 1874 when

25 Calderón, Julio, *La ciudad ilegal: Lima en el siglo XX* (Lima, 2005), pp. 66–67.

the sawmill of Croatian Lorenzo Ciurlizza merged with the furniture factory of Swiss Louis Maurer,[26] introducing industrial processes into its production line.[27] The Swiss Theodor Cron was later commissioned by this family for his first Peruvian work (see IV.3.).

In continuity with what had begun at the end of the nineteenth century, the growth of the city of Lima was directed towards the sea along two axes: to the first east-west axis, the historical link between Lima and the port of Callao, was added a second north-south link, towards the seaside towns of Miraflores, Barranco and Chorrillos. The land along this second development axis belonged to the *latifundia* of Jesús María, Desamparados, Orrantia, San Isidro, Lince and Lobatón, the latter two owned by the Risso family. Manuel and Roberto Risso Dignone, sons of the Italians Manuel Risso and Esther Dignone, donated part of the land of the Lobatón estate to allow the extension of the road linking the old town and the seaside towns. The Avenida Leguía crossed these lands from north to south, forming a direct link between Lima and Miraflores.[28] The construction of this road resulted in an increase in the value of the agricultural land concerned, also reinforcing the process of urbanisation towards the south.

In addition to the presence of the historical colonies of European origin, which experienced considerable economic growth between the nineteenth and twentieth centuries, the arrival of new groups of political migrants during the 1930s and 1940s favoured the inclusion of compatriot professionals who would design and build their residences and headquarters in Peru. For example, there is the case of the Ursuline nuns Caritas Knickenberg and Gertrudis Neugebauer, who moved to Latin America in the late 1930s because of the rise of National Socialism in Germany. The building complex of their institute would be designed and built by Bauhäusler Paul Linder, one of the most prolific European architects who moved to Lima in the first half of the twentieth century (see II.3.).

The reception of these designers in Lima society was influenced by the foreign policies of the United States of America. The good-neighbourly strategies of the North American country in the second quarter of the last century exploited the historical relations between Europe and Latin America, facilitating the relationships established between European architects exiled there and Peruvian intellectuals trained in Western countries. With their activities in the political, professional and academic fields, professionals such as the Peruvian architect Fernando Belaúnde Terry worked to promote urbanism and architecture in Peru.

26 Adelboden, Canton Bern, 1855 – Lima, 1933.

27 See Centurión, Enrique, *El Perú actual y las colonias extranjeras: la realidad actual y el extranjero en el Perú a través de cien años, 1821–1921* (Bergamo, 1924).

28 Günther, Juan, *Planos de Lima, 1613–1983* (Lima, 1983), table 21.

I.2. Fernando Belaúnde Terry and the Europeans who migrated to the United States of America

25 years of *El Arquitecto Peruano*
Cover of the magazine with a photo of Fernando Belaúnde Terry
1963
El Arquitecto Peruano (April–June 1963)

In Latin America, a continent where the formation of modern nation-states began later than in Western Europe and the United States of America, modernisation and modernism (where the latter term refers to the culture that later emerges from the former) tend to occur simultaneously.[29] Modernisation implemented from above and below, as defined by the philosopher Marshall Berman, becomes in the Peruvian case an elite modernism that refers to foreign models and a popular modernisation that has deep local roots. Thus, in the first half of the twentieth century, the figure of the intellectual became consolidated throughout Lima and its environs, a modern subject of which the Peruvian architect Fernando Belaúnde Terry[30] is a clear example. After his return to Peru, he founded the magazine *El Arquitecto Peruano* (1937). He also participated in the foundation of the Sociedad de Arquitectos del Perú (1937) and the Instituto de Urbanismo (1944). Belaúnde was Director of the Department of Architecture at the Escuela Nacional de Ingenieros (1950), and Dean of the Faculty of Architecture at the Universidad Nacional de Ingeniería (1955). In political life, he was deputy for Lima (1945–1948) and twice president of the Republic (1963–1968 and 1980–1985).

I.2.1. The role of intellectuals in the planning of Lima after the 1940 earthquake (1937–1940)

A key figure in the political and professional relations established between Peru, the United States of America and Europe in the twentieth century, Belaúnde returned to Peru in 1936 after a 12-year exile: his father, a political opponent of Augusto B. Leguía, had been deported to France together with his family. Under those circumstances, Belaúnde attended university in Paris until 1930 after which he went to the United States of America, where he completed his architectural studies at the University of Texas at Austin[31] in 1935.

Upon returning home, having worked briefly in Mexico, Belaúnde soon realised how the embryonic condition of the professional figure of the architect in Peru compared unfavourably to other countries in the region. This led him in 1937 to start a magazine specialising in urban planning, architecture, construction and interior design: *El Arquitecto Peruano.*[32] Through the topics explored in its pages, this periodical would involve architects, engineers, builders and the wider public, consolidating the new professional discipline in Lima.

29 See López Soria, José Ignacio, *Filosofía, arquitectura y ciudad* (Lima, 2017).

30 Fernando Isaac Sergio Marcelo Marcos Belaúnde Terry (Lima 1912–2012) was born into a family that had been exiled to France for political reasons. In Paris, he attended the Sainte-Marie de Monceau school and after began his engineering studies at the École Nationale Supérieure d'Électricité et de Mécanique. The family later moved to the United States, where Belaúnde began his architectural studies at the University of Miami in 1930, completed them in 1935 at the University of Texas at Austin.

31 Atoche Intili, Javier, *La revista El Arquitecto Peruano y el rol de la fotografía en la conformación del discurso contemporáneo latinoamericano*, in Alcolea, Rubén, Tárrago, Jorge (eds.), *inter photo arch – Congreso internacional* (Pamplona, 2016), p. 11.

32 Ibid., p. 12.

EL ARQUITECTO
peruano
309, 310, 311

El Arquitecto Peruano magazine gave ample space to the modernisation and expansion of the Peruvian capital through urban planning and public housing, especially after the Peruvian census and the Lima earthquake of 1940: on 24 May, a seismic movement was recorded beneath the Peruvian central coast, measuring 8.2 on the Richter scale, the strongest in the twentieth century. The epicentre was 120 kilometres north-east of Lima, affecting the city and other smaller towns along the coast, such as Callao, Miraflores and Chorrillos.[33]

The devastating effects of this earthquake rekindled the debate concerning construction materials suitable for urban environments, as *adobe* and *quincha* (unfired earth technologies) structures suffered serious damage; whereas reinforced concrete buildings, even the tallest ones, behaved better in the face of the dynamic loads produced by the tremors. Because of this, Belaúnde illustrated extensively in his journal the devastating effects of the earthquake on buildings constructed with traditional technologies, as compared to the behaviour of structures considered to be earthquake-resistant.[34]

The generation of professionals led by Belaúnde found a unity of purpose in the search for solutions to the problems inherent in the urban and social spheres of the Peruvian capital, aggravated by the calamitous events of 1940. The founders of the Sociedad de Arquitectos del Perú also wrote in the magazine, greatly influencing local intellectual circles.[35] The most influential members of the Sociedad's board of directors were foreign-trained architects, who were able to involve established and emerging professionals. The honorary president Ricardo Malachowski,[36] a Polish architect trained at the École des

Effects of the earthquake on outdated buildings
Callao
1940
El Arquitecto Peruano (June 1940)

Architects' lunch at La Cabaña
Event organised by the Sociedad de Arquitectos del Perú for the award given by the Municipality of Lima to the architects Emilio Hath-Terré, José Alvarez Calderón, Luis Miró Quesada, Luis Solimano and Enrique Seoane Ros
Lima
1940
El Arquitecto Peruano (August 1940)

Beaux-Arts in Paris and who moved to Peru in 1911, was the coordinator of the Sección Especial de Arquitectos Constructores of the Escuela Nacional de Ingenieros from 1912. President Rafael Marquina,[37] who had studied at Cornell University in New York, was both a lecturer in architecture at the Escuela and a respected professional among his colleagues for his work in the urban and architectural fields. Vice President Héctor Velarde,[38] also an Escuela professor, trained in Switzerland and France, was one of the first to bring to Peru – through his work, his teaching and his writings – the new architecture that was being realised in Europe. Secretary Belaúnde, after his studies at the University of Texas at Austin, maintained contact with the United States of America, facilitating the visit of architects and urban planners who moved there, including Paul Lester Wiener, Richard Neutra and Josep Lluís Sert (see I.2.2.).

I.2.2. Good Neighbour Policy and Peruvian urban planning legislation (1942–1946)

As a publisher, Belaúnde played a key role in the local introduction of the United States of America's urban planning guidelines,[39] largely disseminated by European planners who moved to the North American country (see I.3.3.). The good-neighbourly foreign policies, adopted by the US in the 1930s, aimed to present other American countries with the benefits of the democratic form of government, namely, economic development and political stability. US interests coincided with those of influential Peruvian politicians and intellectuals eager to establish cooperation agreements with their northern neighbour.

Proof of this is the official visit of the President of the Peruvian Republic Manuel Prado[40] to his US counterpart Roosevelt in 1942. After the presidential meeting, the Prado administration introduced policies that affected some Peruvian industrial and mining activities, using the experience of the Tennessee Valley Authority for Regional Development (1933–1938) as their model for the creation of the Peruvian Corporaciones del Estado (1942–1946). In this way, with foreign technical support, three state corporations were created: the Corporación Peruana del Amazonas, for the exploitation of natural resources in the Peruvian east; the Corporación Peruana del Santa, for the metallurgical development of the northern Peruvian region; and the Corporación Peruana de Aviación Comercial, for the regulation of commercial aviation in the national sphere.[41]

The policies adopted during Prado's liberal government encouraged foreign capital investment and laid the foundation for the capitalist development of Peru's economic system in the second half of the twentieth century.

33 See 'El terremoto de ayer en Lima, Callao y balnearios', *El Comercio* (25 May 1940); 'El sismo en Perú ha originado consternación en Argentina y Chile', *La Prensa: Edición extraordinaria* (25 May 1940); 'Lima después del sismo', *La Crónica: Diario de la mañana* (25 May 1940).

34 See Belaúnde Terry, Fernando, 'Puntos de vista... El sentido de la reconstrucción', *El Arquitecto Peruano* (June 1940).

35 Zapata, Antonio, *El jóven Belaunde: historia de la revista El Arquitecto Peruano: 1937–1963* (Lima, 1995), p. 13.

36 Ryszard Jaxa-Małachowski Kulisicz (Odessa, 1887 – Lima, 1972), from a wealthy family that owned large agricultural estates, was educated in Paris at the École Centrale d'Architecture (1907–1910) and the École des Beaux-Arts (1909–1910). In 1911 he moved to Lima and from 1912 oversaw coordination of the section of architect-builders at the Escuela Nacional de Ingeniería. Malachowski, Ricardo Jaxa, *Lecciones de elementos y teoría de la arquitectura* (Lima, 2015), pp. 26–27.

37 Rafael Ernesto Marquina y Bueno (Lima, 1884 – 1964) began his studies at Cornell University in Ithaca, New York in 1905.

38 Héctor Ángel Velarde y Bergmann (Lima, 1898 – 1989). Peruvian architect, trained at the École des Travaux Publics du Batiment de l'Industrie, from 1917 to 1919, then at the École des Beaux-Arts, both in Paris.

39 See Zapata, Antonio, *El joven Belaúnde: historia de la revista El Arquitecto Peruano: 1937–1963* (Lima, 1995).

40 Manuel Carlos Prado y Ugarteche (Lima, 1889 – Paris, 1967). A Peruvian politician, he was president of the Republic for two terms: from 8 December 1939 to 28 July 1945 and then from 28 July 1956 to 18 July 1962.

41 Kahatt, Sharif, *Utopías construidas: las unidades vecinales de Lima* (Lima, 2015), pp. 66–67.

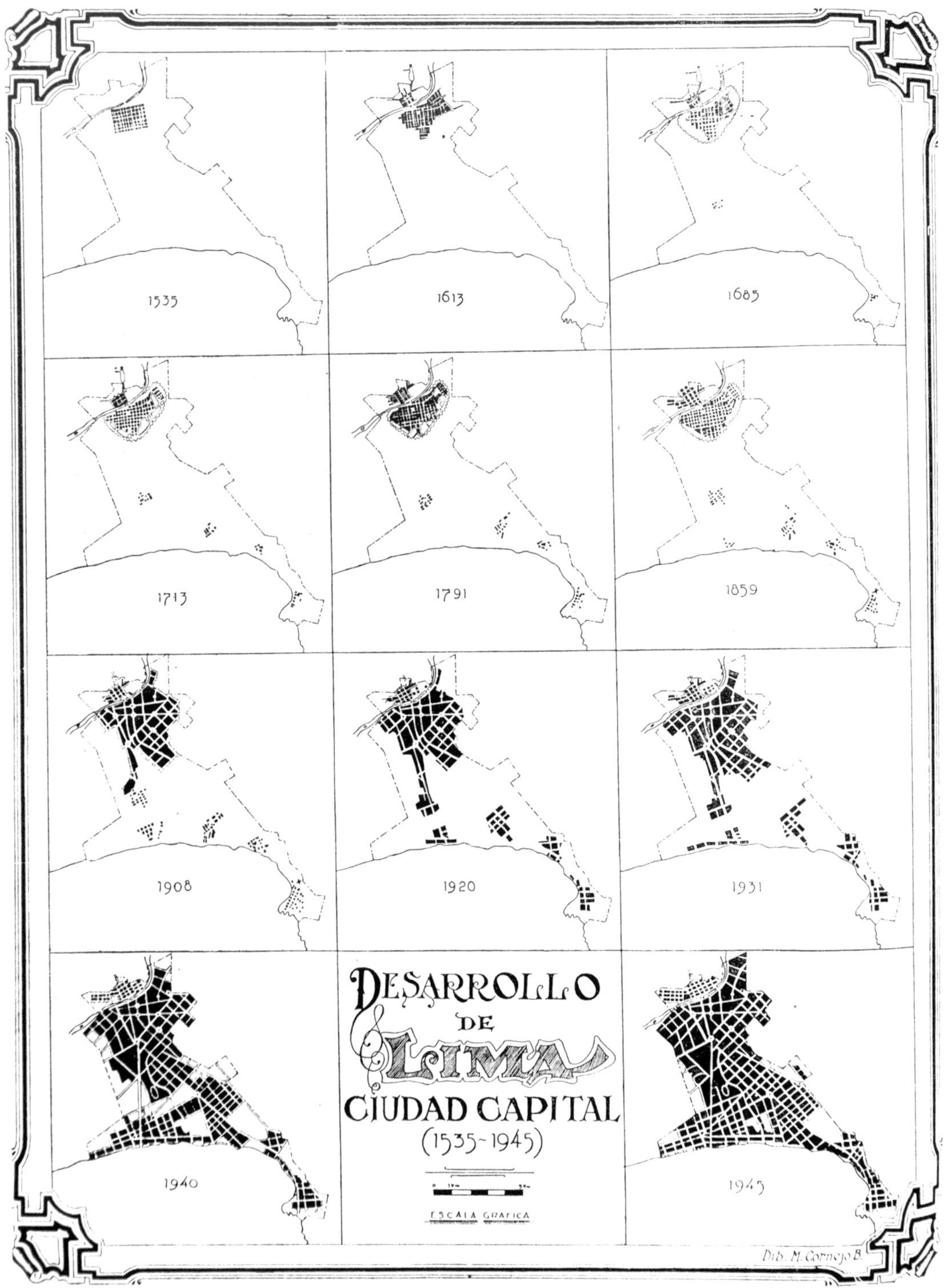

Representation of the urban evolution of the city, in phases
Lima
1944
José Barbagelata, Juan Bromley in *El Arquitecto Peruano* (August 1945)

Luncheon of the Instituto de Urbanismo del Perú
Lima
1945
El Arquitecto Peruano (April 1945)

The US presence in agriculture, mining and manufacturing was accompanied by European participation in the energy, financial and insurance sectors. The increase in foreign presence in Peru during the Prado government was consolidated: in the economic sphere, by the policies adopted by the administration of José Luis Bustamante y Rivero[42] and in the cultural sphere by foreign-trained Peruvian architects, who facilitated the visit of European planners, most of whom had been exiled to the US.

In the aftermath of the Second World War, specifically between 1944 and 1956, several internationally renowned figures visited Peru for professional and academic activities. These included Paul Lester Wiener (1944–1949 and 1956), Richard Neutra (1945), Josep Lluís Sert (1947–1949 and 1953–1954), Ernesto Nathan Rogers (1949), Josef Albers (1953) and Walter Gropius (1953–1954 and 1954). It is therefore of particular interest to study: the cause-effect relationship concerning these visits; the creation of the Instituto de Urbanismo del Perú; and the enactment of 1946's town planning legislation.

42 José Luis Bustamante y Rivero (Arequipa, 1894 – Lima, 1989). Peruvian lawyer, jurist, politician, diplomat, and writer. He was President of the Republic of Peru from 28 July 1945 to 29 October 1948, when he was dismissed in a coup d'état by General Manuel A. Odría. He was President of the International Court of Justice between 1967 and 1969.

Cidade dos Motores
Rio de Janeiro
Town Planning Associates
1943–1946

Town Planning Associates in *L'Architecture d'Aujourd'hui* (September 1947)

Belaúnde and other Peruvian architects – mostly from European or North American backgrounds, such as Luis Dorich, Carlos Morales, Alfredo Dammert and Luis Ortiz de Zevallos – organised and collaborated assiduously with the magazine *El Arquitecto Peruano* from 1937 and created the Instituto de Urbanismo del Perú[43] in 1944. The Instituto had a clear European and North American influence from its inception. On the one hand, the theoretical framework and

43 Huapaya, José Carlos, *Fernando Belaúnde Terry y el ideario moderno: arquitectura y urbanismo en el Perú entre 1936 y 1968* (Lima, 2014), p. 185.

practical courses of the curriculum reflected the foreign experiences of the founders.[44] On the other, the visits of professionals such as Francis Violich[45] and Chloethiel Woodard Smith[46] to the Andean country, funded by the United States Department of State, had begun to make the discipline of US regional planning known in Peru.

Pan-American cultural penetration initiatives, developed during the Roosevelt administration, continued under Harry Truman. Parallel to the creation of the Peruvian institute, visits and lectures by European architects and urban planners who moved there were financed by the US Department of State. That was the case with the German-born architect Paul Lester Wiener, a founding partner of the New York firm Town Planning Associates, together with the well-known Spanish town planner Josep Lluís Sert. Prior to the publication of Sert's book, *Can our cities survive?*[47] (1942), Wiener met with Cordell Hull, Secretary of State of the US, and received an offer to participate in a lecture series in South America.[48]

The first destination was Brazil. The choice of the inaugural destination had a precise objective: political rapprochement between the two countries. With the inauguration of the Estado Novo[49] on 10 November 1937, the Brazilian government, led by Getúlio Vargas, had initiated policies inspired by European authoritarian models. The two Town Planning Associates members gave a series of university lectures, arousing considerable interest given the correspondence received afterwards.[50] In addition to his well-known assignment for the Cidade dos Motores project[51] (1943–1946), the trips to Brazil gave Wiener the opportunity to establish contacts with other intellectuals in the South American region.

Belaúnde, then a candidate for deputy of Lima, saw in Wiener an important personality for his political campaign, which focused on the urban development of the Peruvian capital. In December 1944, he coordinated with the central government to invite Wiener for a series of lectures in Lima, promoted by the Instituto de Urbanismo, the Sociedad de Ingenieros, as well as the Sociedad de Arquitectos, and publicised by *El Arquitecto Peruano*. These experiences were documented and trumpeted by Belaúnde, due to the particular interest they aroused among his colleagues.[52] In fact, the Peruvian architect suggested to Wiener the topics – in keeping with those of the electoral season, such as housing and urban planning – to be dealt with. At the same time, contact with the Peruvian authorities would have allowed Wiener to offer his professional services to the Corporación Nacional del Santa for the *Plan Piloto de Chimbote*, a planned settlement for 40,000 inhabitants, located on the northern Peruvian coast.[53]

El pensamiento creador en arquitectura y urbanismo
Image included in Peruvian magazine article. From left to right: Luis Dorich, Paul Lester Wiener, Fernando Belaúnde Terry
Lima
1945
El Arquitecto Peruano (April 1945)

44 Ibid., pp. 187–188.
45 San Francisco, California, 1911 – Berkeley, California, 2005.
46 Peoria, Illinois, 1910 – Washington, DC, 1992.
47 See Sert, José Luis, *Can our cities survive?: an ABC of urban problems, their analysis, their solutions* (London, 1942).
48 Rovira, Josep María, *José Luis Sert (1901–1983)* (Milan, 2000), p. 113.
49 Liernur, Jorge Francisco, *Escritos de arquitectura del siglo XX en América Latina* (Madrid / Seville, 2002), pp. 143–144.
50 Rovira, Josep María, José *Luis Sert (1901–1983)* (Milan, 2000), p. 114.
51 Town Planning Associates' project for a model city in Rio de Janeiro, with state participation, to produce engines for military and agricultural purposes, as well as the massive construction of public housing. Ibid., p. 116.
52 See 'El Pensamiento creador en arquitectura y urbanismo', *El Arquitecto Peruano* (April 1945).
53 Ibid., pp. 127–137.

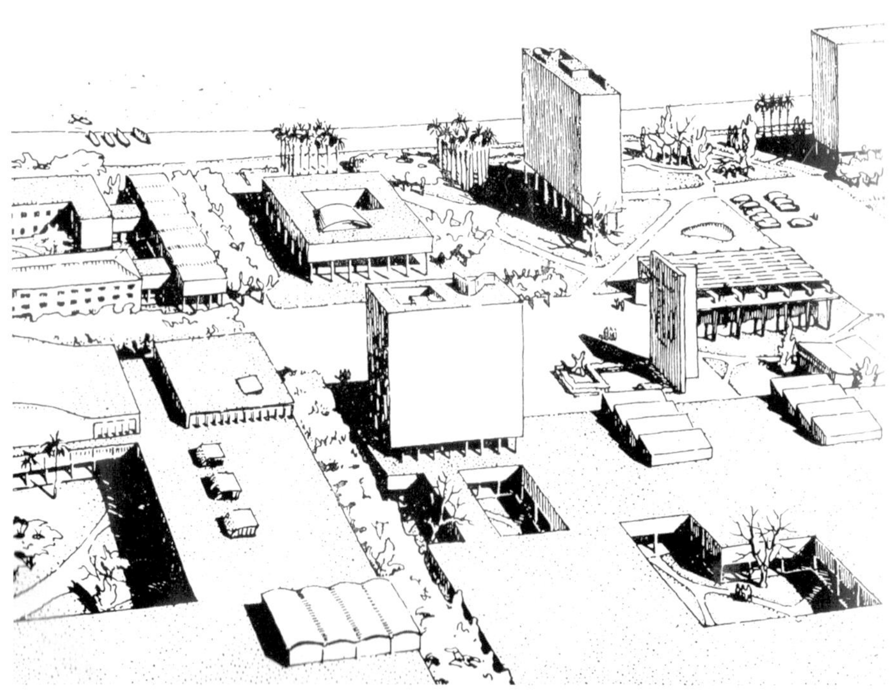

Plan Piloto
Chimbote
Town Planning Associates
1947–1948

Town Planning Associates in *The Heart of the City* (1952)

The architect-candidate had detailed knowledge of US domestic policies, made possible by his education in North America. Most importantly, he documented in *El Arquitecto Peruano* how the middle-class housing policies implemented through the Federal Emergency Administration of Public Works were responsible for the creation of greenbelt communities (satellite towns based on the English model of garden cities).[54] In 1944 he published in *El Arquitecto Peruano* an article, entitled *El barrio-unidad, instrumento de descentralización urbana*, in which he illustrated how the English (garden cities) and American (greenbelt communities) examples could be applied to the case of Lima.[55]

Through their actions, Belaúnde and Wiener aimed to illustrate the potential of urban planning as a tool for economic development and social improvement. In this respect, previously signed cooperation agreements

54 See Renard, Carmen, 'Los pueblos Greenbelt en los Estados Unidos', *El Arquitecto Peruano* (May 1944).

55 See 'El barrio-unidad, elemento de descentralización urbana', *El Arquitecto Peruano* (June 1944).

La visita de Richard J. Neutra
Portrait of Richard J. Neutra in a Peruvian magazine article with extracts from his lecture in Lima.
El Arquitecto Peruano (September 1945)

between the Peruvian and US administrations had enabled the participation of North American technical consultants in some of Peru's most important infrastructure projects. In urban planning matters, the exchanges that took place with foreign colleagues would have allowed Belaúnde to identify the main Western references useful in the planning of the Peruvian capital.

The architect-candidate saw in the realisation of neighbourhood units, which he translated as *barrio-unidad* and later as *unidades vecinales*, an instrument for the expansion of the Peruvian capital. Foreign models of urban planning indicated several useful conclusions for Lima: the development of the city should not focus solely on the consolidated core but more so on urban growth, through the realisation of satellite cities, planned and built with the participation of the state.

Belaúnde's political success reinforced his influence as far as the strategies for Lima's urban development were concerned. Elected as a deputy for the Frente Democrático Nacional in the vote held on 10 June 1945, Belaúnde played a major role in defining the legal and public financial framework for the implementation of the *Plan de Vivienda* he had proposed. As a parliamentarian and son of the Prime Minister of the incumbent government,[56] his actions had an obviously major impact on urban planning in the Peruvian capital.

Besides his communications with the director of the US Department of State, Wiener wrote to Richard Neutra[57] informing him that there was a cultural climate in Lima that was favourable to the dissemination of CIAM principles.[58] Neutra toured Latin America starting in August 1945, financed by the US Department of State which coordinated his various activities in Peru, where he gave a series of lectures on urban planning and contemporary architecture.[59] In a talk entitled *Metropolitan Future of a City with a Great Historical Heritage*, Neutra developed urbanistic ideas espoused by the participants of CIAM and applied them to Lima's historical context. As with Wiener, Neutra helped develop and support Belaúnde's electoral proposals.

The town planning legislation of 1946, which came into force during the democratic government of President José Luis Bustamante y Rivero, became the main legal instrument for Peru's major cities in the second half of the twentieth century. Taking the publications of CIAM as a reference, Belaúnde established the regulatory basis enabling Peruvian cities to fulfil the main contemporary activities of housing, work, recreation and circulation.[60] As a result, four laws were enacted to encourage the involvement of public and private actors: the Ley de Propriedad Horizontal; the Ley de la Oficina Nacional de Planeamiento y Urbanismo; the Ley de la Corporación Nacional de Vivienda; and the Ley de los Centros Climáticos de Esparcimiento. In this way, under the guidance of

56 Juan Rafael Atalo Belaúnde Diez-Canseco (Arequipa, 1886 – Lima, 1972), father of Fernando Belaúnde Terry, was President of the Council of Ministers during the presidency of José Luis Bustamante y Rivero (1945–1946).
57 Vienna, 1892 – Wuppertal, 1970.
58 Rovira, Josep María, *José Luis Sert (1901–1983)* (Milan, 2000), pp. 127–137.
59 Kahatt, Sharif, *Utopías construidas: las unidades vecinales de Lima* (Lima, 2015), p. 87.
60 See 'Algunos principios de urbanismo aprobados por el IV Congreso de Arquitectura Moderna (CIAM) celebrado en Atenas en 1933, con participación de notables personalidades de la arquitectura y urbanismo', *El Arquitecto Peruano* (November 1946).

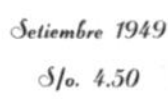

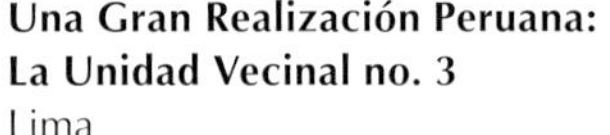

Una Gran Realización Peruana:
La Unidad Vecinal no. 3
Lima
Corporación Nacional de Vivienda
1945–1949
El Arquitecto Peruano (September 1949)

Centro Climático de Huampaní
Lurigancho-Chosica
Corporación Nacional de Vivienda
1947–1955
El Arquitecto Peruano (January–February 1955)

a democratic government and with the participation of private capital and technical specialists, the architect-deputy of Lima would put his urban development plans into practice through the realisation of works of national interest.[61]

I.2.3. **The VI Congreso Panamericano de Arquitectos (1947)**

The VI Congreso Panamericano de Arquitectos, held in Peru between 15 and 25 October 1947, was organised by the Permanent Committee of the Pan-American Congresses and the Sociedad de Arquitectos.[62] Its outcomes document a reorientation in Pan-American architectural practice between the war and the years immediately following: on the one hand, a change in the attitude of architects compared to previous editions translated into the awarding of proposals far removed from historical references, such as the project for the

61 Atoche Intili, Javier, 'Lima la moderna (1937–1969): Expansion of modern culture and multi-storey buildings in Peru', in Jordá Such, Carmen et al. (eds.), *Modern Design: Social Commitment & Quality of Life* (Valencia, 2022).

62 See Congreso panamericano de arquitectos, *Actas del VI. Congreso Panamericano de Arquitectos: Lima, 15 de octubre de 1947, Cuzco 25 de octubre de 1947* (Lima, 1953).

63 Ibid., p. 207–212.

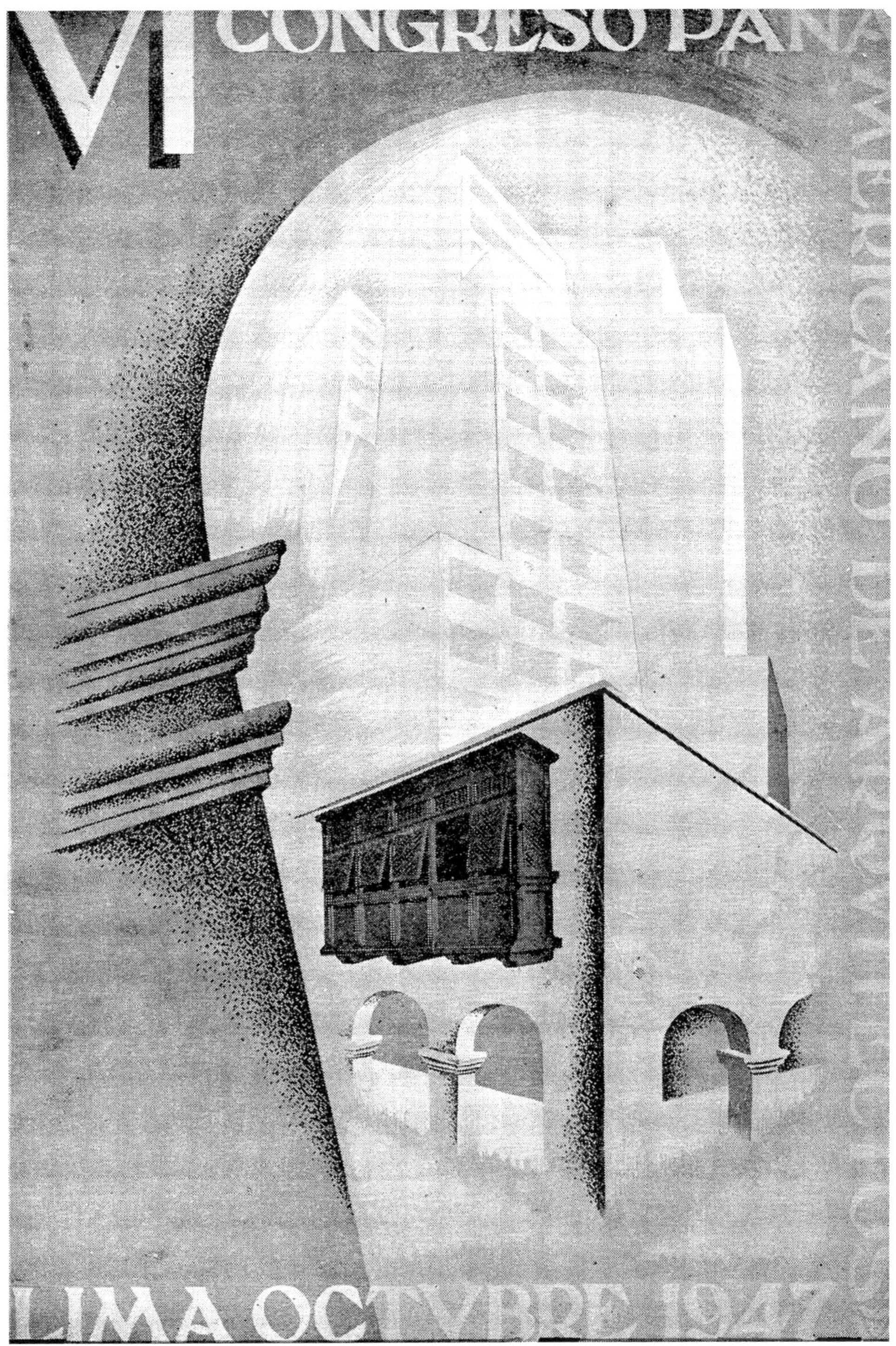

Poster
VI Congreso Panamericano de Arquitectos
Lima
1947

Permanent Committee of the Pan-American Congresses and Sociedad de Arquitectos del Perú in *El Arquitecto Peruano* (September 1947)

Hospital de Antituberculosos de Bravo Chico[63] (Héctor Velarde, 1943–1950, Chavín Prize 1949); on the other, the figure of the architect-planner became instrumental on the path of peace and international development undertaken after the Second World War.[64]

During the opening ceremony, which counted among its participants the President of the Peruvian Republic José Luis Bustamante y Rivero and other esteemed public dignitaries, architect Héctor Velarde illustrated the European presence in Latin American architecture at that time. On a regional level, he cited the recent participation of European masters in Brazil, creating 'formas auténticas y directas que serán como guías para los arquitectos brasileños.'[65] Although the quotation was implicit, he was most likely referring to the recent participation of Town Planning Associates in the drafting of the Cidade dos Motores project (illustrated by Paul Lester Wiener during his visit to Lima in 1944, see I.2.2.), or the recently constructed Ministerio da Educação e Saúde Pública (Affonso Reidy et al., with the advice of Le Corbusier, Rio de Janeiro, 1937–1942, see V.1.).

As described in the articles of the magazine *El Arquitecto Peruano*, published between September and November 1947, the organisers of the congress gave priority to the study of masterplans and neighbourhood units, identified as fundamental tools for the functional development of the city. Of the seven commissions in which the work of the Pan-American congress was organised,[66] those concerning urban planning were highly visible. The principles disseminated by the *Charte d'Athènes* of 1933 were consolidated in the Latin American sphere by the travels of some of its best-known proponents: among them, Le Corbusier's trips begun in 1929[67] and the Latin American conferences of Wiener and Sert, throughout the 1940s.

Particularly intense were Josep Lluís Sert's relations with South American countries: entrusted with the organisation of the CIAM VI in Bridgewater (1947) in which he was to be appointed president, he left for England after Town Planning Associates had already received the order for their drafting of the *Plan Piloto de Chimbote*, one of the many commissions given to them by various countries in the region. The Peruvian commission came after Town Planning Associates' proposal for Rio de Janeiro known as Cidade dos Motores (1943–1946, see I.2.2.), and before the commissions for the drafting of: the *Plan Piloto de Tumaco* (1948–1949); *Plan Piloto de Medellín* (in collaboration with Le Corbusier, 1948–1952); *Plan Piloto de Bogotá* (in collaboration with Le Corbusier and H. Ritter, 1949–1953); Ciudad Piar (in collaboration with Carlos Guinand Baldo, Moisés Bencerraf, 1951–1953); Conjuntos Habitacionales en Pomona (in Maracaibo, in collaboration with Carlos Guinand Baldo, Moisés

64 Ibid., p. 76.

65 'authentic and clear forms that will be like guides for Brazilian architects'. Ibid., pp. 68–69.

66 Ibid., pp. 185–195.

67 In Argentina and later in Brazil and Colombia. Argentinians Jorge Ferrari-Hardoy and Juan Kurchan had worked with Le Corbusier on the *Plan Director de Buenos Aires* between 1937 and 1938. See Liernur, Jorge Francisco, *Escritos de arquitectura del siglo XX en América Latina* (Madrid / Seville, 2002).

Nuevo Palacio Municipal de Lima
Image of the new municipal palace of Lima on the cover of the Peruvian magazine
Lima
1944
El Arquitecto Peruano (August 1944)

Bencerraf, 1952–1953); Centro Cívico de Puerto Ordaz (1951–1953); and finally, the *Plan Piloto de La Habana* (in collaboration with Seeyle, Stevenson, Value, Knecht, 1955–1958).[68]

These precedents explain the wide acceptance of Western urban planning instruments among Peruvian architects: the inclusion of the contents of the 1946 urban planning legislation in the final recommendations of the VI Congreso Panamericano de Arquitectos was supported not only by the professionals organised around the Instituto de Urbanismo del Perú, such as Fernando Belaúnde Terry, but also by the younger members of Agrupación Espacio, whose figurehead was the Peruvian architect Luis Miró Quesada Garland. The members of Espacio occupied managerial positions in charge of public planning and housing policies in Peru – especially in the Oficina Nacional de Planeamiento y Urbanismo and the Corporación Nacional de Vivienda – which in 1947 were fully operational, already developing master plans and housing projects for the main cities of the Andean country, as was the case in the *Plan Piloto de Lima* (1947–1949).

The success of the democracy-development-planning triad, promoted by European planners who moved to the United States of America (Richard Neutra, Paul Lester Wiener and, above all, Josep Lluís Sert), can be explained in the historical relationship between Latin America and Western Europe.

I.3. Agrupación Espacio and the European architects who migrated to Peru

In the second quarter of the twentieth century, foreign and domestic publications played an important role in the dissemination of the new architecture in Peru. From the articles and monographs that reported on examples from other American countries, the students of the Sección Especial de Arquitectos Constructores of the Escuela Nacional de Ingenieros learnt about the overcoming of the Peruvian late-eclectic architectural repertoire. The Escuela's library had architectural magazines from Europe and the United States in its catalogue.[69] Together with these, *El Arquitecto Peruano* had begun, in 1937, to inform the wider public about architectural production beyond the border[70] (see I.2.1.). The Peruvian magazine was characterised in the first years of its existence by a very heterogeneous choice of published projects. The ambiguous critical direction in the magazine's editorial choices was highlighted by Luis Miró Quesada,[71] an architect who graduated from the Escuela Nacional de Ingenieros in 1937, his well-to-do family associated with politics and publishing.

68 Rovira, Josep María, *José Luis Sert (1901–1983)* (Milan, 2000), pp. 115–166.
69 Rodríguez, Katya, *Historia de la Universidad Nacional de Ingeniería: La apertura a espacios nuevos (1930–1955), vol. III* (Lima, 1999), pp. 85–86.
70 Huapaya, José Carlos, *Fernando Belaúnde Terry y el ideario moderno: arquitectura y urbanismo en el Perú entre 1936 y 1968* (Lima, 2014), p. 93.
71 Luis José Antonio Miró Quesada Garland (Lima, 1914–1994). A teacher, journalist, art critic and essayist, he wrote the book *Espacio en el tiempo* in 1945 and led the formation of *Agrupación Espacio* in 1947, structuring the theoretical foundations and then publishing several articles in *Espacio*, the Peruvian collective's magazine of the same name.

I.3.1. **Luis Miró Quesada, mentor of Agrupación Espacio (1943–1949)**

In one of his writings, published by *El Arquitecto Peruano* in 1943, Miró Quesada claimed the potential role of the architect in the dissemination of modern European culture. Since Belaúnde, as the magazine's editor, had the opportunity to illustrate new developments in architectural trends to a wide audience, Quesada's contribution implicitly denounced the uncritical choice of works to be published. As a response to *El Arquitecto Peruano*'s editorial direction, Miró Quesada's work, entitled *Espacio en el tiempo: La arquitectura moderna como fenómeno cultural*,[72] was published in 1945.

The volume collected the contributions on architecture that Quesada had published since the second half of the 1930s in the Peruvian newspaper *El Comercio*, where he claimed the need for artistic expressions that reflected modern culture. A supporter of the ideals of the modern movement and a scholar of the thought and work of some of its main figures (including Sigfried Giedion, Le Corbusier, Henry-Russell Hitchcock, Philip Johnson, Frank Lloyd Wright, Ludwig Mies van der Rohe, etc.), the Peruvian architect drew on their work to support his theses.[73]

As such, the architectural examples selected by Miró Quesada illustrated the innovations in the field of sanitation, such as sunlight, ventilation and minimum living space. The projects presented in *Espacio en el tiempo* also emphasised the use of a spatial distribution and a structural scheme permitted by the adoption of the free plan, as well as a formal composition of floors and volumes without ornamentation. In addition to the work of the modern masters, Miró Quesada included a collection of images of archetypes (such as the Colosseum and the Parthenon) and elements taken from tradition (such as the *moucharabiehs*), proposing a historical continuity in contemporary architectural production. In this way, Miró Quesada's text sought to re-evaluate elements of culture and place, criticising the systematic copying of academicism and the uncritical use of the linguistic repertoire of the International Style.[74]

Luis Miró Quesada's message was also particularly convincing because the theories expounded in his writings found direct application in his professional practice. That was the case in the construction of the Casa Huiracocha (Lima, 1947–1948).[75] Unlike other architectural typologies, in which economic or social reasons permitted the use of a modern language, in 1940s Peru the single-family dwelling of the bourgeoisie was still associated with an eclectic style of historical origin.[76] In this context, the construction of Casa Huiracocha became a cultural manifesto that brought the work of European and North American architects closer to the younger generation of Peruvian colleagues.

Espacio en el Tiempo
Cover of the book by Luis Miró Quesada, published in Lima in 1945
Lima

Espacio en el tiempo: La arquitectura como fenómeno cultural (1945)

72 See Miró Quesada, Luis, *Espacio en el tiempo: la arquitectura moderna como fenómeno cultural* (Lima, 1945).

73 Miró Quesada, Luis, 'Testimonios y Reflexiones: Inicios de la Arquitectura Moderna en Lima', *Documentos de arquitectura y urbanismo* (1987), pp. 41–47.

74 Miró Quesada, Luis, *Espacio en el tiempo: la arquitectura moderna como fenómeno cultural* (Lima, 1945), p. 75.

75 'Casa en San Felipe', *Espacio* (April 1950), p. 7.

76 See 'Residencia en La Punta', *El Arquitecto Peruano* (August 1937); 'La Vivienda Obrera en el Perú', *El Arquitecto Peruano* (September 1939).

DESDE LA CALLE. La solución de problemas de vistas y asoleamiento ha llevado al arquitecto a una expresión básicamente significativa. El balcón enmarcando el ventanal, enseña, con acertado tratamiento plástico, el logro de las funciones propuestas: vista, protección.
Tratamiento de las superficies y colorido empleados como elementos de composición —que los son, a despecho de quienes los suplantan con cornisas, portadas y pegotes— dan un mentis a da equivocada idea de que la arquitectura contemporánea descuida los valores estéticos en aras de un frío mecanicismo.

The spatial organisation and volumetric composition of this dwelling find inspiration in works by Frank Lloyd Wright (such as his Prairie Houses, with their use of two-colour exposed brick in horizontal bands, as well as the adoption of differences in height to define spaces); by Ludwig Mies van der Rohe (whose Tugendhat House, with its arrangement of a curved, full-height wall delimits the rooms) and Le Corbusier (in the Maison Cook, with the use of broken parts, created by the retreat of its façade, or even his Villa Savoye, with its curvilinear dividers on the roof-garden). To these, Miró Quesada combined local references, such as the exposed stone plinth and the wooden jalousies on the roof.

The Casa Huiracocha represented one of the first attempts to blend Western and local elements, bringing North American architecture and the European avant-garde of the inter-war period closer to the students at the Escuela Nacional de Ingenieros at that time.

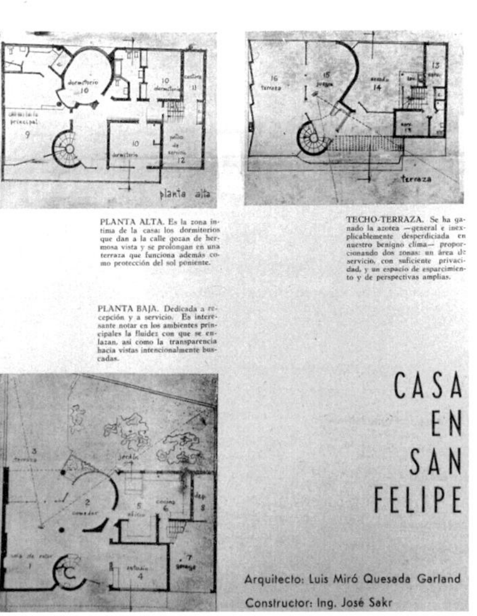

PLANTA ALTA. Es la zona íntima de la casa: los dormitorios que dan a la calle gozan de hermosa vista y se prolongan en una terraza que funciona además como protección del sol poniente.

TECHO-TERRAZA. Se ha ganado la azotea —general e inexplicablemente desperdiciada en nuestro benigno clima— proporcionando dos zonas: un área de servicio, con suficiente privacidad, y un espacio de esparcimiento y de perspectivas amplias.

PLANTA BAJA. Dedicada a recepción y a servicio. Es interesante notar en los ambientes principales la fluidez con que se enlazan, así como la transparencia hacia vistas intencionalmente buscadas.

CASA EN SAN FELIPE

Arquitecto: Luis Miró Quesada Garland
Constructor: Ing. José Sakr

Casa en San Felipe
Article about the Casa Huiracocha by Luis Miró Quesada
Espacio (April 1950)

I.3.2. The manifesto *Expresión de Principios de la Agrupación Espacio* (1945–1947)

Agrupación Espacio was a Peruvian group of intellectuals, engaged in the mid-twentieth century dissemination of contemporary cultural production, their fields being the arts, architecture and urbanism. Formed largely by young architects (but also plastic artists, musicians, anthropologists, writers, etc.), this collective was formed as a response to the late-eclectic cultural manifestations then present in the Peruvian context. The awareness of the decay of historicist languages in various Latin American countries, brought to fruition by Peruvian architecture students, was translated into several initiatives undertaken by them in the immediate post-war period.

One of the first public stances against late-eclectic architecture took place during a study trip to southern Peru between September and October 1946 by four architecture students (Adolfo Córdova, Julio Ferrand, José Polar and Carlos Williams). In Cusco, in September of that year, Córdova and Williams wrote an open letter to the newspaper *El Sol* in response to an article that proposed the prescriptive use of a visual language of pre-Hispanic and viceregal origin, known as neo-Cusqueño. The young students contested the adoption of this style in the new buildings in the historic centre of the Andean city.[77] Soon after, in Arequipa, Polar, Córdova and Williams were commissioned by the Club Internacional to design their institutional headquarters. The project[78] (1946–1947, and its extension, 1954–1955) was to become an emblematic

77 See Córdova, Adolfo and Williams, Carlos, 'El Cuzco Monumental e Intangible', *El Sol* (30 September 1946).

building of the rationalist creed, due to its spatial layout, the seriality of the structure expressed in its forms and the use of industrial materials, such as reinforced concrete and glass.

Belaúnde's uncritical selection of works to be published in *El Arquitecto Peruano*, which presented buildings with modern designs alongside eclectic works, prompted the architecture students to involve Luis Miró Quesada in publishing a new periodical. At Miró Quesada's suggestion, they formed a group to share their principles. They took a public stance with a document, published on 15 May 1947 in the Peruvian national newspaper *El Comercio*, entitled *Expresión de Principios de la Agrupación Espacio*.[79] It was a manifesto in which the collective denounced Peru's indifference to the contemporary cultural revolution taking place internationally.

Following a second publication of the manifesto in the *El Arquitecto Peruano* magazine,[80] the members of Espacio started their first cultural activities embracing the fields of music, theatre, painting, literature, architecture and, later, urbanism. They used two channels for this: first came the organisation of seminal public events in the year of its creation (among them a cycle of live and radio lectures, as well as the publication of their activities in the newspaper *El Comercio*, between 1947 and 1950) and the creation of the magazine *Espacio*, published between 1949 and 1951 (see III.3.).

Proyecto para el Club Internacional de Tiro al Blanco en Arequipa
Adolfo Córdova, José Polar, Carlos Williams
1946–1948
El Arquitecto Peruano (June 1948)

Arequipa construye el moderno Club Internacional
Adolfo Córdova, José Polar, Carlos Williams
1954–1955
El Arquitecto Peruano (May–June 1956)

Illustration from the book *Lecciones de Elementos y Teoría de la Arqutitectura*
1944
Ricardo de Jaxa Malachowski Kulisicz in *Lecciones de Elementos y Teoría de la Arqutitectura* (2015)

I.3.3. Espacio's participation in the dissemination of European culture in Peru, from the Reforma Universitaria to the exhibition *Latin American Architecture Since 1945* (1945–1955)

Espacio had two important objectives: the first encompassed the overcoming of cultural production based on historical-ornamental repertoires, in favour of references drawn from international trends and specific Peruvian characteristics (geographical, climatic, historical); and then came the identification of urban planning as a discipline, as a fundamental tool for the development of Peruvian cities. The acceptance of these objectives in local intellectual and professional circles, facilitated by the visits of European architects to the Latin American region financed by US governments (see I.2.2.), allowed many members of Espacio to increase their presence in the training of new architects, in the planning of Peruvian cities and in architectural criticism.

The information that architecture students at the Escuela received from national publications, most notably the *El Arquitecto Peruano* and *Espacio en el Tiempo*, clashed with a professional education centred on the

78 See 'Proyecto para el Club Internacional de Tiro al Blanco en Arequipa', *El Arquitecto Peruano* (June 1948); 'Arequipa construye el moderno Club Internacional', *El Arquitecto Peruano* (May–June 1956).

79 See 'Expresión de principios de la Agrupación Espacio', *El Comercio* (15 May 1947).

80 See 'Expresión de principios de la Agrupación Espacio', *El Arquitecto Peruano* (June 1947).

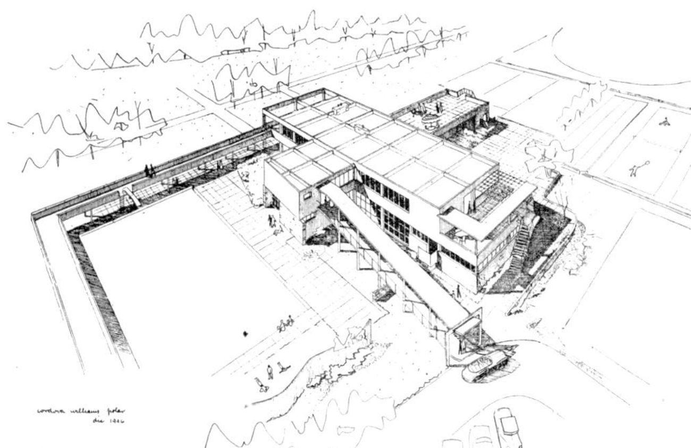

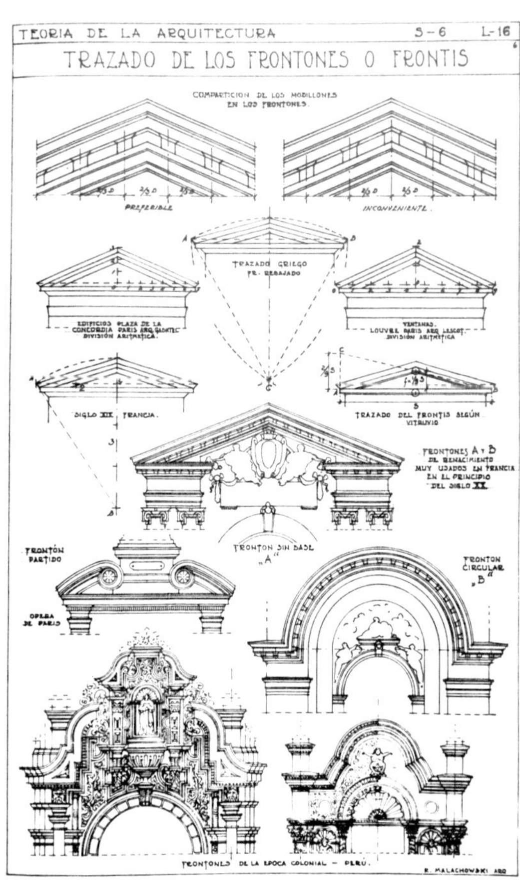

81 The Polish Ryszard Jaxa-Małachowski Kulisicz, having trained at the École des Beaux-Arts (1909–1910), moved to Peru in 1911 and began teaching at the Escuela Nacional de Ingenieros from 1912. He organised the Architectural Composition course (Elementos y teoria de la Arquitectura) following his own Parisian training experience. Alvarez, Syra, *La formación en arquitectura en el Perú: antecedentes, inicios y desarrollo hasta 1955* (Lima, 2006), pp. 131–148.

study of classical antiquities, themselves modelled on the Parisian École des Beaux-Arts.[81] This growing awareness led young Peruvian undergraduates to demand a change in the architecture curriculum, from a model that favoured theoretical courses, to one based on laboratory teaching, as was the case in other Latin American countries in the second half of the 1940s. In Chile, the effects of university reform, which affected the curricula of the Universidad de Chile (1945) and the Universidad Católica (1949), resulted in the re-founding of the Valparaiso School of Architecture, one of the most radical Latin American pedagogical experiments. In Cuba, the School of Architecture of the Universidad de La Habana, two years after the protests of architecture students in 1947, invited Walter Gropius for a lecture series.[82]

In Peru, the Reforma Universitaria (1945–1946) was implemented in 1946 at the Escuela Nacional de Ingenieros. The renewal in the academic sphere, which had seen the participation of Adolfo Córdova, a future founding member of Espacio, included new subjects related to housing policy and urban planning. The drawing workshop, which at the time was the bedrock subject for the entire course of studies – modelled on the École des Beaux-Arts in Paris – was rechristened as a design workshop. Another important change: there would no longer be only one teacher from the second to the fifth year, as two workshops were established in 1946, and later five, beginning in 1955.

With the support of then-director Rafael Marquina, several members of Espacio (such as Córdova) participated in the changes to the architecture curriculum envisaged by the university reform. These changes made it possible for Luis Miró Quesada and other signatories of the collective's manifesto, such as Luis Dorich (Teoría y Práctica de la Composición Urbana) and the German Paul Linder (Estética de la Arquitectura) to join the teaching staff. With the reform, Fernando Belaúnde Terry himself was made Professor and, from 1950, Director

***Plan Piloto*'s survey of existing built-up areas and proposal**
Lima
Oficina Nacional de Planeamiento y Urbanismo (ONPU)
1949

ONPU in *Al Rescate de Lima* (1997)

82 See Pérez Oyarzún, Fernando, *Chile*, in Bergdoll, Barry et al. (ed.), *Latin America in Construction: Architecture 1955–1980* (New York, 2015), p. 158; Luis Rodríguez, Eduardo, *Cuba*, Ibid., p. 191.

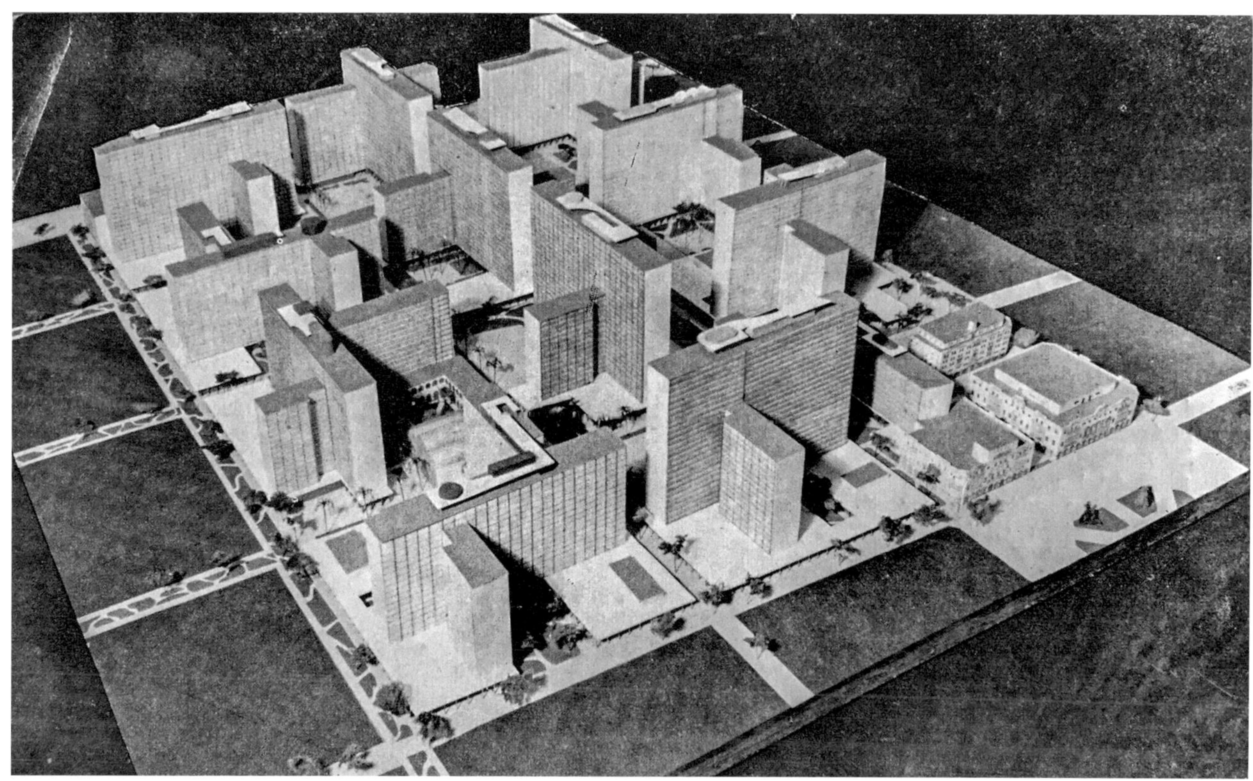

***Plan Piloto*'s volumetric study for the historic centre**
Lima
Oficina Nacional de Planeamiento y Urbanismo (ONPU)
1947–1949
ONPU in *Plan Piloto de Lima* (1949)

of the Department, contributing decisively to the adoption of these curricular changes. In 1955 the design laboratories were directed by Adolfo Córdova in the first year; Santiago Agurto in the second; Luis Miró Quesada in the third; Javier Cayo in the fourth; and the Italian Mario Bianco in the fifth: all were members of Espacio.

Similarly, members of Espacio occupied managerial positions in ONPU (Oficina Nacional de Planeamiento y Urbanismo, see I.2.2.), including Luis Dorich (director) and Mario Bianco (head of the project office), who participated in the drafting of the *Plan Piloto de Lima* (ONPU, with advice from Josep Lluís Sert and Ernesto Nathan Rogers, 1947–1949).

The ONPU identified the *Plan Regulador de la Gran Lima*, of which the *Plan Piloto* was an integral part, as the key instrument for applying the precepts of the Functional City to the Peruvian reality.[83] The figure of Le Corbusier was one of the seminal European references since the birth of Espacio. Two months after the publication of *Expresión de Principios de la Agrupación*

83 See Belaúnde Terry, Fernando, 'Puntos de vista… Un gran paso adelante', *El Arquitecto Peruano* (June 1947).

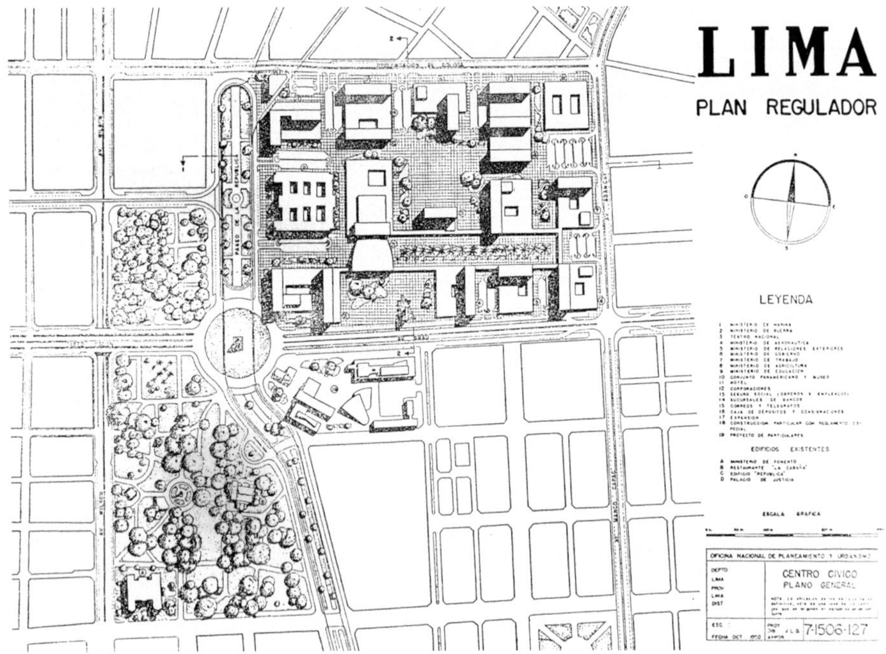

***Plan Piloto*'s proposal for the Civic Centre**
Lima
Oficina Nacional de Planeamiento y Urbanismo (ONPU)
1950
ONPU in *Al Rescate de Lima* (1997)

Espacio, Adolfo Córdova, Carlos Williams y Samuel Pérez-Barreto wrote to the Franco-Swiss master to invite him to Peru. Although there is no record of a reply, Le Corbusier's influence on the members of Espacio, in the form of the modern master's writings and statements, never ceased.[84]

The *Charte d'Athènes* had a considerable influence on Espacio's ideas. The primary objectives discussed in the CIAM VI – sunshine, minimum standards for open spaces and housing – were identified as crucial issues for improving the living conditions of the inhabitants of large cities such as Lima. Josep Lluís Sert, who became a consultant to ONPU in 1948–1949 during the gestation of the *Plan Piloto de Lima*, further facilitated the adoption of CIAM urban planning principles in the planning of the Peruvian capital. For Sert, who until then had worked on newly founded Latin American cities – in the cases of Rio de Janeiro or Chimbote (see I.2.2.) – intervention in a historical city like Lima represented an important professional opportunity. As a result, at the beginning of 1948, he proposed to ONPU the development of an urban planning study, which greatly influenced the state agency's plans for the Peruvian capital.[85]

The ONPU incorporated some of the conclusions reached by Town Planning Associates in its studies for the *Plan Piloto de Lima* and the Sector Central,[86] the consolidated core of the city: the creation of a pedestrian area in

84 See Le Corbusier (Charles-Édouard Jeanneret-Gris), '¡Cuando las catedrales eran blancas!', *Espacio* (May 1949), p. 1; 'La morada del hombre', *Espacio* (August 1949), p. 1; 'Foro sobre el Cusco', *Espacio* (1950), p. 2.
85 Huapaya, José Carlos, *Fernando Belaúnde Terry y el ideario moderno: arquitectura y urbanismo en el Perú entre 1936 y 1968* (Lima, 2014), p. 255.
86 Area bounded by the Rímac River to the north, Avenida Abancay to the east, Avenida Bolivia to the south and Avenida Wilson and Avenida Tacna to the west.
87 See ONPU, 'La Hoja de Urbanismo', *El Arquitecto Peruano* (July 1949).
88 Ibid.
89 Huapaya, José Carlos, *Fernando Belaúnde Terry y el ideario moderno: arquitectura y urbanismo en el Perú entre 1936 y 1968* (Lima, 2014), p. 253.
90 See 'Agrupación Espacio 1947–1949', *El Comercio* (19 May 1949).
91 Ludeña, Wiley, *Tres buenos tigres. Piqueras – Belaunde – La Agrupación Espacio. Vanguardia y urbanismo en el Perú en el siglo XX* (Huancayo, 2004), p. 152.

Luis Miró Quesada G.

Premio Chavín de la Arquitectura

El Premio Chavín de la Arquitectura de 1954 ha sido adjudicado al Arquitecto Luis Miró Quesada Garland por su contribución profesional en la obra "Edificio Radio El Sol" recientemente construído en esta capital por la firma Graña y Montero.

Con este trofeo nacional se ha rendido homenaje justiciero a un profesional destacado y a un prestigioso maestro de arquitectura. Miró Quesada Garland egresó de la Escuela Nacional de Ingenieros hace unos dieciocho años y desde entonces ha hecho una labor decidida y tenaz en pro de la arquitectura contemporánea, auspiciando todo lo que significara adelanto y renovación en esta rama del saber. Al frente de su propia oficina profesional así como funcionario de la Beneficencia Pública de Lima ha desempeñado y desempeña importantes misiones dedicando además buena parte de su tiempo al dictado de las cátedras "Análisis de la función arquitectónica" y "Diseño arquitectónico de 3er. año" que con el mayor acierto y dedicación regenta en la Facultad de Arquitectura, a cuyo desarrollo y progreso ha contribuído notablemente.

Entre los muchos cargos de honor a que ha sido frecuentemente llamado por su prestigio profesional, su capacidad y hombría de bien, se cuenta la Presidencia de la Sociedad de Arquitectos (1952-1954).

Goza también Miró Quesada de merecido prestigio como crítico de arte, colaborando a menudo con los principales diarios y revistas de la capital, habiendo sido presidente y fundador de la Agrupación "Espacio".

"El Arquitecto Peruano", estrechamente vinculado al establecimiento del Premio Chavín, se complace de que, en acto de estricta justicia, haya sido adjudicado en esta oportunidad, como en las anteriores, con el mayor acierto.

Luis Miró Quesada G. / Premio Chavín de la Arquitectura
Article on Luis Miró Quesada's work, awarded with the Chavín Prize
Lima
1955
El Arquitecto Peruano (May 1955)

it; the widening of all streets along its perimeter; the provision of parking areas close by; the construction of a civic centre on the land formerly occupied by the old penitentiary, toward the southern city's expansion area. In this way, ONPU proposed for the Sector Central the strengthening of its historical administrative functions by the densification of the city's fabric.

From an architectural point of view, this plan favoured the spread of the multi-storey building type, endowing Lima's historic centre with an extremely uneven skyline, still a fixture of its urban profile today. The construction of these buildings was the structuring part of a process of urban regeneration based on increasing the scale of constructions in the centre of Lima: the reference building regulation contemplated the formation of consortia of owners, to allow for the amalgamation of building land,[87] and the adoption of territorial building indices, to define the urban parameters to be used in new constructions.[88]

The influence of Le Corbusier's theories on the organisation of the city by functions was explicitly recognised by Sert, who also reported to the Swiss-French master on the usefulness of the 'Modulor,' for establishing the maximum dimensions of buildings and distances between them, in drafting the *Plan Piloto de Lima.*[89] However, this was not the only modern influence on Lima's planning: the regional framing of this urban proposal shows similarities with the Italian experience of the ABRR group for the *Piano Regionale Piemontese* (Giovanni Astengo, Mario Bianco, Nello Renacco, Aldo Rizzotti, 1944–1946). The presence of Mario Bianco, a member of Espacio, would contribute to the dissemination of the Turin study (see III.2, III.6.). Given Bianco's Italian experiences, his participation in ONPU would become important for the affirmation of the discipline of town planning on a local level. This was, after all, one of the objectives recognised as a priority by the Peruvian collective in a note dated 19 May 1949[90] (see III.3.).

The dissemination of contemporary architecture, the primary objective of the collective, saw its greatest effort in the participation of some Espacio members in the organisation of the US exhibition *Latin America Architecture Since 1945* (1955). The collaboration of Espacio members in the Latin American exhibition took place in 1954, one year before the Peruvian collective disbanded.[91] Held in 1955, the exhibition organised by the Museum of Modern Art (MoMA) in New York offered an overview of architecture in the region through the works of 56 firms from 11 countries. Interest from the US in the architectural production of the southern countries was increased with the start of the Good Neighbour Policies adopted by the administration of Democrat Franklin D. Roosevelt's administration mentioned above (see I.2.2.).

US foreign strategies and the activities organised around them thus found important points of convergence, reinforced by the presence of figures responsible for the organisation of these exhibitions, who held positions both in the museum and in US government institutions. On the MoMA Board of Trustees appeared several people who also worked in the Department of State. Such was the case of Nelson D. Rockefeller, head of The Office of the Coordinator of Inter-American Affairs. Reporting to Rockefeller in the Department of State were John E. Abbott, Executive Vice President of MoMA, and Monroe Wheeler, Director of MoMA's Exhibitions Department.[92]

Latin American Architecture Since 1945 represented a concluding point in the Pan-American architecture exhibitions organised by MoMA during the first half of the century and inaugurated with *Modern Architecture: International Exhibition* (1932).[93] Following the experience of the New York exhibition *Early Modern Architecture: Chicago 1870–1910*[94] (1933), in 1955 Hitchcock emphasised the spread of multi-storey buildings throughout Latin America. Towards the end of the exhibition catalogue, Hitchcock presented a section called *Urban Façades*, a collection of such buildings constructed between 1945 and 1955 in major cities.

It is interesting to highlight the curatorial synergy between Belaúnde and Henry-Russell Hitchcock, since both Peruvian multi-storey buildings featured – the Edificio Ostolaza (Enrique Seoane Ros, Lima, 1952–1954, Chavín Prize 1953) and the Edificio Radio El Sol (Luis Miró Quesada, Lima, 1953–1954, Chavín Prize 1954) – were reviewed in both the Peruvian magazine and the North American catalogue.[95]

By contrast, examples of Latin American architectural production attributable to regionalism found very little space. This lack of interest was reflected in the small representation of Peruvian works characterised by a synthesis of local traditions and international innovations. Despite the great interest coming from members of Agrupación Espacio, Peruvian housing production, which boasted multiple examples during those years, was not selected. Buildings that were widely disseminated in specialist publications, such as Luis Miró Quesada's Casa Huiracocha (see I.3.1.) or the conspicuous number of residences designed by the Swiss Theodor Cron (see IV.3., IV.4.), were omitted from the 1955 New York overview.

The importation of modern movement principles into urban planning and architecture did not depend exclusively on the relationships established between Peruvian intellectuals and European designers who had emigrated to the United States of America, such as Josep Lluís Sert or Paul Lester Wiener. The acceptance and integration of these principles into local practices is also,

92 Liernur, Jorge Francisco, *Escritos de arquitectura del siglo XX en América Latina* (Madrid / Seville, 2002), p. 166.

93 See *Modern Architecture: International Exhibition* (New York, 1932); Goodwin, Philip Lippincott, *Brazil Builds: architecture new and old, 1652–1942* (New York, 1943); Museum of Modern Art, *Built in USA: 1932–1944* (New York, 1944); *Two cities: planning in North and South America* (New York, 1947).

94 Museum of Modern Art exhibition in which Hitchcock collaborated with Philip Johnson, held in New York between 18 January and 23 February 1933.

95 See Hitchcock, Henry-Russell, *Latin American Architecture Since 1945* (New York, 1955).

and to a large extent, attributable to the presence of European professionals who moved to the Andean country. It is the latter who, by providing their expertise and getting involved personally in local institutions and practices, have contributed to the development of Peruvian architecture and urbanism in their areas of expertise: to the renewal of university teaching, in the experience of the German Paul Linder; to the affirmation of territorial planning, as in the case of the Italian Mario Bianco; and to the development of regional architecture, by the Swiss Theodor Cron. The following three chapters investigate the international relations cultivated by these designers, who were the most prolific of the Europeans who emigrated to Peru in the mid-twentieth century, to better understand the dynamics that facilitated their professional affirmation and the consolidation of modern architecture in this country.

PAA

PART II

On European designers working in Peru in the twentieth century

PAUL LINDER (1897–1968): A BAUHÄUSLER AT THE ESCUELA NACIONAL DE INGENIEROS

1897

Paul Linder's birth (Lennep, Remscheid, Germany)

1914

First World War

1916

Linder takes part in the First World War as a pilot in the Luftstreitkräfe

1919

Linder attends Baugewerkschule and Staatliche Bauhaus

1921

SPAIN Linder, Ernst Neufert and Kurt Löwengard, on the advice of Walter Gropius, collaborate with the Institut d'Estudis Catalans

1924

ITALY Linder's six-month stay

SPAIN *La construcción de rascacielos en Alemania* (Paul Linder, Madrid)

1925

Linder works with Alfred Breslauer

1927

SPAIN Linder's second stay

1928–1929

Linder works with Taut and Hoffmann

Linder marries Ruth Breslauer

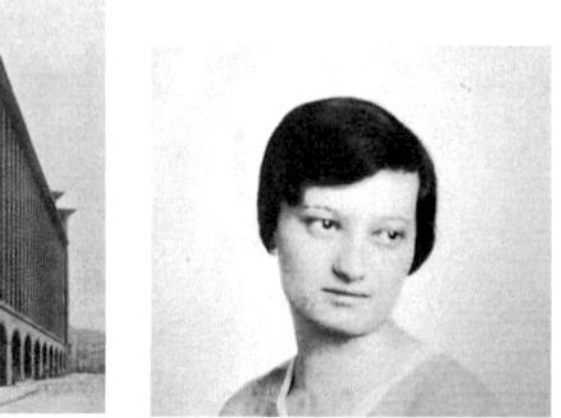

1890s

1910s

1920s

1931

Birth of Linder's first child (Alfredo)

Apartment in Berlin (Paul Linder, Berlin, 1931)

1932

Birth of Linder's second child (Gaspar)

St. Thomaskirche (Paul Linder, Berlin, 1930–1932)

1933

House in Zehlendorf (Paul Linder, Berlin, 1932–1933)

1936–1939

Spanish Civil War

1939

Beginning of the Second World War

1940

Mussolini declares war on the Allies

1945

End of the Second World War

USA Good Neighbour Policy (1933–1945)

1930s

1940s

1930

Edificio Gildemeister (Werner Benno Lange, Lima, 1928–1930)

1937

El Arquitecto Peruano's first issue

Establishment of the Sociedad de Arquitectos del Perú

1938

Establishment of the Consejo Nacional de Urbanismo

1939

Paul Linder moves to Peru

1940

Earthquake and tsunami in Lima and Callao

1940

National Census

GERMAN, EUROPEAN, AMERICAN EXPERIENCES

1947

UK CIAM VI (Bridgewater)

1952

Linder makes a stay in Europe, between May and September, with stops in the UK, The Netherlands, Germany, France, Switzerland and Italy

1953

CHILE Linder travels to Santiago

1955

USA *Latin American Architecture Since 1945* (Museum of Modern Art, New York)

1940s

PERUVIAN EXPERIENCES

1942

Linder starts teaching at the Pontificia Universidad Católica del Perú

Nueva Residencia de la Nunciatura Apostólica (P. Linder, H. Velarde, Lima, 1939–1942)

1946

Reforma Universitaria. Linder starts teaching at Escuela Nacional de Ingenieros

1947

Iglesia de San Felipe Apóstol (Paul Linder, Lima, 1945–1947)

Manifesto Expresión de principios de la Agrupación Espacio

VI Congreso Panamericano de Arquitectos (Lima and Cusco)

1948

Parroquia de Nuestra Señora de Lobatón (Paul Linder, Lima, 1941–1948)

1950s

1950

Edificio Arnodi (Paul Linder, Lima, 1950)

1950

Clínica y convento Stella Maris (Paul Linder, Lima, 1948–1950)

Colegio Santa Ursula (Paul Linder, H. Velarde, Lima, 1939–1950)

1953

Josef Albers in Peru

Walter Gropius and Josep Lluís Sert in Peru

1954

Walter Gropius in Peru

Henry-Russell Hitchcock in Peru to gather material for the exhibition *Latin American Architecture Since 1945*

1968

Paul Linder dies (Haar, Germany)

1957

MEXICO Linder travels to Mexico City

1960s

1958

Colegio y convento Santa María Goretti (Paul Linder, Lima, 1956–1958)

1959

Cervecería San Miguel (Paul Linder, Piura, 1957–1959)

1960

Colegio Alexander von Humboldt (Paul Linder, Lima, 1958–1960)

1962–1964

Linder stops university teaching

1963

Laboratorios Hoffmann-La Roche (Paul Linder, Lima, 1960–1963)

Chapter II
Paul Linder (1897–1968), a Bauhäusler at the Escuela Nacional de Ingenieros

II.1. **Training in Germany, trips to Spain (1916–1924)**

Paul Linder,[1] a German architect, critic and university lecturer, had a long and complex education, conditioned by a political framework that led him at the end of the inter-war period to emigrate to the American continent. During this phase, from 1916 to 1931, he made several trips to Spain and Italy, encountering Latin cultures and learning Spanish, a language that would be useful to him during his long stay in Peru (1939–1968). Educated in Aachen, Weimar and Munich, he shared experiences with German colleagues, including Ernst Neufert, and established relationships with several prominent figures, including the then director of the Staatliches Bauhaus, Walter Gropius, who would influence his training and professional work.

The early Bauhaus presents aesthetic experiences, frequently in stark contrast that hinged on the opposition between the *Gemeinschaft* (community, as the expression of an organic life) and the *Gesellschaft* (society, as the result of a mechanical organisation).[2] The Italian historian Francesco Dal Co identifies, in the period between the end of the Bismarckian era and the collapse of the Weimar Republic, the desire for harmony in a world experienced through laceration and difference.[3] Linder's experience speaks to that tension between culture (internal, organic) and civilisation (external, mechanical).

German-Spanish exchanges in the first half of the twentieth century largely reflected Germany's foreign policies. Motivations, at once economic, political and cultural, led in 1907 to the founding of the Deutscher Werkbund, the most important and prestigious pre-war cultural institution in Germany, aimed at balancing the needs of art with those of industry.[4] Companies that had participated in its creation turned to artists to take care of their image in an effective and homogenous way, as was the case in the collaborations between Peter Behrens and the Allgemeine Elektricitäts-Gesellschaft (AEG), a company that had a considerable presence in pre-war Spain. The Deutscher Werkbund's programmes fostered a cultural development driven by the extraordinary economic growth of imperial Germany and had noteworthy consequences in the architecture that was being built in the Iberian country in those years.

The outbreak of the First World War had a great effect in Germany: several avant-garde artists saw their enlistment as an opportunity for spiritual renewal in a Nietzschean sense, while Wilhelm II and most of the population saw German participation as an opportunity to definitively consolidate the country's role as a leading power. But the ominous consequences changed the attitude of intellectuals towards the war, leading architects and artists to gather around the figure of Bruno Taut, who had founded the Arbeitsrat für Kunst, a workers

1 Paul Linder Lob (Lennep, Remscheid, 10 December 1897 – Overath, Cologne, 16 October 1968). The son of Philipp Linder, headmaster of the Catholic school in Lennep, he remained in the district of the German town of Remscheid until 1916, moving that year to Munich after completing his studies in the Real-gymnasium.

2 Dal Co, Francesco, *Abitare nel moderno* (Rome / Bari, 1985), p. 13.

3 Dal Co, Francesco, *Teorie del moderno: architettura, Germania, 1880–1920* (Roma / Bari, 1982), pp. 3–5.

4 There is a vast bibliography on the subject, Droste's work from 1990 is particularly noteworthy. See Droste, Magdalena, *Bauhaus: 1919–1933* (Cologne, 1990), p. 12.

council for art, after the November Revolution. A year earlier, Walter Gropius had emphasised the 'necessity of a new alignment of intellectuals,'[5] and he later became head of the council.[6]

At this juncture, his years as a pilot in the Luftstreitkräfte, the air force component of the German Empire's army, left a deep mark on Linder: in 1916, he had to interrupt his studies in architecture, which had begun in Aachen, at the Königlich Rheinisch-Westphälische Polytechnische Schule.[7] In 1918, Linder resumed his studies in Munich, at the Königlich Bayerische Technische Hochschule,[8] although he had to suspend them again for political reasons: namely, the rise in power of the National Socialists. Around this time, he left the Bavarian capital for Weimar. In 1919, he attended the Baugewerkschule, a construction school led by Paul Klopfer – with Ernst Neufert[9] and Kurt Löwengard[10] – and the Bauhaus, then directed by Gropius. He would remain in contact with the German master, even after their respective expatriations.

Gropius identified the redemption of the entire society in the revaluation of the unity of the arts in the Middle Ages, traceable to the images of the Gothic cathedral and the Bauhütte (masons' lodge). For this reason, it was the German master himself who encouraged Linder, Neufert and Löwengard to organise a study trip to Spain. Following in the footsteps of a similar learning experience Gropius himself had undertaken on the Iberian Peninsula between 1907 and 1908,[11] his students were to deepen an identity discourse based on the idealisation of Gothic art.

Once established in Spain in 1920, Linder and Neufert, by way of Gropius, got in touch with the politician, archaeologist, and architect Josep Puig i Cadafalch,[12] who commissioned them on behalf of the Institut d'Estudis Catalans to survey Gothic monuments in various Catalan locations.[13] This experience allowed Linder to make comparisons with German Gothic architecture. Above all, Linder's reflections on European art were enriched by his encounter with Antoni Gaudí,[14] whose art would leave its mark on the German designer's later works. In 1922, when Neufert had already returned to Germany, Linder extended his stay on the Iberian Peninsula, exploring Seville and Madrid.[15]

In the Spain of those years, architects such as Luis Lacasa[16] disseminated the different theories and practices of German architecture as an attempt to revitilise local production.[17] Linder, who had already returned home in the summer of 1923 and resumed his architectural studies in Munich, was visited by him. It was documented in an article entitled *Un interior expresionista*,[18] published in *Arquitectura*, the official periodical of the Spanish Sociedad Central de Arquitectos. The contribution, in which Lacasa presented Linder's design for the arrangement of his student room, initiated a long collaboration of

5 Droste, Magdalena, *Bauhaus: 1919–1933* (Köln, 1990), p. 16.

6 Among the numerous monographs dedicated to Gropius, in addition to those mentioned above, see Nerdinger, Winfried, *Walter Gropius: complete works* (Milan, 1988), p. 244; Argan, Giulio Carlo, *Walter Gropius e la Bauhaus* (Turin, 1974); Medina Warmburg, Joaquín, *Walter Gropius – proclamas de modernidad: escritos y conferencias, 1908–1934* (Barcelona, 2018).

7 Current Rheinisch-Westfälische Technische Hochschule Aachen.

8 Current Technische Universität München.

9 Freyburg , 1900 – Rolle 1986.

10 Hamburg, 1895 – London, 1940.

11 Medina Warmburg, Joaquín, *Irredentos y conversos. Presencias e influencias alemanas: de la neutralidad a la postguerra española (1914–1943)*, in Pozo, José Manuel and López, Ignasi (coords.), *Modelos alemanes e italianos para España en los años de la postguerra* (Pamplona, 2004), p. 22.

12 Mataró, 1867 – Barcelona, 1956.

13 Such as Barcelona, Vich, Poblet, Santa Creus, Tarragona, Gerona, Lérida, Mauresa and Reus. See Ludowieg Telge, Cecilia, *Paul Linder: su obra* (Lima, 1984).

14 Linder, Paul, 'Encuentros con Antonio Gaudí', *Mar del sur: Revista peruana de cultura* (1950), pp. 1–11.

15 Medina Warmburg, Joaquín (ed.), *Paul Linder, 1897–1968: de Weimar a Lima: antología de arquitectura y crítica* (Madrid, 2019), p. 422.

16 Luis Lacasa Navarro (Ribadesella, 1899 – Moscow, 1966) was a Spanish architect, urban planner and promoter of rationalist architecture in Spain. Together with Josep Lluís Sert, author of the *Pabellón de la República Española* in the 1937 International Exhibition in Paris, he had to exile himself to Moscow after the rise of Francisco Franco's totalitarian regime. Vicente Garrido, Henry, *Arquitecturas desplazadas: arquitecturas del exilio español* (Madrid, 2007), pp. 200–201.

Paul Linder as a Luftstreitkräfte pilot
Second half of the 1910s
Archivo de Arquitectura PUCP, Paul Linder Fund

Paul Linder (left) with Luis Lacasa (second right) and others reading the Catholic newspaper *El Debate*
Munich
1923
Archivo de Arquitectura PUCP, Paul Linder Fund

the then German student with the magazine. Linder would go on to become *Arquitectura*'s correspondent in Germany, publishing a total of 12 articles between 1924 and 1933.[19]

In 1924, towards the end of his architectural studies in Munich, he was awarded the Diplom-Ingenieur (with distinction in architecture); his professors were Theodor Fischer,[20] an architect detached from historicist currents (as well as a co-founder and the first President of the Deutscher Werkbund) and German Bestelmeyer,[21] whose work was in a more traditionalist style.

17 Medina Warmburg, Joaquín, 'Irredentos y conversos. Presencias e influencias alemanas: de la neutralidad a la postguerra española (1914–1943)', in Pozo, José Manuel and López, Ignasi (coords.), *Modelos alemanes e italianos para España en los años de la postguerra* (Pamplona, 2004), p. 22.

18 Lacasa, Luis, 'Un interior expresionista', *Arquitectura: órgano oficial de la Sociedad Central de Arquitectos* (1924), pp. 174–176.

II.2. **Professional practice and German works (1924–1938)**

After his university training period, between 1924 and 1929, Linder deepened his relations with southern European countries and undertook two professional collaborations, with Alfred Breslauer and Bruno Taut, which were decisive factors in his later departure for the American continent. Linder and Alfred Breslauer, a Berlin-based neoclassical designer of Jewish origin, shared experiences in the Iberian lands, albeit at separate times. In fact, Breslauer was part of that group of German designers who, thanks to the economic expansion of the Wilhelmine era, worked in pre-Francoist Spain. The search for the Spanish essence in the Kocherthaler House, designed by the Berlin architect in 1921 for the headquarters of AEG in Madrid, was part of the cultural expansion policies advanced by the Werkbund.[22] Linder collaborated with Breslauer in his Berlin studio between 1925 and 1927. There, he met the architect's daughter Ruth, who was to become his wife in 1929.

Between 1928 and 1929, Linder worked with the Taut brothers and Franz Hoffmann in their Berlin studio, collaborating on social housing projects such as the Siedlung Britz and the Siedlung Zehlendorf, encountering their ideals of transforming society through new architecture. Taut's social commitment, along with his liberation from the superfluous, had a great effect on the young architect. In 1929, he published two articles in the Spanish magazine *Arquitectura* with the titles *Arquitectos, pensad y construid con sentido social*[23] and *El arquitecto Max Taut*,[24] which idealised the role of the designer as a builder of modern, ethical and aesthetic dwellings, both useful and artistic at the same time.

In 1929, Linder opened his own practice in the German capital, where he worked until his departure for the American continent in 1938.[25] In his projects realised in Germany, both the ideals of social transformation and the essentiality of the new architecture, not to mention the historicist references acquired during his trips to Spain and his collaborations with Breslauer, can be found. In the magazine *Bauwelt*, for example, Linder published the design for his apartment in Berlin (1931), employing the same method of representation as Bruno Taut had adopted in 1924 in his book *Die Neue Wohnung: Die Frau als Schöpferin*.[26] The use of before and after photographs made it possible to document clearly the desire to eliminate all ornamentation, in an aesthetic quest through the essentiality of objects.[27]

The St. Thomaskirche (1930–1932), built in Berlin's Charlottenburg district[28] after winning first mention in an architectural competition, was Linder's most popular German achievement in the specialist press. The church took

Apartment in Berlin
View of the living area before and after renovation (top and bottom, respectively)
Berlin
Paul Linder
1931

Archivo de Arquitectura PUCP, Paul Linder Fund

19 Linder, Paul, 'La construcción de rascacielos en Alemania', *Arquitectura: órgano oficial de la Sociedad Central de Arquitectos* (1924), pp. 310–313; 'Tres ensayos sobre la nueva arquitectura alemana. Primer ensayo. A manera de introducción', Ibid. (1926), pp. 20–22; 'Tres ensayos sobre la nueva arquitectura alemana. Segundo ensayo. Los tectónicos', Ibid. (1926), pp. 235–241; 'El nuevo Bauhaus en Dessau', Ibid. (1927), pp. 110–112; 'La exposición

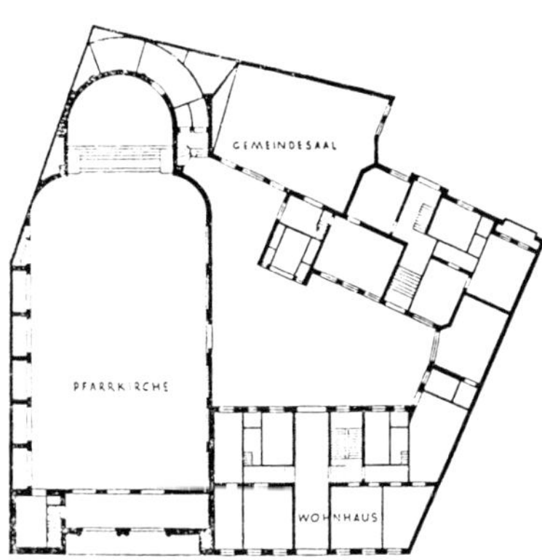

Grundriß von: St. Thomas-Kirche, Gemeindehaus, Wohnhaus

St. Thomaskirche
Floor plan and main view (top and right, respectively)
Charlottenburg, Berlin
Paul Linder
1930–1932

Archivo de Arquitectura PUCP, Paul Linder Fund

"Werkbund Ausstellung" en Stuttgart', Ibid. (1927); 'El arquitecto Max Taut', Ibid. (1929), pp. 422–430; 'Arquitectos, pensad y construid con sentido social', Ibid. (1929), pp. 12–22; 'El arquitecto Wilhelm Riphahn', Ibid. (1930), pp. 75–81; 'Sobre especialistas, sobre arquitectura universal y sobre el arquitecto hamburgés Karl Schneider', Ibid. (1930), pp. 333–339; 'Walter Gropius', Ibid. (1930), pp. 245–254; 'Exposición berlinesa de la construcción', Ibid. (1931), pp. 287–295; 'Acerca de la plástica en arquitectura. Obras de Georg Kolbe', Ibid. (1933), pp. 80–84.

up two of the guidelines learnt by the German designer during his formative period: the elimination of all superfluous elements in the work and the removal of all spatial barriers to allow the active participation of the faithful, restoring the centrality of the altar as the place for celebrating the Eucharist. The structural solution identified – the use of metal trusses that disappeared behind clinker infills – allowed for an easily identifiable volume from the outside and a completely free space inside. The design choices for this building demonstrated a profound knowledge of the written work of the Catholic priest and theologian Romano Guardini and the sacred architecture of the German expressionist architect Dominikus Böhm inspired by it.[29]

In the House in Zehlendorf (1932–1933), Linder reintroduced the same idea of a space purified of any redundant elements for the living room, just as he had done in the Berlin flat designed two years earlier. But Linder did not make strictly functionalist choices, instead dividing the family home into the living area (conceived as a neutral space that could accommodate different furniture arrangements) and other rooms (such as bedrooms) designed according to functional precepts. The collaborations of other artists in this work are noteworthy: the photo reportage was done by Ruth's sister Marianne Breslauer,[30] one of the main figures of Das Neue Sehen (New Vision); in the same photo reportage, a detail of the terrace with Georg Kolbe's sculpture,[31] *Javanese Dancer* (1920), was captured. The relations developed between Kolbe and Linder allowed the latter to plan the extension of the Berlin studio-house and to publish an article on the sculptor's work.[32]

In this early professional phase, Linder's work was characterised by the coexistence of transitional proposals towards a renewed architecture of expressionist derivation and projects marked by a far more historicist language.

St. Thomaskirche
Internal view, during assembly of the metal structure (top and bottom left, respectively)
Charlottenburg, Berlin
Paul Linder
1930–1932

Archivo de Arquitectura PUCP, Paul Linder Fund

House in Zehlendorf
Rear elevation with the sculpture by Georg Kolbe called *Javanese Dancer*
Zehlendorf, Berlin
Paul Linder
1932–1933

Marianne Breslauer in Archivo de Arquitectura PUCP, Paul Linder Fund

II.3. Trips to the American continent and the arrival in Peru (1938–1939)

The correspondence between Paul Linder and Walter Gropius in the second half of the 1930s documented the plight of the many European intellectuals who were forced to emigrate following the rise to power of the Nationalsozialistische Deutsche Arbeiterpartei. From his influential position at Harvard University, after his 1937 expatriation to the United States, Gropius sought to bring in as many designers as possible who, like Linder, could work toward the dissemination of new architecture on the American continent.[33]

Gropius wrote a letter in July 1937 informing Linder that he had nominated him for a professorship at the University of Oregon.[34] The prompt reply in a letter sent a few days later testified to the necessity and urgency for Linder, a figure not in line with the regime, to leave Germany. In thanking him for his recommendation, Linder informed Gropius of his readiness to leave for this or any other possible job offer in the US.[35]

The possibility of teaching in Oregon did not materialise, as can be deduced from a letter from Linder to his teacher in November 1937.[36] Despite this, the anti-Semitic policies of the extreme right-wing German government led the Bauhäusler to organise a trip to Princeton on his own initiative in January of the following year to meet the German art historian Hanns Swarzenski[37] and to assess the possibilities of joining a North American university. Following his stay in the USA, Linder received an offer in August 1938 of a lectureship at the Carnegie Institute of Technology in Pittsburgh, which eventually fell through due to the German architect's inability to relocate in time for the start of the academic year.[38]

In the end, the possibilities of expatriation came not from the North American academic environment, but from the South American professional one. In a letter written to Gropius at the beginning of 1940 from Lima,[39] we learn that on the occasion of the one-year leave granted by the Reich, Linder had left for Chile: the German sisters of the congregation of Saint Ursula had planned to open houses of their order in Latin American countries and had entrusted Linder with the planning of a complex in Chile. In the same year, the Ursulines Caritas Knickenberg and Gertrudis Neugebauer, who had moved to Peru, commissioned Linder to draw up the plans for a school in Lima (see I.1.3.).

On 2 February 1939, Paul Linder left National Socialist Germany and sailed to the American continent.[40] The reasons for this decision can be attributed to his closeness to socialist ideas and his wife's Jewish origin,[41] both

20 Schweinfurt, 1862 – Munich, 1938.
21 Nuremberg, 1874 – Bad Wiessee, 1942.
22 Medina Warmburg, Joaquín, *Irredentos y conversos. Presencias e influencias alemanas: de la neutralidad a la postguerra española (1914–1943)*, in Pozo, José Manuel and López, Ignasi (coords.), *Modelos alemanes e italianos para España en los años de la postguerra* (Pamplona, 2004), p. 23.
23 Linder, Paul, 'Arquitectos, pensad y construid con sentido social', *Arquitectura: Órgano Oficial de La Sociedad Central de Arquitectos* (1929), p. 12.
24 Linder, Paul, 'El arquitecto Max Taut', *Arquitectura: Órgano Oficial de La Sociedad Central de Arquitectos* (1929), p. 422.
25 Ludowieg Telge, Cecilia, *Paul Linder: su obra* (Lima, 1984), p. 11.
26 Linder, Paul, 'Umwandlung von Altwohnungen', *Bauwelt* (1931), pp. 1370–1372.
27 Medina Warmburg, Joaquín, 'Paul Linder, arquitecto, crítico, educador: del Bauhaus a la Escuela Nacional de Ingenieros de Perú', *RA: revista de arquitectura* (2004), p. 73.
28 See Linder, Paul, 'Die St. Thomaskirche in Berlin-Charlottenburg. Architekt Paul Linder, Berlin', *Bauwelt* (1933).
29 Medina Warmburg, Joaquín (ed.), *Paul Linder, 1897–1968: de Weimar a Lima: antología de arquitectura y crítica* (Madrid, 2019), p. 74.
30 Berlin, 1909 – Zollikon, 2001.
31 Waldheim, 1877 – Berlin, 1947. Medina Warmburg, Joaquín (ed.), *Paul Linder, 1897–1968: de Weimar a Lima: antología de arquitectura y crítica* (Madrid, 2019), pp. 407–410.
32 Linder, Paul, 'Acerca de la plástica en arquitectura. Obras de Georg Kolbe', *Arquitectura: Órgano Oficial de La Sociedad Central de Arquitectos* (1933) pp. 80–84.
33 The Bauhaus-Archiv holds the correspondence between Paul Linder and Walter Gropius in the period 1937–1940. Thanks are due to Joaquín Medina Warmburg for the kind permission of this material. Gropius, Walter, 'Letter to Paul Linder', *Bauhaus-Archiv* (14 July 1937).
34 Ibid.
35 Linder, Paul, Letter to Walter Gropius, *Bauhaus-Archiv* (26 July 1937).

Proposal for the Ursuline Mother Convent
Model
Santiago de Chile
Paul Linder
1939

Archivo de Arquitectura PUCP, Paul Linder Fund

factors that had led to his exclusion from the Reichskulturkammer. Although he was later rehabilitated by the German Chamber of Culture, at the intercession of the sculptor Georg Kolbe, the political situation all but forced the German designer into self-exile.

Linder's move to Peruvian lands was facilitated by his knowledge of the local language, learnt as a student during his trip to Spain, as confirmed by the architect in a letter to Gropius.[42] In the same 1940 letter, Linder already raised the possibility of a future visit by Gropius to Peru. This meeting, in the Andean country, would not take place until many years later, in 1953[43] (see II.6.).

36 Linder, Paul, Letter to Walter Gropius, *Bauhaus-Archiv* (17 November 1937).
37 Hanns Peter Theophil Swarzenski (Berlin, 1903 – Wielenbach, 1985).
38 Linder, Paul, Letter to Walter Gropius (14 January 1940). Medina Warmburg, Joaquín (ed.), *Paul Linder, 1897-1968: de Weimar a Lima: antología de arquitectura y crítica* (Madrid, 2019), pp. 407–410.
39 Ibid.
40 The National Archives at Washington, DC, *Passenger and Crew Lists (New York State), 1917–1967* (2 January 2023).
41 Medina Warmburg, Joaquín, 'Paul Linder, arquitecto, crítico, educador: del Bauhaus a la Escuela Nacional de Ingenieros de Perú', *RA: revista de arquitectura* (2004), p. 75.
42 Linder, Paul, Letter to Walter Gropius (14 January 1940). Medina Warmburg, Joaquín (ed.), *Paul Linder, 1897–1968: de Weimar a Lima: antología de arquitectura y crítica* (Madrid, 2019), pp. 407–410.
43 'I think that sometimes (since the war will make it impossible to go on holiday to Europe for the next few years) I will eventually go down to the west coast and I will then be a good guide and expert in Inca culture'. Ibid.

II.4. Peruvian works: from enigmatic monumentality to functional legibility (1939–1980)

Much of Paul Linder's activity in Peru was made possible by the prestige of having attended the famous Weimar school in 1919–1920. Nevertheless, upon arrival in the Andean country, this cultural matrix was not evident in his architectural production.

Linder arrived in Lima at a time when the first examples of architecture without historicist references were being built. Their construction was facilitated by the urban expansion of the Peruvian capital and the presence of a large group of Peruvian architects trained abroad (see I.2.2.). However, despite the construction of new neighbourhoods and the influence of European cultural references, Linder's first works had a rather traditionalist approach, most likely linked to the nature of his first clients as well as his familiarity with Peruvian viceregal architecture (thanks to his previous experience in Spain).

The debate around the identity aspects of national architecture was developing in Peru in parallel with the consolidation of the figure of the architect as a profession independent of that of the engineer. The formation of the Peruvian Register of Architects in November 1937 saw the participation of Peruvian architects trained abroad and facilitated Linder's professional integration in Lima (see I.2.1.). The Vice-President of the Register of Architects, Héctor Velarde, who was trained in Europe, supported his candidacy for the Chair of Art History at the Pontificia Universidad Católica del Perú and co-authored his first projects. Velarde's secretary, Fernando Belaúnde Terry, of French and American background, founded the magazine *El Arquitecto Peruano* the same year, in which he published several projects and essays by the German architect.

Linder contributed to the debate on national identity issues through various historical-critical reflections. In an article published in May 1949 in the Peruvian magazine, entitled *Reconocimiento a la Arquitectura Peruana*, he expressed his thoughts on the Peruvian concept of the 'deseuropeización de la importación española.'[44] According to Linder, colonial architecture was to be considered a phenomenon specific to this country, as a unique and non-transferable fusion of pre-Columbian and Spanish cultures. This reading of Peruvian heritage, which was shared by Velarde, characterised the first projects they worked on together, and materialised in the adoption of a markedly traditionalist lexicon.

The first projects developed in the collaboration between Linder and Velarde, from 1939 onwards, were the Colegio Santa Ursula (1939–1950), an Ursuline school, and the Nueva Residencia de la Nunciatura Apostólica

44 'de-Europeanisation of the Spanish model'. Linder, Paul, 'Reconocimiento a la Arquitectura Peruana', *El Arquitecto Peruano* (May 1949).

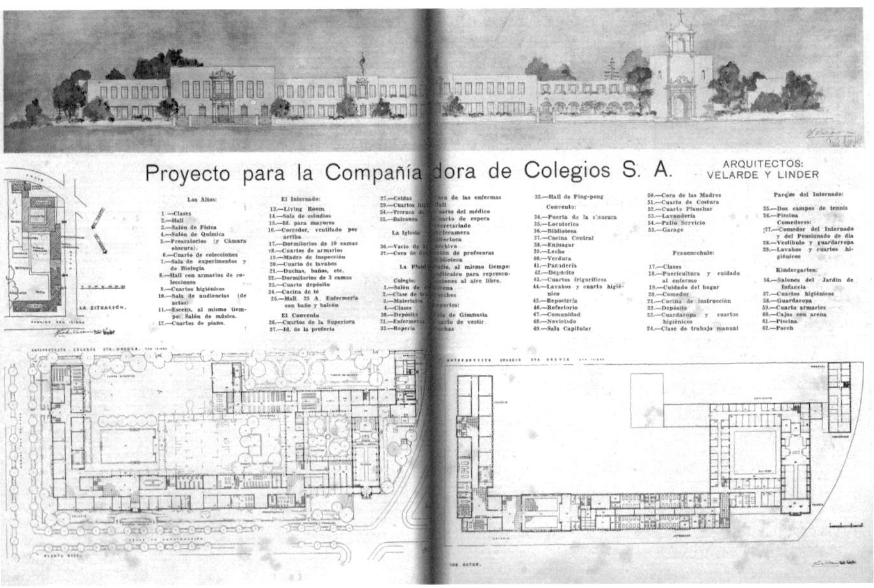

Proyecto para la Compañía dora de Colegios S. A.

ARQUITECTOS: VELARDE Y LINDER

Colegio Santa Ursula
Main elevation, ground and first floor levels
Jesús María, Lima
Paul Linder and Héctor Velarde
1939

Paul Linder and Héctor Velarde in *El Arquitecto Peruano* (May 1939)

Residencia de la Nunciatura Apostólica
Main view
Jesús María, Lima
Paul Linder and Héctor Velarde
1939–1942

Paul Linder and Héctor Velarde in *El Arquitecto Peruano* (August 1942)

(1939–1942), the seat of the Peruvian curia. The design choices for the school and the archbishop's palace, which were conditioned by the respective functions of these buildings, led Linder and Velarde to the use of ponderously asymmetrical volumes adorned with elements of colonial reminiscence, such as portals, balconies and loggias. *El Arquitecto Peruano* documented these collaborations in three issues, published between 1939 and 1942: the preliminary proposal for the Colegio Santa Ursula in an article entitled *Proyecto para la Cía: Edificadora de Colegios SA*[45] in May 1939; the preliminary project and completed work on the Peruvian archbishop's palace in the contributions *Proyecto para la Nueva Nunciatura Apostólica*;[46] and *Nueva Residencia de la Nunciatura Apostólica*,[47] in October 1940 and August 1942 respectively.

The references to historical sources in Linder's work were affected both by a process of progressive purification from ornamental elements as well as by overcoming spatial tripartition. Clearly discernible towards the middle of the century, this process was documented in an article on the Iglesia de San Felipe Apóstol (Lima, 1945–1947), published in the Peruvian magazine in 1947.[48] The neo-Romanesque church, designed by Linder for the Congregation of the Missionaries of the Sacred Heart of Jesus, featured a bell tower and the religious residence (placed on the boundary of the land), the façade of the hall (set back) and a porticoed structure (placed as a link between both bodies). The Iglesia

Iglesia de San Felipe Apóstol
Main view
San Isidro, Lima
Paul Linder
1945–1947

Paul Linder in *El Arquitecto Peruano* (May 1947)

Iglesia de Santa Ursula
Magazine cover
San Isidro, Lima
Paul Linder
1945–1950

Paul Linder in *El Arquitecto Peruano* (December 1950)

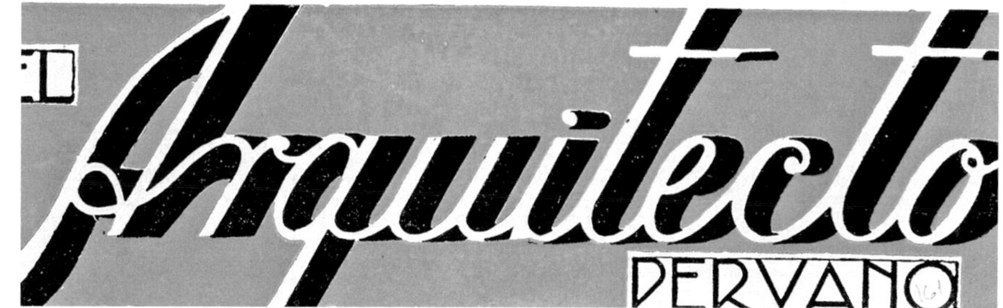

45 See Linder, Paul and Velarde Bergmann, Héctor, 'Proyecto para la Cía. Edificadora de Colegios SA', *El Arquitecto Peruano* (May 1939).

46 See Linder, Paul and Velarde Bergmann, Héctor, 'Proyecto para la Nunciatura Apostólica', *El Arquitecto Peruano* (October 1940).

47 See 'La nueva residencia de la Nunciatura Apostólica', *El Arquitecto Peruano* (August 1942).

48 See 'Iglesia San Felipe Apóstol', *El Arquitecto Peruano* (May 1947).

49 See 'Iglesia de Santa Ursula', *El Arquitecto Peruano* (December 1950).

de Santa Ursula[49] (1945–1950), built in the Ursuline complex previously conceived together with Velarde, revealed a desire for abstraction in a composition of Gothic-Catalan inspiration, with the space of the hall punctuated by large ogival arches in reinforced concrete.

In both cases, despite the simplification of the decorative apparatus, the internal layout of the buildings remained far from a series of halls free of barriers or separations, a solution tried out in Berlin's St. Thomaskirche. The interior space presented divisions between the central nave, side aisles and the choir, and adopted a spatial distribution far removed from the profound liturgical transformations of the early twentieth century.

The rapprochement of Linder's ecclesiastical work toward liturgical renewal ideals, through a liberation from decorativism and spatial tripartition, reached a turning point in his design for a parish church and oratory in Lima, the Parroquia de Nuestra Señora de Lobatón[50] (1941–1948). This complex consisted of three volumes that delimited the perimeter of the lot: the prism of the bell tower, the octagon of the baptistery and the parallelepiped of the missionaries' cells, all three of which were wrapped in wrinkled plaster and painted a dark colour. The different heights of the volumes produced a discontinuous profile in this enclosure, within which stood the body of the hall, marked

Iglesia de Santa Ursula
Interior view
San Isidro, Lima
Paul Linder
1945–1950

Paul Linder in *El Arquitecto Peruano* (December 1950)

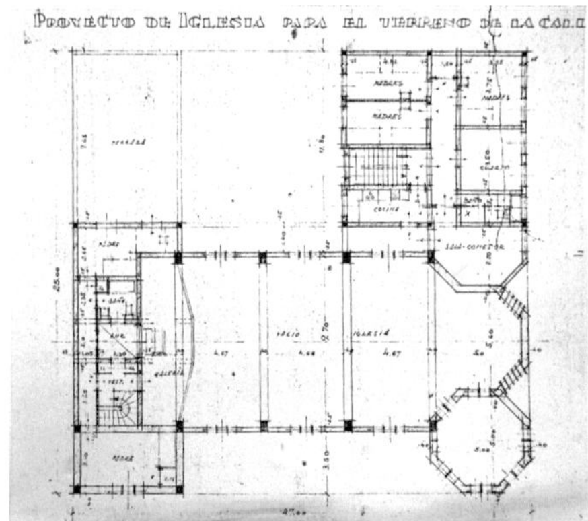

Nuestra Señora de Lobatón
Ground plan level
Lince, Lima
Paul Linder
1941–1948

Archivo de Arquitectura PUCP, Paul Linder Fund

Nuestra Señora de Lobatón
Main view
Lince, Lima
Paul Linder
1941–1948

Archivo de Arquitectura PUCP, Paul Linder Fund

Casa Matriz MSC
y Clínica Stella Maris
Magazine cover
Pueblo Libre, Lima
Paul Linder
1948–1950

Paul Linder in *El Arquitecto Peruano* (May 1939)

50 Linder, Alfredo, 'Las Iglesias de Paul Linder', *Habitar: Revista del Colegio de Arquitectos del Perú* (1980), pp. 3–10.

by vertically arranged windows. The proximity of the central-vertical and perimeter-horizontal bodies had the baptistery and apse as their only point of contact. The interior contradicted this reading: the volumes merged into a single space, devoid of separations, extending to the limits of the property, integrating the side naves with the central one. This dichotomy between exterior and interior had already been experimented with by Linder in the St. Thomaskirche in Berlin. Thus, Nuestra Señora de Lobatón can be seen as a continuation of the research he had begun with the Berlin place of worship, this time crystallised in a reinforced concrete structure instead of metal elements.

A last project published in *El Arquitecto Peruano*, documenting the transition to the new architecture, is the main house of the Misioneros del Sagrado Corazón, named Casa Matriz MSC y Clínica Stella Maris'[51] (1948–1950). The building presents a singular mixture of avant-garde and traditional elements. The spaces, organised around a central courtyard, were contained in a white, neutral, measurably asymmetrical body. Ornamented openings, balconies and galleries stood out from the red clinker elements added externally. These projecting bodies, with arched mirrors, contained the loggias, stairwells and a bell gable. A portico, supported by round arches, defined the fourth façade of the courtyard. The language used in this part of the complex contrasted with the clinic proper: a modern, multi-storey curtain wall building that made its functions explicit in the volumetry.

In the 1950s, Linder's articles published in the Peruvian press were not only about his projects. He also wrote several articles on Bauhaus-related figures, published in the magazine *El Arquitecto Peruano*[52] and the newspaper *El Comercio,*[53] which contributed to the architect's identification with the German school's language.[54] The subdivision of different functions into individual volumes distinguishable by materials and construction solutions, which references Gropius's building in Dessau, became more and more evident in Linder's later projects. In his proposals for hospitals, laboratories, offices, factories, shopping centres and schools, he began to move away from the enigmatic monumentality of the religious buildings he had designed up to that point.

El Arquitecto Peruano dedicated four articles to him, between 1958 and 1963, on four different projects, all for European clients. The first concerned industrial buildings and his last school buildings. The Cervecería San Miguel[55] (Piura, 1957–1959), incorporating all the brewery's activities under a plastered skin punctuated by *moucharabies*, had German-born Klaus Ahrens as its director. The Laboratorios Farmaceuticos Hoffman-La Roche[56] (Lima, 1960–1963), whose volumetry clearly differentiates the executive and representative area from that of production, was the Peruvian headquarters of the

Cervecería San Miguel
Main view
Piura
Paul Linder
1957–1959
Archivo de Arquitectura PUCP, Paul Linder Fund

Laboratorios Hoffman-La Roche
Main view
San Borja, Lima
Paul Linder
1960–1963
Archivo de Arquitectura PUCP, Paul Linder Fund

Colegio y Convento Santa María Goretti
Main view
La Victoria, Lima
Paul Linder
1956–1965
Archivo de Arquitectura PUCP, Paul Linder Fund

Colegio Alexander von Humboldt
Aerial view
Miraflores, Lima
Paul Linder
1958–1960 (first phase)
Archivo de Arquitectura PUCP, Paul Linder Fund

Swiss pharmaceutical firm of the same name. The Colegio y convento Santa Maria Goretti[57] (Lima, 1956–1965) was a complex that saw the coexistence of the school and convent of the religious order of the Franciscan Sisters of Bramberga. Finally, the Colegio Alexander von Humboldt[58] (Lima, first phase 1958–1960), came to be the most ambitious work of the designer, in terms of the size of the complex and the type of client, the Bundesbaudirektion of the Federal Republic of Germany.

The Colegio presented an organisation of volumes by addition, explicitly manifesting the functional programme contained therein. The different wings organised around courtyards, as well as the use in the elevations of solids and voids, glazed façades and vaulted pergolas, took the functional breakdown and reorganisation of the Bauhaus in Dessau as a reference. The distribution of the spaces, defined by rational choices related to circulation, sunlight and ventilation, was to be reflected in the external volumetry, resulting in an architectural complex perfectly responding to functional requirements.

51 'Casa Matriz MSC y Clínica Stella Maris', *El Arquitecto Peruano* (February–March 1952), p. 38.
52 See Linder, Paul, 'Homenaje a Walter Gropius', *El Arquitecto Peruano* (March–April 1953).
53 See Linder, Paul, 'Josef Albers, artista y educador', *El Comercio, Suplemento Dominical* (July 1953).
54 Medina Warmburg, Joaquín, *Walter Gropius – proclamas de modernidad: escritos y conferencias, 1908–1934* (Barcelona, 2018), p. 70.
55 'La nueva cervecería Piura', *El Arquitecto Peruano* (July–August–September 1959), pp. 34–35.
56 'Hoffman-La Roche, Lima', *El Arquitecto Peruano* (October–November–Dicember 1963), pp. 40–47.
57 'Colegio y convento Santa María Goretti en La Victoria', *El Arquitecto Peruano* (January–February–March 1958), pp. 25–28.
58 'Colegio A. von Humboldt', *El Arquitecto Peruano* (July–August–September 1960), pp. 23–29.

Edificio Arnodi
Main view and
internal view
Lima
Paul Linder
1950

Archivo de Arquitectura
PUCP, Paul Linder Fund

II.5. Edificio Arnodi: reference to local traditions and exclusion from the exhibition *Latin American Architecture Since 1945* (1950–1955)

Since his arrival in Peru, Paul Linder continued his activities as an architectural theorist which had been initiated in Europe. He actively participated in cultural debates, as can be seen in writings published in the pages of the magazine *El Arquitecto Peruano* between 1939 and 1961.[59] His contributions were included in the editions of newspapers with national circulation, such as *El Comercio*, or cultural periodicals, such as *Las Moradas* and *Mar del Sur*.[60] In 1947, he signed the manifesto and participated in the first activities of Agrupación Espacio, inaugurating a cycle of lectures organised at the Sociedad de Arquitectos, with a speech entitled *Acerca de la plástica en arquitectura*[61] (see I.3.2.). As a result of his affirmation as an architectural critic, his relationship with Walter Gropius, as well as his acquaintance with the most active members of Agrupación Espacio, Linder was able to get in touch with Henry-Russell Hitchcock, curator of *Latin America Architecture Since 1945*. He collaborated in the organisation of this New York exhibition, together with Espacio members Luis Miró Quesada and Santiago Agurto (see I.3.3.).

On the US delegation's visit to Peru in October 1954, Hitchcock met Linder and remained in contact thereafter, as documented in correspondence between December 1954 and January 1955.[62] In these letters, the projects preselected for the exhibition were described in detail, of which multi-storey pieces constituted the majority. Four of the six works, including the Edificio Arnodi, designed by Linder himself, belonged to this type.

The Edificio Arnodi (1950) represents the only known multi-storey project among Linder's output. The seven-storey building, the ground floor of which is used for commerce and the remainder for flats, was constructed close to the historical centre of Lima. This work picks up on the themes of Americanism and the appropriateness of vertically developed buildings in predominantly horizontal urban environments, discussed by Linder in 1924 in an article published in the Spanish magazine *Arquitectura* entitled *La construcción de rascacielos en Alemania*: the debate was as topical and polemical in Europe as it was in mid-twentieth century Peru, a period in which its capital city saw a significant increase in multi-storey construction.

One of the earliest precedents of tall buildings in Peru dates back to the 1920s and relates to the Peruvian experience of another German designer, Werner Benno Lange. In 1926, Lange moved to Lima to work on the modernisation of the capital, the *Plan de la Gran Lima* (see I.1.3.), where he also

59 Art reviews were published in various articles (with titles such as *Balance de la pintura moderna, Se puede entender el arte moderno, Ideas acerca de la pintura abstracta, El 37° Salón anual de la Escuela de Bellas Artes* and *Visita sumaria de la Biennale 1952 de Venecia*), as well as essays on architecture and iconic architects (such as *La fuerza de la emoción en arquitectura, La situación de la vivienda en la Alemania de hoy día, Homenaje a Walter Gropius*, and *Frank Lloyd Wright visto desde Europa)*.

60 Ludowieg Telge, Cecilia, *Paul Linder: su obra* (Lima, 1984), pp. 226–228.

61 Córdova Valdivia, Adolfo, 'European architects and Agrupación Espacio', *Interview* (13 September 2016)

62 The MoMA archives in New York hold two missives from Linder to Hitchcock dated 21 December 1954 and 19 January 1955, and one from Hitchcock to Linder dated 14 January 1955. Thanks are due to Joaquín Medina Warmburg for the kind permission to use this material.

built the administrative headquarters of the agricultural estate belonging to the German-born Gildemeister family.[63] The Casa Gildemeister (1928–1930), a building characterised by its then unusual height of six storeys, is an early example of both the administrative function of the historical centre of Lima and a multi-storey Art Deco building.

The Edificio Arnodi, built about twenty years later, is part of the renewal phase of Linder's architectural language: it presents the overcoming of the classical basement-body-coronation composition and the mixing of traditional and contemporary materials. Completed in 1950, this building was constructed in the period following the introduction of the 1946 town planning regulations, which encouraged the adoption of the multi-storey type regulated by the Horizontal Property Law (see I.2.2.).

Although the Edificio Arnodi appeared among the works Hitchcock examined for the exhibition, there were other examples of multi-storey buildings included in the 1955 MoMA exhibition catalogue: the Edificio Ostolaza (Enrique Seoane, Lima, 1952–1954) and the Edificio Radio El Sol (Luis Miró Quesada, Lima, 1953–1954). Hitchcock's choice of architecture for the exhibition highlighted the great interest in the spread of the multi-storey architectural type in Latin America. Indeed, the American historian's attention was limited to those examples that adhered to Western models, as was the case with the architecture of Miró Quesada and Seoane. But Linder's work – which united a typically modern functional differentiation of volumes, with references to local Spanish and Peruvian traditions (translated in the Edificio Arnodi into the use of mosaic facings and brick *moucharabies*) – did not fit into the canons of the International Style and was chosen neither for the exhibition nor its catalogue.[64]

La Casa de Chile
Main view published in a magazine article
Hamburg
Fritz Höger
1924

Fritz Höger in *Arquitectura*

63 See Gonzales, Michael, *Plantation Agriculture and Social Control in Northern Peru, 1875–1933* (Austin, 2014).

64 Atoche Intili, Javier, 'Tres cartas desde Lima. Paul Linder y los arquitectos europeos', in Medina Warmburg, Joaquín (ed.), *Paul Linder, 1897–1968: de Weimar a Lima – antología de arquitectura y crítica* (Madrid, 2019), pp. 80–91.

Casa Gildemeister
Main view
Lima
Werner Benno Lange
1928–1930
La Página Perdida

II.6. Paul Linder's university activities and his efforts to spread modern culture in Peru (1942–1966)

Paul Linder during one of his lectures at the Department of Architecture of the Escuela Nacional de Ingenieros
Lima
Early 1950s
Archivo de Arquitectura PUCP, Paul Linder Fund

The European designers who moved to Peru inserted themselves into the culture-producing apparatuses – public education and administration – in order to spread modern culture from their seats. And Paul Linder was not an exception.

His built work, coupled with his articles published in various specialised magazines of the time, had a considerable influence on generations of young architects in the second half of the twentieth century. His university experiences began in 1942, at the Pontificia Universidad Católica del Perú, through the intermediary of Héctor Velarde.[65] From 1945, Linder held the Chair of Art History at that university,[66] where he taught until 1966.[67] In 1946, following the Reforma Universitaria, he became Professor of Architectural Aesthetics and Philosophy of Art in the Departament of Architecture at the Escuela Nacional de Ingenieros,[68] followed by Professor Emeritus in the Facultad de Arquitectura of today's Universidad Nacional de Ingeniería until his resignation in 1964.[69]

The teaching materials prepared by Linder for university lectures, as well as the examination registers containing the evaluations of aspiring architecture students, show his profound knowledge of the topics covered in the classroom and his great dedication to teaching. In 1951, an aptitude test was introduced in the Department of Architecture, the purpose of which was to select future students for a career in architecture.[70] Linder, together with Agrupación Espacio members Adolfo Córdova and Luis Miró Quesada, was commissioned to assess the candidates' skills deemed important for these studies.[71]

Lecture by Josef Albers at the Department of Architecture of the Escuela Nacional de Ingenieros
Lima
1953
Archivo de Arquitectura PUCP, Paul Linder Fund

Linder's education in Weimar most certainly contributed to this assignment. His approach as an architect was directly connected to the Bauhaus and, consequently, to his own experience with Walter Gropius. In the 1950s, Linder wrote several articles about Gropius's visits to Lima between 1953 and 1954, and about other promoters of Bauhaus-related artistic and social ideas. Most were published in the magazine *El Arquitecto Peruano* and in the newspaper *El Comercio*.[72] His relations with Fernando Belaúnde Terry, Director of the Department of Architecture and founder of the Peruvian magazine (see I.2.), as well as his contacts with Luis Miró Quesada, himself a key figure in Agrupación Espacio and son of the Director of *El Comercio* (see I.3), allowed him to promote Josef Albers' trips to Peru from their pages. An article was published in the journal, entitled *Josef Albers, Artista y Educador*, in conjunction with a lecture the German artist and lecturer gave at Department of Architecture in the second half of that year.[73]

Arrival of Walter Gropius and Josep Lluis Sert at Limatambo Airport
Lima
1953

Archivo de Arquitectura PUCP, Paul Linder Fund

Linder paid tribute to Walter Gropius in 1953, on his 70th birthday, from the pages of *El Arquitecto Peruano*. On this occasion, recalling the lessons he had received at the Bauhaus, he presented him as a 'brillante modelo entre los educadores al arte.'[74] Linder's efforts to promote Gropius's visit to Peru were successful, as documented in a letter the German architect wrote to Belaúnde in 1953.[75] In December of 1953, Walter Gropius, together with Josep Lluis Sert, stopped in Lima as part of his itinerary on a trip to the Bienal de São Paulo. A photograph taken on 28 December of that year, upon arrival of the US delegation in the Peruvian capital, is historically significant for two reasons. On the one hand, it documents the meeting of three European architects exiled to the

American continent in the inter-war period (Linder, Gropius and Sert), a meeting facilitated by US foreign policies (see I.2.2.); on the other, it illustrates the relationships established by Linder with some of the most influential Peruvian intellectuals, which enabled him to disseminate Gropius's works and thoughts within the Escuela Nacional de Ingenieros: Rafael Marquina (Director of the Department of Architecture); Héctor Velarde (designer, historian and writer) and Fernando Belaúnde Terry (architect, publisher and politician, as well as the future President of Peru).

Gropius's trip represented an opportunity for Linder to bring to Peru a leading promoter of the unifying project of the arts – both aesthetic and social. Nevertheless, the celebratory atmosphere of the visit (Gropius, who was to be awarded a prize at the second international architecture exhibition in São Paulo, attended the graduation ceremony of Linder's son in Lima) offered no public opportunity either to discuss the pedagogical principles that Linder had experienced first-hand during his attendance at the Weimar School, nor to debate the social commitment of architecture: two topics of primary importance in the Andean country.[76]

Paul Linder, architect, critic and lecturer, gave up teaching at the Universidad Nacional de Ingeniería in 1964 and at the Pontificia Universidad Católica del Perú in 1966. These decisions, which came after twenty years of teaching and active participation in cultural exchanges between Peru and Europe, were linked to health reasons that forced the German architect to limit all his activities.[77] Two years later, in 1968, during a trip to Germany for treatment, Linder died suddenly and was buried in Overath.

65 Medina Warmburg, Joaquín, 'Paul Linder, arquitecto, crítico, educador: del Bauhaus a la Escuela Nacional de Ingenieros de Perú', *RA: revista de arquitectura* (2004), p. 79.

66 Ludowieg Telge, Cecilia, *Paul Linder: su obra* (Lima, 1984), p. 12.

67 Alarco, Gerardo, Letter to Paul Linder, *Archivo de Arquitectura PUCP, Paul Linder Fund* (5 May 1966).

68 Martuccelli, Elio, *Conversaciones con Adolfo Córdova* (Lima, 2012), p. 67.

69 Linder, Paul, Letter to Jorge del Busto, *Archivo de Arquitectura PUCP, Paul Linder Fund* (1964).

70 See Linder, Paul, *Examen Vocacional para estudiantes de arquitectura. Experiencias adquiridas* (Lima, 1959).

71 Alvarez Ortega, Syra, *La formación en arquitectura en el Perú: antecedentes, inicios y desarrollo hasta 1955* (Lima, 2006), pp. 207–210.

72 Valenzuela, Hildebrando, Letter to Paul Linder, *Archivo de Arquitectura PUCP, Paul Linder Fund* (26 May 1953)

73 Ibid.

74 'an illustrious example of an art educator.' See Linder, Paul, 'Homenaje a Walter Gropius', *El Arquitecto Peruano* (March–April 1953).

75 Linder, Paul, Letter to Fernando Belaúnde, *Archivo de Arquitectura PUCP, Paul Linder Fund* (18 June 1953)

76 Medina Warmburg, Joaquín, *Walter Gropius – proclamas de modernidad: escritos y conferencias, 1908–1934* (Barcelona, 2018), p. 71.

77 Linder, Paul, Letter to Jorge del Busto, *Archivo de Arquitectura PUCP, Paul Linder Fund.*

Paul Linder and Fernando Belaúnde Terry
Lima
About 1960
Archivo de Arquitectura PUCP, Paul Linder Fund

La Promoción 1953 posa con los Huéspedes de Honor Gropius y Sert
Architects Walter Gropius, Josep Lluis Sert and Fernando Belaúnde Terry accompany the group of graduates
Lima
1953
El Arquitecto Peruano
(November–December 1953)

MARIO BIANCO (1903–1990): FROM THE *PIANO REGIONALE PIEMONTESE* TO THE *PLAN PILOTO DE LIMA*

ITALIAN, EUROPEAN, AMERICAN EXPERIENCES

1903

Mario Bianco's birth (Varallo Sesia, Vercelli, Italy)

1921–1922

Bianco joins the National Fascist Party and participates in the March on Rome

1926

Bianco concludes engineering studies at the Regia Scuola Politecnica di Torino

S.M. VITTORIO EMANUELE III

1933

USA Tennessee Valley Authority (1933–1938)

1934

Bianco marries Laura Melloni

Palazzo Grisolia (Mario Bianco, Turin, early 1930s)

1936

Birth of Bianco's first child (Lorenzo). His wife dies

1930s

Palazzo Olivetti-Tabacchi (Mario Bianco, Urbano Carboni, Turin, 1935)

1937

FRANCE *Plan de Paris* (Le Corbusier, Parigi, 1937)

Piano regolatore della Valle d'Aosta (BBPR et al., 1936–1937)

Bianco obtains his teaching qualification

Palazzo Fariselli (Mario Bianco, Turin, second half of the 1930s)

1939

Start of the Second World War

Bianco marries Rhena Ghidoni

Bianco obtained the Chair of Technical Architecture (Gabinetto di ingegneria) and was appointed Head of the Project Office at the Regia Scuola Politecnica di Torino

1900s

1920s

1930s

PERUVIAN EXPERIENCES

1937

El Arquitecto Peruano's first issue

Establishment of the Sociedad de Arquitectos del Perú

1938

Establishment of the Consejo Nacional de Urbanismo

1940

Mussolini declares war on the Allies

1941

Title of Cavaliere dell'Ordine della Corona d'Italia to Bianco

1942

Bianco becomes assistant to G. Muzio in the Architectural Composition course

1944

Bianco collaborates on the second edition of the Dizionario tecnico industriale enciclopedico

Foundation of ABRR (G. Astengo, M. Bianco, N. Renacco, A. Rizzotti)

Piano regolatore milanese (Architetti Riuniti – Franco Albini et al., 1944–1945)

1945

Agricoltura e urbanistica (G. Astengo, M. Bianco)

Sistema ABC (G. Astengo, M. Bianco, A. Ceratto)

1946

Sul soleggiamento degli edifici di abitazione (G. Astengo, M. Bianco, Metron)

Piano regionale piemontese (ABRR, G. Astengo, M. Bianco, N. Renacco, A. Rizzotti, 1944–1946)

1947

FRANCE *Piano Regionale Piemontese* at the Exposition Internationale de l'habitation et de l'urbanisme di Parigi

USA The Sistema ABC is published in *Architectural Forum*

UK CIAM VI (Bridgewater)

1940s

1940

Earthquake and tsunami in Lima and Callao

National Census

1944

Establishment of the Instituto de Urbanismo del Perú

Paul Lester Wiener in Peru

1946

Reforma Universitaria

Peruvian urban planning regulations: Ley de propiedad horizontal, Oficina Nacional de Planeamiento y Urbanismo, Corporación Nacional de Vivienda, Centros Climáticos de Esparcimiento

1947

Bianco moves to Peru

Expresión de Principios de la Agrupación Espacio

VI Congreso Panamericano de Arquitectos (Lima, Cusco)

Mario Bianco, Adolfo Córdova, Carlos Williams associates

Josep Lluís Sert in Peru

MARIO BIANCO (1903–1990): FROM THE *PIANO REGIONALE PIEMONTESE* TO THE *PLAN PILOTO DE LIMA*

ITALIAN, EUROPEAN, AMERICAN EXPERIENCES

1948

ITALY Cino Calcaprina, Luigi Piccinato, Ernesto Nathan Rogers and Enrico Tedeschi move to Argentina

I piani urbanistici (Giovanni Astengo et al.)

ARGENTINA Mario Bianco, Luigi Piccinato and Ernesto Nathan Rogers as consultants for the *Estudio del Plan de Buenos Aires* (EPBA, 1948–1954)

1951

COLOMBIA Bianco as consultant for the Centro Interamericano de Vivienda (Organization of American States, Bogota, 1951–1952)

1952

ITALY *I piani regionali* (edited by del Ministero dei lavori pubblici, Roma, 1953–1954)

1953

BRAZIL Publication of the *Piano regionale piemontese* in the magazine *Acrópole*

1954

CHILE Bianco is granted Arquitecto Honorario by the Universidad de Chile

1955

USA The catalogue of the exhibition *Latin American Architecture Since 1945* (MoMA, New York, 1955) includes the work of Bianco

1940s

1950s

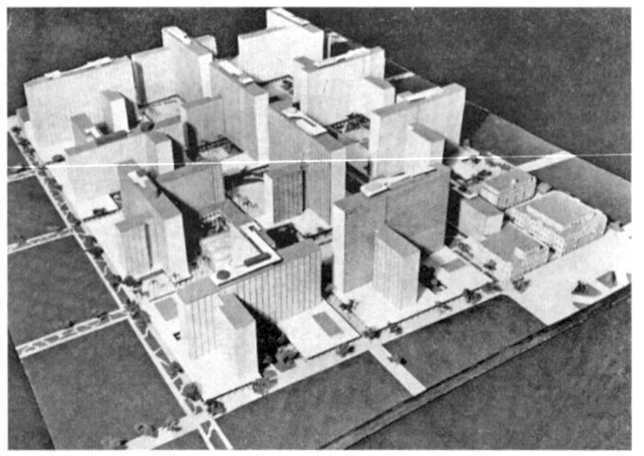

Nota a Vallejo

¡Cuando las catedrales eran blancas!

ESPACIO

PERUVIAN EXPERIENCES

1948

Bianco was appointed professor (Escuela Nacional de Ingenieros) and head of the project office (Oficina Nacional de Planeamiento y Urbanismo)

1949

Bianco and Enrico Tedeschi travel to Cusco

Casa D'Onofrio (Mario Bianco et al., Lima, 1948–1949)

Plan Piloto de Lima (ONPU, E. N. Rogers, J. L. Sert, 1947–1949)

1950

First issue of *Espacio* magazine

Birth of Bianco's second child (Marḥena)

1952

Unidad Vecinal Santa Marina (Junta de Obras Públicas del Callao, Mario Bianco project leader, Callao, 1949–1952)

1953

Department of Architecture (Mario Bianco et al., Lima, 1951–1953)

Enrico Tedeschi in Peru

Walter Gropius and Josep Lluís Sert in Peru

1954

Henry-Russell Hitchcock in Peru

1959

ITALY Bianco stays in Italy

1960

White and his family move to Turin

1962

ITALY The Akropolis 9 group (of which Bianco is a member) receives first prize in the Concorso per il centro direzionale di Torino

1963

ITALY Bianco receives the honour of Gran Maestro de la Orden del Sol at the Embassy of Peru in Italy

1965

ITALY Bianco is recognised as an Arquitecto Honorario by the Colegio de Arquitectos del Perú

1990

Mario Bianco dies (Turin, Italy)

1960s

1990s

1957

Hotel Savoy (Bianco, Lima, 1954–1957)

Bianco receives the honour of Cavaliere dell'Ordine al merito della Repubblica Italiana

1959

Lecture by Bianco entitled *Impresiones sobre una decada de arquitectura italiana* (Lima, 1959)

1963

Architect Fernando Belaúnde Terry is elected president of the Republic of Peru

Chapter III
Mario Bianco (1903–1990): from the *Piano Regionale Piemontese* to the *Plan Piloto de Lima*

III.1. Teaching at the Regia Scuola di Ingegneria di Torino and professional practice in Italy (1926–1944)

Mario Bianco[1] was an urban planner, designer and university professor for several generations of Italian and Peruvian architects and engineers. In the early years of his professional career, he established a close relationship with representatives of the Italian Novecento style and then, towards the end of the Second World War, he became one of the leading European researchers on post-war reconstruction, having conducted studies on prefabrication, sunlighting and territorial planning.

Mario Bianco
Lima
1955
Ing. Prof. Mario Bianco
Private Archive

1 Mario Bianco Zanaldo (Varallo Sesia, Vercelli, 27 February 1903 – Turin, 24 October 1990).

Palazzo Fariselli
Turin
Mario Bianco
Second half of 1930s
Javier Atoche Intili (2018)

Unlike Paul Linder, who had self-exiled from National Socialist Germany, Bianco left Italy for professional reasons: having started out with the idea of exporting a prefabricated construction system, in the Andean country he initially found work in the sphere of urban planning, largely due to the promotional work carried out by Peruvian and foreign intellectuals (see I.2.2.). As can be seen from his Peruvian projects, the urban planning-architectural design combination was a particularly important aspect of Bianco's professional career, which began in Italy in the inter-war period.

Bianco was an early member of the National Fascist Party, becoming a squad member and taking part in the March on Rome in 1922.[2] He undertook training at the Regia Scuola di Ingegneria in Turin, graduating in civil engineering in 1926.[3] From the following year until 1947, when he left for Latin America, he worked assiduously on teaching at the Politecnico. His commitments at the Turin school allowed him to remain in contact with professors and students of engineering and architecture (some of whom he would later collaborate with) and not interrupt his academic and professional activities during the war.[4]

In the Gabinetto di Ingegneria (today's Faculty of Engineering) he became, in 1927, an assistant in the Technical Architecture course of Professor Enrico Bonicelli,[5] whom he succeeded in 1939, inheriting his chair.[6] At the same

2 'Cartella personale di Mario Bianco. Dichiarazione del Fascio di combattimento di Chieri, *Museo del Politecnico di Torino, Archivio Storico Docenti* (26 February 1931).

3 Curriculum vitae of Mario Bianco. Certificato di conseguimento del titolo di Dottore in ingegneria civile del Regio istituto superiore di ingegneria di Torino, *Ing. Prof. Mario Bianco Private archive* (11 May 1936).

4 'Dichiarazione del direttore del Politenico di Torino', *Museo del Politecnico di Torino, Archivio Storico Docenti* (11 May 1939).

Honour of Cavaliere dell'Ordine della Corona d'Italia given to Mario Bianco
Turin
22 April 1941

Ing. Prof. Mario Bianco
Private Archive

S. M. VITTORIO EMANUELE III

PER GRAZIA DI DIO E PER VOLONTA' DELLA NAZIONE

RE D'ITALIA E DI ALBANIA

IMPERATORE D'ETIOPIA

Gran Mastro dell' Ordine della Corona d'Italia

In considerazione di particolari benemerenze;
Sentita la Giunta degli Ordini dei Santi Maurizio e Lazzaro e della Corona d'Italia;

Sulla proposta del Duce del Fascismo, Capo del Governo e del Segretario del P.N.F. Ministro Segretario di Stato;

Con Decreto in data Zona di Operazioni 22 aprile 1941 XIX ha conferito l'Onorificenza di:

Cavaliere

dell'Ordine della Corona d'Italia con facoltà di fregiarsi delle insegne stabilite per tale grado onorifico.

al Sig. Mario Bianco di Sebastiano

Il Cancelliere dell'Ordine della Corona d'Italia incaricato della esecuzione di tale Decreto, dichiara che questo venne registrato alla Cancelleria dell'Ordine predetto e che:

il Sig. Mario Bianco

fu inscritto nell'Elenco dei Cavalieri (Nazionali) al n° 105430 (Serie 3ª)

Il Cancelliere dell'Ordine

Il Direttore Capo della Divisione I.

time, in the Sezione di Architettura (today's Faculty of Architecture), Bianco was recognised as an extraordinary assistant in the academic activities of Professor Giovanni Muzio.[7] During this period, in addition to meeting students and future members of the ABRR group (Giovanni Astengo, Mario Bianco, Nello Renacco and Aldo Rizzotti), the Piedmontese designer took on professional assignments linked to the activities of the Politecnico. Thus, the collaborations with Muzio within the Regia Scuola would mark an important point in Bianco's professional development, influencing his early projects. Of the currents present in early twentieth century Italian architecture, from historicist to avant-garde and transitional, Bianco's repertoire presented examples of all three groups, with a preference in the inter-war period for an extremely simplified classicism, of which Muzio was one of its main proponents.

In 1939, Bianco was appointed by the Ministry of Public Works as head of the design office of the Turin school. In this role, he was part of the design team for the Politecnico headquarters in Corso Duca degli Abruzzi,[8] a proposal on which Muzio was working as a consultant. As office manager of the technical area, Bianco drew up the plans for the aeronautics laboratory, the thermoelectric power station and annexed offices, until 1943, when he left the post.[9] However, due to the war, these projects were never realised.

His various assignments at the Politecnico had allowed Muzio to appreciate Bianco's teaching abilities and design skills to the point that, in the commission appointed in 1942 to report on his suitability for teaching,[10] the Milanese architect emphasised that his aptitude for teaching was diligent and that he was passionate in the care of his students. Concurrently, Muzio also reported on Bianco's skill in drawing up the project for the Scuola.[11]

His many activities in the professional and academic spheres, as well as his political affiliation, earned Bianco the title of Cavaliere dell'Ordine della Corona d'Italia in 1941.[12] These political convictions were, however, cast into doubt by the war's development, with the alliance established between Fascist Italy and Nazi Germany and the outcome of Italy's entry into the war. Similarly, a *caesura* can be seen in his design work: until the second half of the 1930s he employed the Novecento style; from 1944, he adhered to the principles of the modern movement with a public gesture: namely, his participation in the drafting of the *Piano Regionale Piemontese* for the ABRR professional association. This turning point would be reaffirmed by his subsequent membership of the Piedmont section of the Associazione per l'Architettura Organica (APAO), of which Bianco remained a full member even after his departure for Peru.[13]

5 'Appointment as voluntary assistant', Ibid. (24 February 1927).

6 Curriculum vitae, Ing. Prof. Mario Bianco Private archive (s.d.).

7 Milan, 1893 – 1982.

8 Brunelli, Pietro Enrico, 'Dichiarazione del direttore del Politenico di Torino', *Museo del Politecnico di Torino, Archivio Storico Docenti* (11 May 1939).

9 Ibid. (4 December 1946).

10 Ministero dell'educazione nazionale, 'Decreto di abilitazione alla libera docenza in Composizione Architettonica', *Museo del Politecnico di Torino, Archivio Storico Docenti* (10 March 1937).

11 See 'Estratto del verbale di adunanza del Consiglio della Facoltà di ingegneria', Ibid. (25 June 1942); Muzio, Giovanni, Letter to the Director of the Politecnico di Torino, Aldo Bibolini, Ibid. (15 July 1942).

12 Onorificenza di Cavaliere dell'Ordine della Corona d'Italia, Ing. Prof. Mario Bianco Private archive (22 April 1941).

13 'Executive Board of Associazione Piemontese Giuseppe Pagano per una Architettura Organica', *Bruno Zevi Archive* (November 1947).

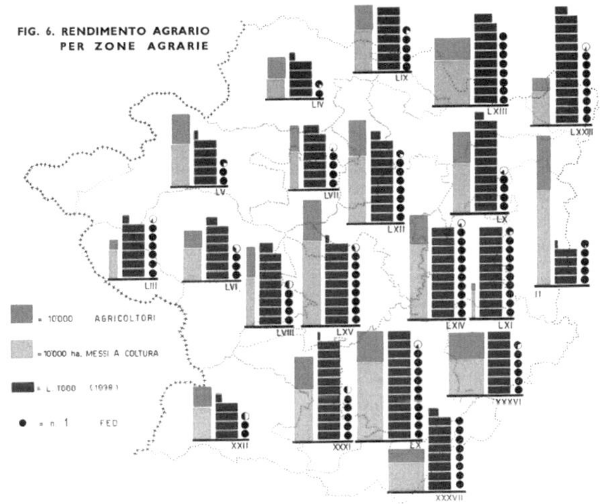

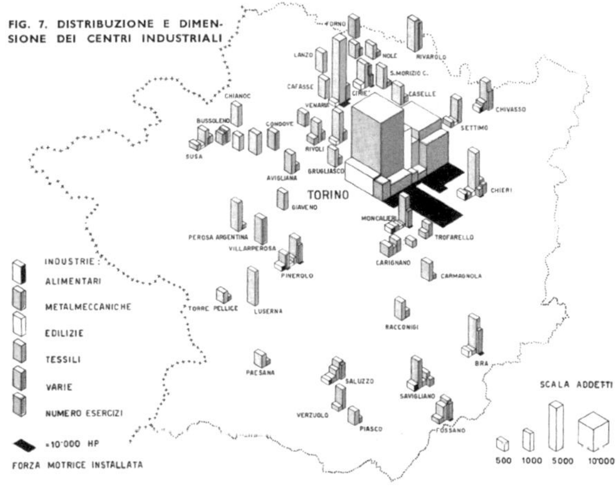

Piano Regionale Piemontese
Agrarian performance by agricultural zones and distribution and size of industrial centres
Piedmont
ABRR (Giovanni Astengo, Mario Bianco, Nello Renacco, Aldo Rizzotti)
1944–1946
ABRR in *Metron* (1947)

III.2. The contributions to post-war reconstruction, the *Piano Regionale Piemontese* and the departure for Peru (1944–1947)

In Italy, the tension of the Fascist regime's years had been replaced by a reconstructive concern for the huge devastated urban areas left at the war's end.

From 1944, Bianco was part of the ABRR group, together with those who had been his students in the Architectural Composition course held by Muzio: Astengo, Renacco and Rizzotti. Within two years, they had drawn up, on their own initiative, the *Piano Regionale Piemontese* (1944–1946), an instrument for the reorganisation of the territory's economic and social activities. In the study, they proposed the improvement of living conditions by replacing the buildings destroyed by the war with ones that were more efficient in their use of land, in their exploitation of natural light and in their spatial distribution.[14]

The Plan was the first serious territorial planning effort attempted in Italy.[15] Made public in 1947 in the pages of *Metron*,[16] it had three important precedents: the *Piano Regolatore della Valle d'Aosta* (1937); the *Piano Regolatore Milanese* (1945); and, in the international sphere, the experience of the Tennessee Valley Authority. As in the Peruvian case (see I.2.2.), the latter was taken as a model and became the first step towards national planning.

The need for a state reconstruction plan was raised by several authoritative voices. In December 1945, the Italian architects Ernesto Nathan Rogers and Ignazio Gardella organised the First National Conference for Building

14 Astengo, Giovanni, 'Piano Regionale Piemontese', *Metron: rivista internazionale d'architettura* (1947), pp. 3–76.
15 Dal Co, Francesco, *Storia dell'architettura italiana: il secondo novecento* (Milano, 1997), pp. 113–116.
16 See Astengo, Giovanni, 'Piano Regionale Piemontese', *Metron: rivista internazionale d'architettura* (1947).

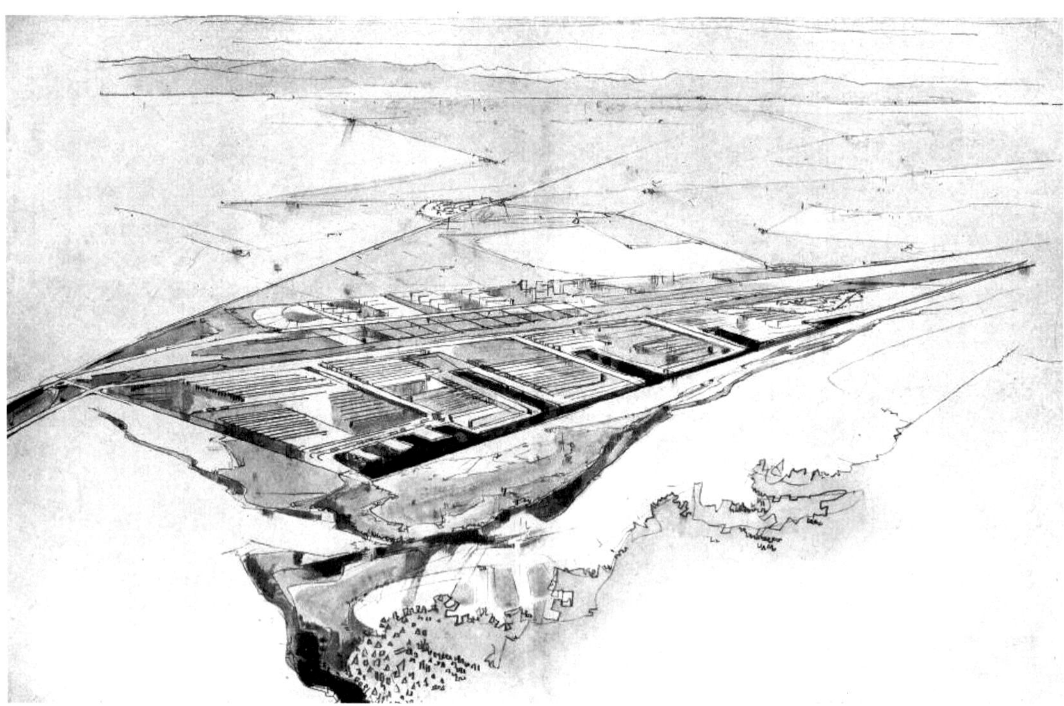

Piano Regionale Piemontese
View of the new unit from Stura to Settimo
Piedmont
ABRR (Giovanni Astengo, Mario Bianco, Nello Renacco, Aldo Rizzotti)
1944–1946
Università IUAV di Venezia, Archivio Progetti, Giovanni Astengo Fund

Reconstruction in Milan, during which intellectuals discussed the urgency of a territorial reorganisation, both in urban and rural areas. Here, Rogers and Enrico Peressutti highlighted the urgent need for a national plan, while Bruno Zevi suggested adopting the US model. The ABRR group presented the developments of the plan they were working on and the possibilities of its application in other Italian regions.[17]

The *Piano Regionale Piemontese* thus became one of the first Italian scientific proposals for territorial analysis and diagnosis. In the authors' forecasts of the region's development over the next 30 years, the river Po was seen as its structuring element. This major artery allowed for the creation of a natural communication network, by means of navigable canals, like the Lombard *navigli*, which connected the Canton Ticino with the Veneto region. The settlements established along this route would have been urban cores of between 5,000 and 20,000 inhabitants.[18]

The ABBR group carried out further studies at the time to support the river communication of the new settlements with road and rail communication: in *Arteria di Attraversamento Nord-Sud di Torino*,[19] they proposed a system

17 See Tafuri, Manfredo. *Storia dell'architettura italiana: 1944–1985* (Turin, 1986).

18 See Astengo, Giovanni, 'Piano Regionale Piemontese', *Metron: rivista internazionale d'architettura* (1947).

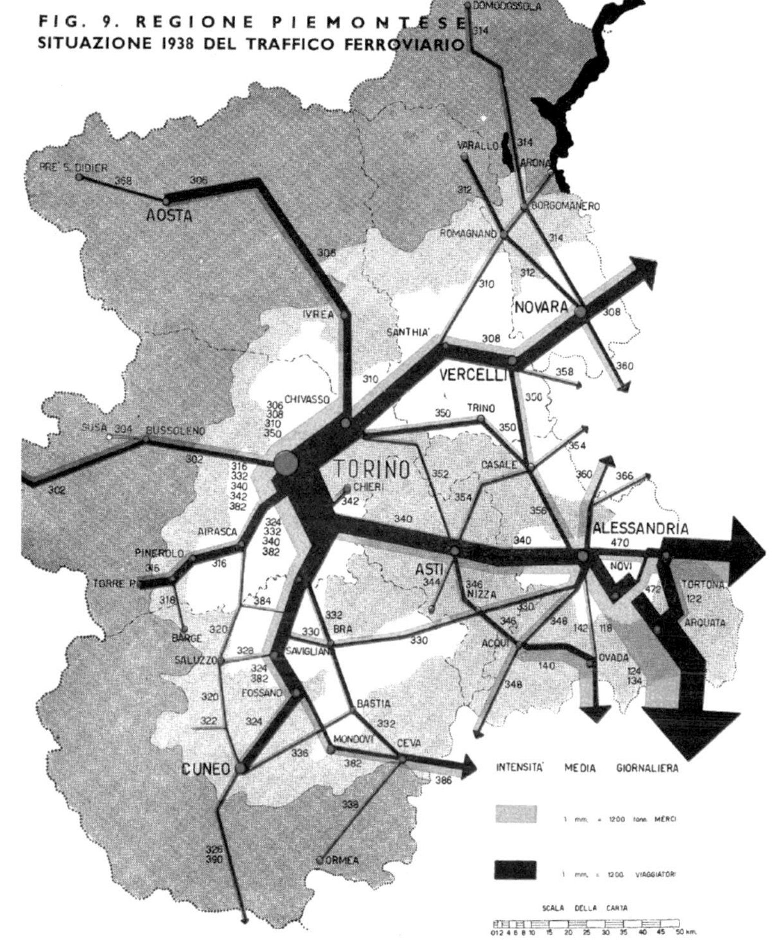

Piano Regionale Piemontese
Railway traffic situation in 1938
Piedmont
ABRR (Giovanni Astengo, Mario Bianco, Nello Renacco, Aldo Rizzotti)
1944–1946
Università IUAV di Venezia, Archivio Progetti, Giovanni Astengo Fund

of level crossings to allow the fast flow of urban vehicular transit. In *Sistema Ferroviario di Torino*,[20] the creation of an extra-urban railway line was proposed, which would allow efficient communication between Turin and its hinterland, connecting it more efficiently to the stations of Porta Nuova and Porta Susa.

Bianco and his fellow ABRR members soon became aware of the historical responsibility of the task they had voluntarily taken on. In February 1946, the professional association was officially commissioned by the local government to draw up a regional plan.[21] In the same year, the central government, noting the urgent need for a plan to reorganise the Italian territories devastated by the war and recognising the originality and depth of the work of the Piedmontese planners, chose them as consultants.

19 ABRR, 'Arteria di attraversamento Nord-Sud di Torino', *Atti e rassegna tecnica della società degli Ingegneri e degli Architetti in Torino* (1947), pp. 236–241.

20 Astengo, Giovanni, 'La sistemazione ferroviaria di Torino', *Cronache economiche* (1947), pp. 12–14.

21 See Astengo, Giovanni et al., *Cenni sul piano regionale piemontese. Relazione al sindaco di Torino* (Turin, 1946).

Sistema ABC
Modular houses with pressed sheet metal elements. Overall view of the collective housing type with balcony
Turin
Giovanni Astengo, Mario Bianco, Armando Ceratto
Mid-1940s
Università IUAV di Venezia, Archivio Progetti, Giovanni Astengo Fund

For the *Piano Regionale Piemontese*, the initial support of the Italian government was followed by a phase of bureaucratic stalemate and state inertia. Despite the inactivity of the Italian government, Bianco's relocation to Peru, as well as the early international dissemination of the Plan, allowed its teachings to reach the Latin American region. In 1947, in addition to a monographic issue of the magazine *Metron*,[22] the Exposition Internationale de l'habitation et de l'urbanisme in Paris gave considerable space to the Turin proposal. On that occasion, *L'architecture d'aujourd'hui* also published the study in two editions: one in French, the other in Spanish.[23] In 1948, *Urbanistica e edilizia in Italia*, a book edited by the National Institute of Urban Planning, published the material presented by ABRR in the Paris exhibition.[24] By 1953, the magazine

22 See Astengo, Giovanni, 'Piano Regionale Piemontese', *Metron: rivista internazionale d'architettura* (1947).
23 Letourneau, Jean, 'L'exposition internationale de l'urbanisme et de l'habitation', *L'architecture d'aujourd'hui* (1947), pp. 120–135.

Sistema ABC
Interior view of the prototype
Turin
Giovanni Astengo, Mario Bianco, Armando Ceratto
1945
Università IUAV di Venezia, Archivio Progetti, Giovanni Astengo Fund

Acrópole, an important voice on issues of Brazilian architecture and urbanism, included the Piedmontese plan in a comparative analysis of American and European town planning.[25]

During the same years in which they wrote their contributions on spatial planning, Bianco and Astengo developed other studies related to post-war reconstruction in Italy. In collaboration with Armando Ceratto (a former student of Bianco's at the Politecnico di Torino), they patented the Sistema ABC[26] (an acronym of Astengo, Bianco and Ceratto) for modular houses with unified elements in moulded sheet metal. It is a prefabricated and modular construction system that allowed housing to be built in a shorter time than with traditional technologies. Bianco and Astengo also prepared a study on the natural lighting of residential buildings, as it applied to this system for multi-storey buildings, which was widely disseminated within and beyond national borders: the study was used in the Quartiere INA-Casa di Falchera (1951–1960) in Turin, designed by a collective led by Astengo, and in the Unidad Vecinal Santa Marina (1949–1952) in Callao, a project led by Bianco (see III.5).

This research was presented in various activities organised in Italy and abroad. Between September and October of 1947, at the International Building Exhibition in Turin, the work of the ABRR was illustrated in the urban planning and architecture sections. As far as territorial planning was concerned, the

24 Astengo, Giovanni, 'I piani urbanistici, in Istituto nazionale di urbanistica' (ed.), *Urbanistica e edilizia in Italia* (Rome, 1948), pp. 37–83.
25 Lodi, Carlos, 'Considerações sobre pontos fundamentais do Planejamento Urbanistico', *Acrópole* (December 1953), pp. 378–382.
26 Astengo, Giovanni and Bianco, Mario, 'Case componibili ad elementi unificati in lamiera stampata', *Metron: rivista internazionale d'architettura* (1945), pp. 74–83.

Plan was exhibited by Bianco and associates; the architectural exhibition, which included the assembly of two prefabricated systems, one of which was ABC,[27] was curated by the Piedmont section of APAO. Between June and November of the same year, the Triennale di Milano was held, where Bianco and his colleagues' patent was exhibited together with the CGT system developed by Aldo Cassinelli, Eugenio Gentili and Enrico Tedeschi. Finally, *Architectural Forum* published the Piedmontese designers' solution in its November 1947 issue, dedicated to prefabricated metal systems.[28] In Italy, however, the need to quickly employ a considerable mass of unskilled workers was one of the main factors that led to a lack of interest in prefabricated metal structures. Mario Ridolfi, in the first edition of the *Manuale dell'Architetto*, omitted these construction systems, preferring the continued use of traditional ones.[29]

In 1947, Bianco accepted an invitation from another engineering alumnus, Renato Ghibellini, to work in Peru with his family construction company (see I.1.3.). This opportunity, together with the possibility of finding application in the Latin American market for the ABC patent and the application of Piedmont's territorial planning studies in South American countries, not to mention the national economic situation as well as that of his family,[30] finally convinced him to leave Italy.

Bianco applied for a one month leave of absence from the Politecnico in April 1947 to travel to Peru as a representative for the prefabricated systems of the Italian company Ceratto.[31] The designer thus joined the group of architects and urban engineers who adhered to the APAO and participated in the editorial activities of the magazine *Metron*: all moved to the Latin American continent between 1947 and 1948, with temporary or permanent stays (see I.2.3., III.6.). As the correspondence of those years testifies, these transfers contributed to the consolidation of the discipline of urban planning as a tool for developing a model for the Latin American city promoted by Europeans on that continent.

III.3. **Bianco's activity in Agrupación Espacio (1947–1951)**

In the second half of 1947, the year of Mario Bianco's arrival in Lima, Agrupación Espacio's first cultural activities began, which covered music, theatre, painting, literature, architecture and, later, urban planning. To this end, following the publication of their manifesto (see I.3.2.), Espacio used two channels to which Bianco actively contributed: the organisation of various public events, including a cycle of lectures, and the publication of these activities and other news related to urban planning, architecture and arts in the newspaper *El Comercio*,

27 Becker, Gino. 'Mostra Internazionale di Edilizia a Torino', *Metron: Rivista Internazionale d'architettura* (1947), pp. 61–66.

28 Martin, Henry T., Letter to Giovanni Astengo, *Università Iuav di Venezia, Archivio Progetti, Giovanni Astengo Fund* (25 June 1948).

29 Abarca, Héctor, 'Una arquitectura a dos voces: Las transferencias arquitectónicas del Piamonte a Latinoamérica', in Montestruque-Bisso, Octavio, and Fabbri García, Martín (eds.), *Mario Bianco: el espacio moderno en el Perú* (Lima, 2017), p. 110.

30 A serious bereavement in the family, the death of his wife in 1936, and his subsequent second marriage in 1939.

31 Perucca, Egidio, Letter to Mario Bianco, *Museo del Politecnico di Torino, Archivio Storico Studenti* (17 April 1947).

between 1947 and 1950, and in the magazine *Espacio*, between 1949 and 1951. As he had done in Italy with APAO and the magazine *Metron*, Bianco shared his Italian professional experiences with a wider audience through the spaces the collective had available in the mainstream and specialised press.

Bianco attended the first lecture of the public events programme, held by Paul Linder in the Sociedad de Arquitectos, entitled *Acerca de la plástica en arquitectura*, on the interaction between architecture and the visual arts (see II.5.). Through the German architect, Bianco met Adolfo Cordova Valdivia[32] and Carlos Williams León,[33] founding members of Espacio. Although the gestation and creation of Espacio took place shortly before Bianco's move to Peru, the designer was soon to become a first-class member of the group. Already by the second year of Espacio's existence, Bianco had become part of its executive committee, as communicated in a brief note in March 1948.[34]

Through his rank, Bianco played an active role in international relations, such as those established with the CIAM organisers.[35] As the group's operational advisor, he signed a letter addressed to the CIAM secretary Sigfried Giedion in which he requested the creation of a Peruvian delegation that could participate in forthcoming congresses. Although this delegation was never formalised, the communications that took place during this period attest to the active participation of the Italian planner in Espacio.

In tune with members of the Peruvian collective, Bianco advocated the necessity of urban planning as an instrument capable of providing answers to the dizzying growth of Peru's major cities, primarily Lima. This strong support from Bianco, which was added to that of other Peruvian and foreign colleagues, had tangible results. In a note published in the newspaper *El Comercio* in 1949, the members of Agrupación Espacio wrote that the consolidation of urban planning would become a priority over architecture and contemporary arts.[36]

In the pages of *El Comercio*, in the section *Colabora la Agrupación Espacio* (1947–1950), Bianco found ample opportunity to share his Italian experiences in the fields of prefabrication, university teaching and, above all, regional planning, as demonstrated by the various articles published. In these writings, Bianco's effort to popularise his Italian experiences in the Peruvian context was evident (see III.2.). Thus, in *El tamaño de Lima*, he spoke to readers about the maximum admissible size of an urban settlement (according to the methodology employed by ABRR in the drafting of the *Piano Regionale Piemontese*); whereas, in *Prefabricación*, he illustrated the advantages of prefabricated and modular construction systems over traditional ones (topics already dealt with in 1945 in the Italian *Metron*.

32 Arequipa, 1924 – Lima, 2022.
33 Lambayeque, 1924 – Lima, 2004
34 'Agrupación Espacio', *El Comercio* (6 March 1949).
35 Agrupación Espacio, Letter to Sigfried Giedion, *ETH Zürich, gta Archiv, CIAM Fund, 42-SG-33-240/241* (11 April 1949).
36 'Agrupación Espacio 1947–1949'. *El Comercio* (19 May 1949).

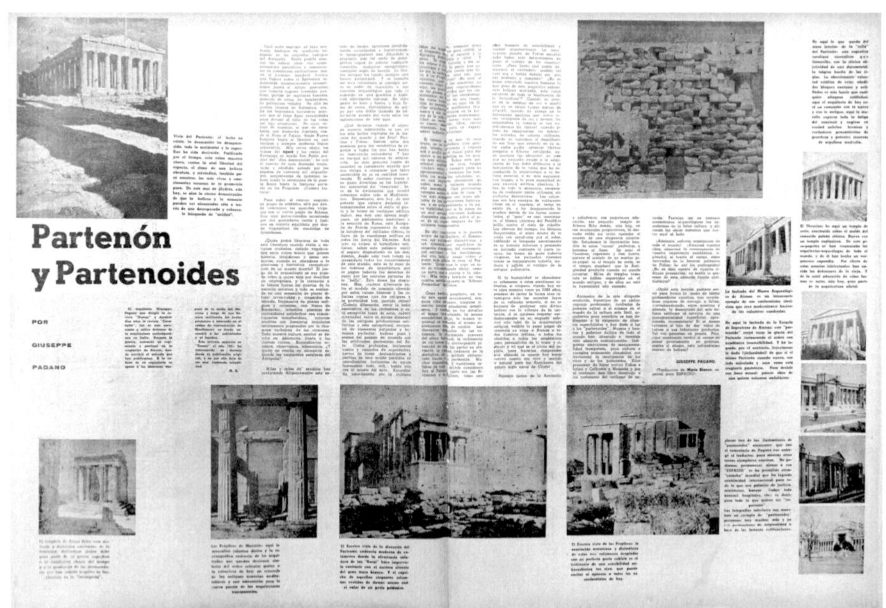
Partenón y Partenoides

POR GIUSEPPE PAGANO

Giuseppe Pagano (translated by Mario Bianco)
Partenón y Partenoides
Lima
1950

Giuseppe Pagano in *Espacio* (1950)

Interest in the rationalisation of building systems was revealed by some of Bianco's Peruvian experiments, conducted until 1951, on prefabricated systems using local materials such as wood and cane. These experiences were published in the trade press. In particular, the magazine *El Arquitecto Peruano* dedicated two articles in 1949 to the realisation of timber-framed residential buildings and the use of universal metal knots for Guayaquil-type cane structures, for which Bianco filed a patent in the Peruvian register in 1951. Despite widespread media coverage, as in the Italian case, they never attracted the interest of the Peruvian market.[37] In the short and intense process of institutionalising Agrupación Espacio, two years after the publication of its manifesto, the official journal was inaugurated. From 1949 to 1951, the specialised magazine of the same name published several articles related to Bianco's early activities in Peru as a cultural populariser, urban planner and designer. In 1950, for instance, Luis Miró Quesada described the Casa D'Onofrio[38] (1948–1949), one of the Italian designer's first Peruvian works also published by *El Arquitecto Peruano*. This project, for an Italian family's suburban villa, carried out in collaboration with Córdova and Williams, repeated the dynamic of the European client and the professional association with local colleagues, which had already been undertaken by Paul Linder with the German Ursuline nuns and the Peruvian architect Héctor Velarde (see II. 4.). The design choices for Casa D'Onofrio – the

37 See Bianco, Mario, 'La Arquitectura y el Medio. La Caña como Elemento Estructural', *El Arquitecto Peruano* (April 1949); 'Stands diversos', *El Arquitecto Peruano* (October 1949); Beingolea del Carpio, José Luis, 'Mario Bianco. Clasicismo y modernidad entre Italia y Perú', *Universidad Nacional de Ingeniería* (Lima, 2007).

38 See Miro Quesada, Luis, 'Residencia en San Felipe', *Espacio* (July 1950), p. 5; 'Residencia del Señor Luis D'Onofrio en Orrantia del Mar, por el Arqto. Mario Bianco y el Constructor José de Bona', *El Arquitecto Peruano* (January-February 1950), pp. 38–44.

Casa D'Onofrio
Magazine cover
San Isidro, Lima
Mario Bianco et al.
1948–1949

El Arquitecto Peruano
(January–February 1950)

Enero 1950
S/o. 4.50

overcoming of the decorative apparatus using proportions, the treatment of surfaces and the choice of colours employed – echoed the themes addressed by Bianco in *Valores Eternos y Valores Perecederos*, published in May 1949 in *Colabora la Agrupación Espacio.*[39]

Thanks to his academic and professional experiences in Italy and the relationships established within Espacio, Mario Bianco received positions in various Peruvian state institutions. The earliest and longest, a lectureship at the Escuela Nacional de Ingenieros, came as a direct consequence of the Reforma Universitaria. This assignment reinforced Bianco's decision to remain in Peru until 1960.

39 Bianco, Mario, 'Valores eternos y valores perecederos', *El Comercio* (12 May 1949).

III.4. Escuela Nacional de Ingenieros, the Department of Architecture and the exhibition *Latin American Architecture Since 1945* (1948–1955)

In 1948, Mario Bianco became the holder of the chair of architectural design in the final year of the course of studies in the Department of Architecture at the Escuela Nacional de Ingenieros. The Reforma Universitaria (1945–1946) and his membership in Agrupación Espacio (1947–1955), two factors that enabled the start of his university career in Peru, were closely linked to each other (see I.3.3.). Several professors participating in the changes to the architecture curriculum envisaged by this reform were members of Espacio. In 1955, for example, all design workshops were directed by professors belonging to the Peruvian collective.

As the leader of the fifth-year design workshop, dedicated to the drafting of these projects, Bianco had the opportunity to train some of the students who were to become first-rate national and international exponents: in the disciplines of urban planning, Eduardo Neira;[40] in architectural design, Walter Weberhofer;[41] in the history of architecture, José García Bryce;[42] and in restoration, Víctor Pimentel.[43] The latter had the opportunity to forge a relationship of esteem and trust with Bianco even before having him as a professor, during the construction of the Department's headquarters. Between 1951 and 1953, the young architecture student was installed as Technical Director at this building site, closely following all phases of construction.[44]

40 Eduardo Neira Alva (Lima, 1924 – 2005).
41 Walter Weberhofer Quintana (San Jerónimo de Tunan, Junín, 1923 – Lima, 2002).
42 José García Bryce (Lima, 1928 – 2020).
43 Víctor Pimentel Gurmendi (Lima, 1928).
44 Pimentel Gurmendi, Víctor. *Víctor Pimentel Gurmendi y el patrimonio monumental: textos escogidos*, in Beingolea del Carpio, José Luis (ed.) (Lima, 2015), p. 43.

Class of 1952
Mario Bianco, in the second row, is third from the left
Department of Architecture at the Escuela Nacional de Ingeniería, Lima
1952
Ing. Prof. Mario Bianco Private Archive

Department of Architecture building of the Escuela Nacional de Ingenieros
Magazine cover
Lima
Mario Bianco et al.
1951–1953

El Arquitecto Peruano (January–February 1955)

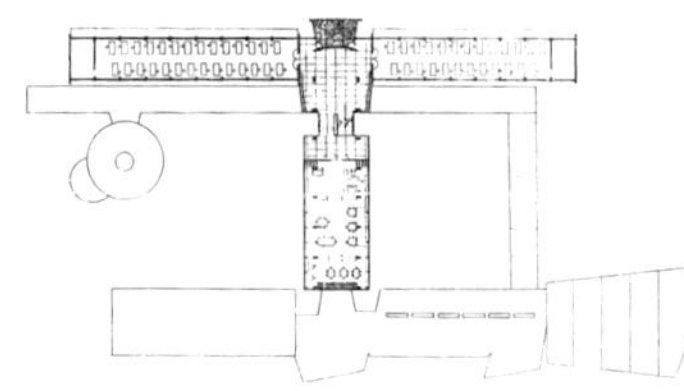

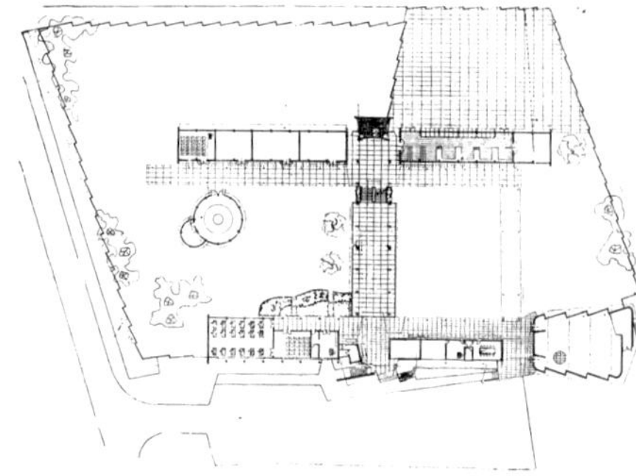

Department of Architecture building of the Escuela Nacional de Ingenieros
Area view from the south and ground and first floor plans
Lima
Mario Bianco et al.
1951–1953

El Arquitecto Peruano (January–February 1955)

The project for the headquarters of the Department of Architecture of the Escuela Nacional de Ingenieros (Lima, 1951–1953) was developed from a scheme proposed by Mario Bianco.[45] In this regard, Fernando Belaúnde Terry recalled that '[Mario Bianco] tenía un gran sentido de la estructura… Para construir nuestra facultad, escogimos el esquema que él presentó.'[46] We can read in the pages of the magazine *El Arquitecto Peruano* how the proposal drawn up by Bianco took into consideration the functional programme presented by Belaúnde and the suggestions made by the other lecturers in the department during meetings held at the school in 1951.[47] Bianco, fresh from his design experience for the new headquarters of the Politecnico di Torino, had no difficulty in developing the layout on which the future seat of architecture would be built.

The building was constructed to the north-west of the historic centre of Lima, on the road leading to the seaside town of Ancón, and was oriented towards the south. A series of volumes delineated the different activities housed there: to the south, beyond the main entrance, there were three bodies containing the administrative offices, the classrooms dedicated to urban planning subjects and the auditorium; to the north, a three-storey building contained the teaching rooms and the materials laboratories. Between these two, the volume of the library, built on pilotis, divided the open space into two courtyards, oriented toward the east and west; in the latter, a circular body was arranged as a classroom for drawing and sculpture. The choice in the volumetric composition testified to the interiorisation of the functionalist creed by the Italian designer. A system of canopies provided covered access to the various buildings.

45 See 'El Departamento de Arquitectura de la Escuela Nacional de Ingenieros', *El Arquitecto Peruano* (January–February 1955).

46 '[Mario Bianco] had a great sense of structure… To build our faculty, we chose the scheme that he presented.' Zapata, Antonio, *El joven Belaunde: historia de la revista El arquitecto peruano: 1937–1963* (Lima, 1995), p. 132.

47 Belaúnde Terry, Fernando, 'Aspiración lograda', *El Arquitecto Peruano* (May–June 1953), pp. 17–18.

Department of Architecture building of the Escuela Nacional de Ingenieros
Library reading room
Lima
Mario Bianco et al.
1951–1953

El Arquitecto Peruano (January–February 1955)

To conceive the spaces of the new department, Bianco made skillful use of the reinforced concrete structure, which allowed for free layouts and façades. The orientation and the use of sunshades throughout displayed the designer's close attention to the issues of sunshine and natural illumination of the buildings.[48]

The completion of work on this building was followed by the visit of numerous illustrious guests (see III.6.). In its first issue of 1953, the magazine *El Arquitecto Peruano* reported on the visit of the Italian architect Enrico

Peruvian delegation from the Department of Architecture of the Escuela Nacional de Ingenieros with Chilean colleagues from the Faculty of Architecture of the Universidad de Chile. Mario Bianco, seated, second from left
Santiago de Chile
1954

Ing. Prof. Mario Bianco Private Archive

Tedeschi,[49] who had moved to Argentina in 1948 (see I.2.3.). In the middle of the same year, Josef Albers gave a lecture at the department. Between 1953 and 1954, Walter Gropius and Josep Lluís Sert visited the Department of Architecture and were appointed honorary professors of the Escuela de Ingenieros.[50] In 1954, two events took place in the international arena which were to have a major impact on the Department of Architecture and the construction of its premises. In October, Henry-Russell Hitchcock visited the Peruvian capital, while he was organising the *Latin America Architecture Since 1945* exhibition on behalf of the Museum of Modern Art (see I.3.3., II.5.). Although Bianco's two projects – the headquarters of the Department of Architecture of the Escuela Nacional de Ingenieros and the Unidad Vecinal Santa Marina – were not shown in the exhibition, the Department of Architecture was included in the catalogue.

In November of the same year, Bianco's activities were also recognised by the Universidad de Chile: on his trip to Santiago, as a representative of the delegation of the Department of Architecture,[51] itself part of a university exchange programme,[52] he was recognised as Miembro Honorario of that university.[53] The precedents of these relationships can be traced back to the experiences of two Peruvian architects, members of Espacio, trained in Chile: Mario Gilardi, who had attended a conference organised by the Peruvian Centro de Estudiantes de Arquitectura in 1945, illustrating the work of emblematic architects of the modern movement, such as Le Corbusier; and later, Javier Cayo, who would be given the chair of the fourth-year design workshop, forming part of the Peruvian Teaching College in 1955.

48 Atoche Intili, Javier, 'Gli apporti europei nella costruzione del Progetto Moderno in America Latina. Mario Bianco e il Perù', in Esposito, Daniela, and Montanari, Valeria (eds.), *Realtà dell'architettura fra materia e immagine. Per Giovanni Carbonara: studi e ricerche* (Rome, 2021), p. 500.

49 See 'Visita de Enrico Tedeschi', *El Arquitecto Peruano* (January–February 1953).

50 See 'Sert y Gropius Profesores Honorarios de La Escuela', *El Arquitecto Peruano* (November–December 1953).

51 Together with Córdova, Carlos Morales Macchiavello and Miguel Cusianovich. See Pimentel Gurmendi, Víctor, 'Víctor Pimentel Gurmendi y el patrimonio monumental: textos escogidos', in Beingolea del Carpio, José Luis (ed.) (Lima, 2015), p. 20.

52 See Alvarez Ortega, Syra, *La formación en arquitectura en el Perú: antecedentes, inicios y desarrollo hasta 1955* (Lima, 2006), pp. 186–201; 'Apuntes a Mano Libre. Ha Llegado La Delegación Chilena', *El Arquitecto Peruano* (January–February 1953).

53 Diploma of Honorary Member of the Faculty of Architecture of the Universidad de Chile, Ing. Prof. Mario Bianco Private archive (11 November 1954).

Agrupación Espacio's sphere of influence, however, involved more than just the university. Starting in 1946, Fernando Belaúnde Terry, along with some of the leading exponents of the Peruvian collective, developed within the Department the lines of thought that were to influence not only architecture in the following decades, but above all Peruvian housing policies. As was the case of the Corporación Nacional de Vivienda (see I.2.2.), as well as the Junta de Obras Públicas del Callao (see III.5.), managerial positions within the public housing bodies were occupied by members of Espacio, including Mario Bianco.

III.5. Junta de Obras Públicas del Callao and the construction of the Unidad Vecinal de Santa Marina (1949–1952)

The contacts established with Agrupación Espacio, as well as the influence of CIAM members on the American continent, enabled Mario Bianco to quickly resume the professional experiences he had begun in his native country. Ever since his arrival in Lima in April 1947,[54] the designer was employed as a consultant to public housing authorities. Together with Adolfo Córdova and Carlos Williams, founders of Agrupación Espacio, Bianco drew up preliminary plans for the cities of Chiclayo, Cajamarca and Trujillo on behalf of the Corporación Nacional de la Vivienda.[55]

Collaborations with public administration in the field of housing continued in those years within the Junta de Obras Públicas del Callao, and this was soon documented by two articles (entitled *La Ricostruzione del Callao, Porto di Lima*[56] and *Nuovi Quartieri Organici al Callao*[57]) published by Bianco in 1950 in the Italian magazine *Urbanistica*. The port locality presented various urban problems related to internal migration, aggravated by the effects of the earthquake and subsequent tidal wave of 1940 (see I.2.1.). In the published articles, Bianco provided details related to management of the reconstruction, as well as reporting his designation as group leader for the drafting of housing proposals. As the chief in charge of the housing policy office, Bianco directed a group of technicians, largely made up of members of Espacio,[58] who were charged with the planning of *unidades vecinales* (see I.2.2.), neighbourhoods equipped with complimentary services. The construction of the new centres became the instrument for an organised expansion of the city, whose organic neighbourhoods gave their title to Bianco's article published in 1950 in *Urbanistica*.[59]

The 3,000 housing units requested by Junta de Obras Públicas del Callao, representing approximately half of the houses needed to replace those rendered uninhabitable by the earthquake of 1940, while at the same time reducing the

54 This air travel document records Bianco's presence in New York on 18 April 1947, in transit from Italy to Peru. See *New York, Passenger Lists, 1820–1957* (2 January 2023).

55 See 'Plan Nacional de La Corporación de La Vivienda'. *El Arquitecto Peruano* (August 1949).

56 Bianco, Mario, 'La Ricostruzione del Callao, Porto di Lima', *Urbanistica* (April–June 1950), pp. 61–62.

57 Bianco, Mario, 'Nuovi Quartieri Organici al Callao', *Urbanistica* (October–December 1950), pp. 49–52.

58 Formed by Adolfo Córdova, Carlos Williams, and Fernando Sanchéz Griñán, signatories of the founding manifesto of Agrupación Espacio.

59 Bianco, Mario, 'La Ricostruzione del Callao, Porto di Lima', *Urbanistica* (April–June 1950), p. 61.

Mario Bianco, Adolfo Córdova and collaborators
Around 1949

Ing. Prof. Mario Bianco Private Archive

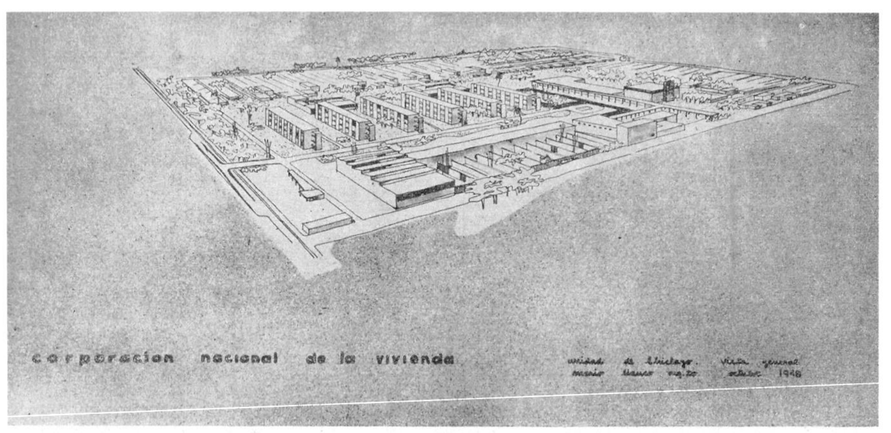

Moderna Unidad Vecinal para Chiclayo
Aerial view of the proposal Corporación Nacional de Vivienda (team leader Mario Bianco)
1949

Corporación Nacional de Vivienda in *El Arquitecto Peruano* (August 1949)

Moderna Unidad Vecinal para Chiclayo

con 545 viviendas en 225·hectáreas

overcrowded ones in Callao,[60] were grouped into smaller neighbourhoods and clusters. The Pescadores neighbourhood (never realised) envisaged 1,080 housing units, with a density of 265 inhab/ha, as well as complimentary services (including laundry, market, primary school, sports and recreation areas, not to mention a church) for a population of 6,900 inhabitants. In the area

60 Bianco, Mario, 'Nuovi Quartieri Organici al Callao', *Urbanistica* (October–December 1950), pp. 49–50.

61 Abarca, Héctor, 'Una arquitectura a dos voces: Las transferencias arquitectónicas del Piamonte a Latinoamérica', in Montestruque-Bisso, Octavio, and Fabbri García, Martín (eds.), *Mario Bianco: el espacio moderno en el Perú* (Lima, 2017), p. 120.

62 Bianco, Mario, 'Nuovi Quartieri Organici al Callao', *Urbanistica* (October–December 1950), pp. 50–52.

Unidad Vecinal de Santa Marina
Highlights, far left, the Santa Marina intervention area
Callao
Junta de Obras Públicas del Callao (Housing team leader Mario Bianco)
1949–1952

Junta de Obras Públicas del Callao in *Urbanistica* (October–December 1950)

designated for the Itsmo de Chucuito neighbourhood (this too never realised), a smaller project was eventually built in the 1960s, occupying only one of the eight projected blocks.[61]

The Unidad Vecinal Santa Marina (1949–1952),[62] the largest of the three planned complexes, was the only one to be built under the direction of Bianco. This neighbourhood unit comprised 1,240 dwellings, with a maximum of 9,600 inhabitants. In addition to two-storey, two-bedroom, single-family buildings, the planner added multi-family blocks of four storeys in height, with two flats accessed by each stairwell. The use of different types of housing units (*casas modelo*) was intended as demonstration of the distributional efficiency and construction effectiveness of the various types designed.

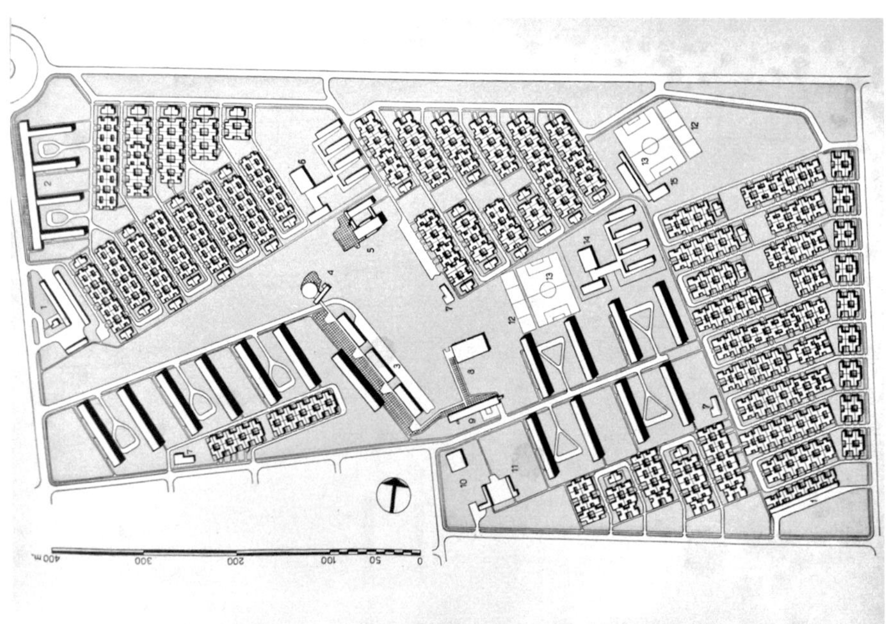

Unidad Vecinal de Santa Marina
General planimetry of the neighbourhood unit
Callao
Junta de Obras Públicas del Callao
(Housing team leader Mario Bianco)
1949–1952

Junta de Obras Públicas del Callao in *Urbanistica* (October–December 1950)

Unidad Vecinal de Santa Marina
Three-bedroom multi-family blocks and one- and two-level modular houses
Callao
Junta de Obras Públicas del Callao
(Housing team leader Mario Bianco)
1949–1952

Ing. Prof. Mario Bianco Private Archive

As in other neighbourhood units built at that time in Peru, the design criteria adopted by Bianco included the creation of a pedestrian island, limiting the traversing of the neighbourhood to service vehicles only. As far as zoning was concerned, three areas (civic, religious and sports) were created, along with public spaces for the different groups of houses, through the introduction of small green areas. An exception, requested by the municipal administration, concerned a group of four-storey buildings placed outwards, at the intersection of the two main streets in the area, to create a gateway to the city for those arriving from the port.

In addition to this variation, the proposal was modified during construction, to adapt to the new road system as well as to the demands for increased housing density. Thus, the redefinition of the lot after the construction of the roundabout (at the intersection of the two arteries already mentioned) and the need to build more housing, forced the planner to revise the orientations and distances between the buildings, which had been scrupulously studied beforehand. Despite changes, Santa Marina remained, in the words of Walter Gropius during his 1954 visit to Lima, an architectural work capable of competing with other newly built neighbourhoods.[63] Bianco himself would confirm this appreciation in a letter written to his colleague Giovanni Astengo in April 1954.[64]

III.6. Oficina Nacional de Planeamiento y Urbanismo, the planning of the *Plan Piloto de Lima* and the construction of the Hotel Savoy (1948–1957)

The promotion in Peru of the triad democracy-development-planning by some members of CIAM, as well as experience in the spheres of urban planning and architectural design in Italy, facilitated Mario Bianco's participation in the preliminary studies necessary for the drafting of the *Plan Piloto de Lima*, as did his consulting job for the *Plan Regulador de Buenos Aires*, in 1949. A letter from Bianco, sent on 25 January 1949 to the then director of the Politecnico di Torino, Eligio Perucca, documented his collaborations with the Oficina Nacional de Planeamiento y Urbanismo (as head of the projects department), including an invitation from the Buenos Aires City Council for a consultancy on the execution of a nationwide study (*Estudio del Plan de Buenos Aires*, 1948–1954).[65]

It stands to reason that the contacts established at the CIAM conference in Bridgewater in 1947, between Ernesto Nathan Rogers and the Argentine delegate Jorge Vivanco, allowed architects Enrico Tedeschi, Cino Calcaprina, Luigi Piccinato and Rogers himself to travel to Argentina and participate in the

63 Héctor Abarca, Ibid.

64 Bianco, Mario, Letter to Giovanni Astengo, *Università Iuav di Venezia, Archivio Progetti, Giovanni Astengo Fund* (28 April 1954).

65 Bianco, Mario, Letter to the Director of the Politecnico di Torino, Eligio Perucca, *Museo del Politecnico di Torino, Archivio Storico Docenti* (6 April 1949).

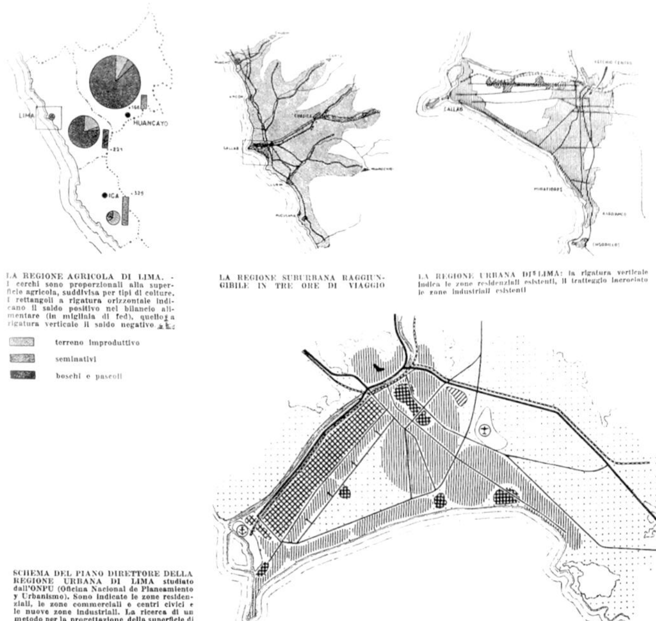

***Urbanistica* no. 2**
Magazine cover
Turin
1949
Urbanistica (September–October 1949)

Il Dimensionamento nell'Urbanistica Regionale
Scheme of the Lima Urban Region Master Plan
Lima
Mario Bianco
1949
Mario Bianco in *Urbanistica* (September–October 1949)

activities of the Instituto de Arquitectura in Tucumán. Piccinato, who became ministerial councillor for urban planning and government representative in the *Plan de Buenos Aires*, managed the Italian group's participation in the drafting of the Plan, on which Argentine architects Bonet, Ferrari-Hardoy and Kurchan were working. All except Calcaprina and Tedeschi, who were engaged on the Tucumán front, were involved in the undertaking[66] (see III.2.).

As with Argentina, collaborations between Italian and Peruvian technicians intensified after the Second World War. In a letter dated 16 March 1949, Giovanni Astengo – in response to a request for collaboration on studies of Italian urban planning legislation made by the director of the ONPU and Espacio member Luis Dorich – sent him *Urbanistica e edilizia in Italia*, a publication promoted by the National Research Council, containing material from the *Piano Regionale Piemontese* presented at the Exposition Internationale de l'habitation et de l'urbanisme in Paris.[67] Concurrently, Ernesto Nathan Rogers visited Lima to advise on the drafting of the *Plan Piloto*, while Bianco completed the studies necessary to draw up the plan for the Peruvian capital. In April 1949, he informed Eligio Perucca of developments regarding his collaboration with the ONPU. The studies by the Piedmontese planner, published also in

66 Their correspondence, exchanged with Astengo at the time, confirmed Bianco's presence in the city of Buenos Aires, Ibid.

67 See Astengo, Giovanni, 'I piani urbanistici', in Istituto nazionale di urbanistica (ed.), *Urbanistica e edilizia in Italia* (Rome, 1948).

68 Bianco, Mario, 'Il Dimensionamento nell'Urbanistica Regionale', *Urbanistica* (September–October 1949), pp. 11–14.

Edificio Irma
Main view
Lima
Gianfelice Fogliani
1946–1948
El Arquitecto Peruano (September 1948)

Urbanistica of the same year,[68] were focused on: the relationship between town planning and agriculture; demographic movements and internal migrations; a national road plan; the agrarian budget; the situation concerning ports; hydroelectric and mining potentials; the possibilities of population growth in the city of Lima; and interventions in its historic centre.[69]

The *Plan Piloto de Lima*, an integral part of the master plan that was drawn up adhering to the precepts of the *Charte d'Athènes*, promoted the construction of multi-storey buildings as part of its strategy for the organisation of the city's growth (see I.2.2.). An early example of a multi-storey building is the work of another Italian designer, Gianfelice Fogliani, in the Edificio Irma[70] (1946–1948), a rationalist work that presents a mixture of commercial activity, offices and housing. This was the context for the Hotel Savoy (1954–1957), conceived by Bianco in the centre of Lima, about which the designer wrote to his colleague Astengo on 28 April 1954:[71] 'Then I want to build a "building" that I am designing, with a parking area on the roof on the 2nd floor, and another eight on stilts.' This was Bianco's architectural response to the requirements of the *Plan Piloto*.

The Hotel Savoy is located in the historical centre of Lima, just two blocks from the Plaza Mayor, on the corner of Jirón Cailloma and Jirón Callao.[72] As in the case of the headquarters of the Department of Architecture, Bianco divided the building into a series of volumes with different functions: the plinth consisting of the first two floors used for the reception of the hotel and related commercial spaces; the tower used for the rooms, having the main view onto Jirón Cailloma; between the two bodies, an open plan contained the parking spaces; the terrace above the tower was dedicated to the Savoy's sky room. The main façade was a composition of solids and voids, created by alternating windows and cupboards in the hotel rooms. These dual volumes testified to the fusion of two sources of inspiration present in Bianco's cultural baggage: first, the viceregal-era balconies, visible in the basement, which recalled the typical colonial-era balconies still present in the centre of Lima; and, of course, modern European architecture, which was present in the tower, a design reminiscent of the proposals made by the New York firm Town Planning Associates for Chimbote (see I.2.2.) and by Josep Lluís Sert for the historical centre of Lima (see I.3.3.), both inspired by the Unité d'Habitation of Marseille in its adoption of pilotis and the use of free-standing plants and a roof-garden.[73]

As in 1941, Bianco's manifold professional and academic activities were recognised in 1957 by the Italian government, which awarded him the honour of Cavaliere. Despite his professional success in Peru, and simultaneously harbouring numerous qualms about returning to his homeland,[74] Bianco decided

69 Bianco, Mario, Letter to the Director of the Politecnico di Torino, Eligio Perucca, *Museo del Politecnico di Torino, Archivio Storico Docenti* (6 April 1949).

70 Gianfelice Fogliani (Milan, 1906 – ?), a civil engineer trained at the Politecnico di Milano, moved to Peru in 1945. The *Edificio Irma*, commissioned by *Compañía de Seguros La Colmena*, has six floors above ground and one basement, of which the first three levels are used for commerce and offices and the remaining four for housing. See 'Edificio Irma, en Lima, propiedad de la Compañía de Seguros "La Colmena"', *El Arquitecto Peruano* (September 1948).

71 Bianco, Mario, Letter to Giovanni Astengo, *Università Iuav di Venezia, Archivio Progetti, Giovanni Astengo Fund* (28 April 1954).

72 See 'Hotel Savoy', *El Arquitecto Peruano* (December 1957).

73 Atoche Intili, Javier, 'Gli apporti europei nella costruzione del Progetto Moderno in America Latina. Mario Bianco e il Perù', in Esposito, Daniela, and Montanari, Valeria (eds.), *Realtà dell'architettura fra materia e immagine. Per Giovanni Carbonara: studi e ricerche* (Rome, 2021), pp. 500–502.

Hotel Savoy
Main view
Lima
Mario Bianco
1954–1957

Ing. Prof. Mario Bianco
Private Archive

Hotel Savoy
Reception
Lima
Mario Bianco
1954–1957

Ing. Prof. Mario Bianco
Private Archive

Letter from Mario Bianco to Giovanni Astengo with details and sketch of the multi-storey hotel that the former was designing in Lima
28 April 1954

Università IUAV di Venezia, Archivio Progetti, Giovanni Astengo Fund

MARIO BIANCO - ARQUITECTO
LIMA

(AÑO DEL LIBERTADOR MARISCAL CASTILLA) 256

28 aprile 1954

Mi querido Gio,
chi é in colpa é il sottoscritto, che da vari mesi pensa de scriverti in risposta alla tua ultima, in ringraziamento per i magnifici volumetti de evidente, seppur celata, paternitá tua. Veramente avrei gradito, lá dove parli del Fed, un cenno riguardo al fratello suo, il coefficente de industrializzazione. Perché non imposto uno studio al proposito, come sé fatto per l'economia agricola; Potremmo farlo in collaborazione a distanza, se credi; io potrei contribuire alle spese per il personale impiegato.

Degli aurei volumi del Ministero, che tu mi mandasti, vorrei altri due esemplari, per la Facoltá e per la Oficina de Planeamiento; un terzo paio di esemplari dovresti farlo inviare al "Ministero de Fomento y Obras Publicas" per tramite dell'Ambasciata. Tutti gli altri Stati danno molta pubblicitá alle loro realizzazioni ed elucubrazione; noi dobbiamo solo esportare pellicle e tenori.

Il corso estivo ventilato da Nerla, é rimasto una delle tante intenzioni di quel bravo giovane, che, come ventilatore, é piuttosto volatile e soffia un pó da tutte le parti, combinando poco. E non se ne puó fargli rimprovero perché in questo paese resta ben poco tempo da dedicare ad attivitá che non sia la routine pecuniaria. Per intanto, tra il lavoro del suo studio e l'impiego de un impiego che ha accettato nel Ministero, dove fa le funzioni di sottocapo de la divisione urbanistica, credo che non gli resti neanche tempo di vedersi con gli amici. Io non lo vedo da mesi. Per quanto riguarda la tua venuta quá, io confidavo piuttosto sull' Un. di Tucumán; ma ho ricevuto da poco una lettera di Tedeschi, che mi dice che si trasferisce a Mendoza, all'Un. del Cuyo, strano tipo di universitá che prende il nome da una regione e che dissemina le sue facoltá in differenti cittá. Per quanto riguarda la tua fermata en Lima, ti confermo quanto ebbi giá a dirti nella mia precedente; due mil soles dalla facoltá, chissá altrettanto da Planeamiento, naturalmente starai a casa mia. In totale sarebbe un 'entrata netta di circa duecento dollari; poco, ma sommato a quello che potrebbe venire dall'Argentina, potrebbe rifonderti le spese di viaggio. Scrivi a Tedeschi che avrei tanto piacere di riavere anche lui in Lima.

Ti sono molto grato delle notizie dei concorsi; non credo che ne faró nulla, per le seguenti ragioni; uno sradicamento é giá sufficente, nella vita; tornerei in Italia(per trapiantarmici), solo se avessi, per esempio, un congruo incarico; ma non mi sento di affrontare le lotte di un concorso, che non potrei neanche seguire da vicino e cercare i corrispondenti appoggi. Di pubblicazioni, qui non se ne fanno, o quel poco che c'é é molto meschino. Se il ministro mi manda a chiamare dall'ambasciatore, offrendomi la nomina a Padova, il passaggio per me e la famiglia masserizie incluse, e tre mesi di stipendio anticipati, forse ci potrei pensare. Siccome poi il ministro dei ll.pp. é di nuovo quel caro bassetto, c'é una ragione in piú per disgustarmi del ritorno. In un paese poi dove non nominano neanche un Astengo per acclamazione alla cattedra de Firenze! No, caro mio, In Italia ci torneró da turista, se ce la faró. Poi voglio costruire un building che sto progettando, con piazzale di stazionamento sul tetto del 2° piano, ed altri otto piani sul palafitte. Ho ormai molto lavoro, e mi sto facendo una solida fama tra gli ebrei, che hanno quattrini a sacchi; ho giá fatto una casa che io chiamo organica, per uno di essi, una casa d'affitto per un altro, che sto finendo, ho poi anche un simpa-

GIRON HUANCAVELICA 470-409
TELEFONO 41858

MARIO BIANCO - ARQUITECTO
LIMA

256

tico cinese, milionario e sarto, al quale ho giá fatto tre case, e ho consegnato ieri il progetto di un'altra, di dodici appartamenti. Sta bollendo in pentola l'affare del terminal terrestre, stazione generale di autolinee, e anche il risanamento del colle di San Cosme, accumulazione di quattromila persone che hanno invaso con le loro capanne una collinetta di propietá privata che ora lo Stato compra per ricostruire le case e venderle per un boccón di pane agli invasori. Come vedi, ci sono parecchie cose sul tappeto, Si termina il padiglione della facoltá, riuscito solo a mezzo, come ti racconteró quando ti manderó le foto, e continuo a insegnare composizione al quinto anno. Gli alunni sono simpatici.

Per ora basta, ti abbraccio, vecchio mio, saluti a Luciana, al Gis, a tutti quanti. Dammi notizie e pettegolezzi dell'ambiente. Ciao

Mario

Dimenticavo di dirti che abbiamo avuto la visita di Gropius, che ci é parso una magnifica persona, pare che quello che abbiamo fatto nel Perú non gli sia dispiaciuto. Insisti con Tedeschi; io per mio conto scriveró a Solow capo della divisione " vivienda y Planeamiento" dell'organizzazione degli Stati Americani in Washington, perché ti procuri un incarico di conferenza al centro di Bogota, che servirebbe a foraggiarti il viaggio, ed a conoscere un p'ó di Colombia

Ciao Mario

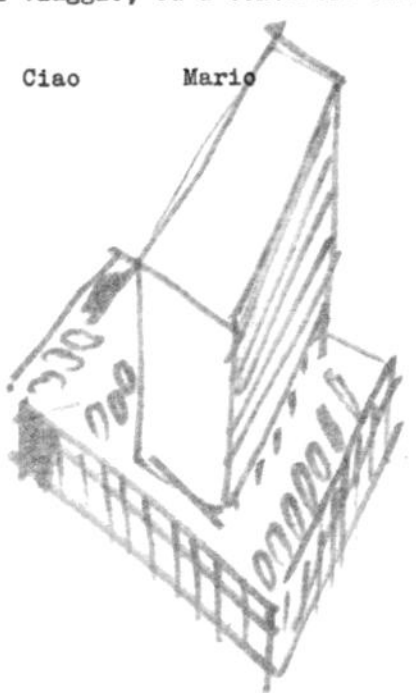

GIRON HUANCAVELICA 470-409
TELEFONO 41858

La più alta onorificenza del Perù riconosce i meriti di un torinese

E' l'architetto Mario Bianco, che, dopo aver insegnato al nostro Politecnico, si trasferì a Lima - Fa parte dell'équipe di architetti che ha vinto il concorso per il Centro direzionale

L'architetto Mario Bianco nel suo studio. Accanto: un palazzo da lui progettato a Lima. Al secondo piano c'è un colossale parcheggio per auto.

La più alta onorificenza del Perù riconosce i meriti di un torinese
Article published on the awarding of the honour of Comendador de la Orden El Sol del Perú to Mario Bianco
Turin
1963

La Stampa (22 November 1963)

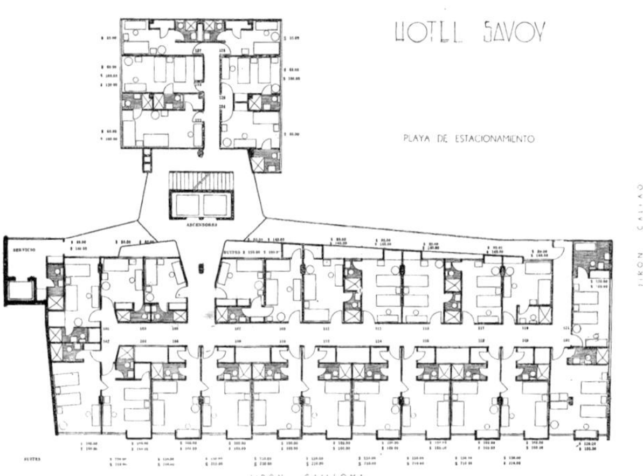

Hotel Savoy
Tower floor plan
Lima
Mario Bianco
1954–1957

Mario Bianco in *El Arquitecto Peruano* (December 1957)

to travel back to Italy. Reasons related to family (his wife's homesickness[75]) and his profession (most notably, the limited space for research dedicated to the discipline of town planning) all contributed to his decision.

A trip to Italy in 1959 enabled Bianco to re-establish the necessary contacts with the authorities at the Politecnico di Torino. In short order, he was able to give a free course, entitled *Urbanistica regionale*, in the academic year 1960–1961, which summarised his experiences in Italy and Peru. Given the possibility of resuming university teaching in his native country, along with the completion of his son Lorenzo's architectural studies in December 1959, Bianco decided to return to his homeland for good in April 1960.[76] Upon return to Italy, an episode marked his professional career: in 1962, he participated with a group, directed by Ludovico Quaroni (motto 'Akropolis 9'), in a competition for the design of the Centro Direzionale di Torino. Their proposal won first place and was widely published in architectural periodicals.

Other participants in the competition for the Centro Direzionale, which remains one of the cornerstones of 1960s Italian architecture, included Giovanni Astengo, Giuseppe Samonà, Carlo Aymonino and Aldo Rossi with Gianugo Polesello.[77] *Domus* magazine dedicated two issues to the competition in November 1963 and February 1964.[78]

The following year, the architect Belaúnde, having since been elected President of the Republic of Peru, honoured him with the title Gran Maestro de la Orden del Sol in recognition of his contributions in the fields of Peruvian town planning and architecture.

74 Bianco, Mario, Letter to Giovanni Astengo, *Università Iuav di Venezia, Archivio Progetti* (28 April 1954).

75 See Córdova Valdivia, Adolfo, 'Los arquitectos europeos y la Agrupación Espacio', *Interview* (13 September 2016); Vella Zardin, Franco, 'Mario Vella Micocci, constructor de arquitectos europeos', *Interview* (22 February 2017).

76 The air travel document records Bianco's presence in Miami on 10 April 1960, in transit from Peru to Italy. *Florida passenger lists, 1898–1963* (2 January 2023).

77 Rogers, Ernesto Nathan, 'Il Concorso per Il Centro Direzionale di Torino', *Casabella Continuità: Rivista Internazionale di Architettura e Urbanistica* (1963), p. 9.

78 'Appunti Sulle Idee al Concorso di Torino', *Domus* (November 1963), pp. 4–10; Ponti, Gio, 'Le Torri Di Torino', *Domus* (February 1964), pp. 1–10.

Ceremony at the Embassy of Peru in Rome for awarding the honour of Comendador de la Orden El Sol del Perú to Mario Bianco
From left to right: Peruvian architect Santiago Agurto, Mario Bianco, Peruvian ambassador to Italy Eduardo Garland
Rome
18 November 1963
Ing. Prof. Mario Bianco Private Archive

Peruvian recognition for the Italian master was reaffirmed in 1965, when the Colegio de Arquitectos del Perú (formerly Sociedad de Arquitectos) declared him an honorary member. The signatories of the diploma – Oswaldo Jimeno, President of the Order, and Hilde Scheuch, Secretary General – represented two generations of Peruvian architects who had been trained, both at the university and professional level, by the Italian architect, engineer, urban planner and professor.

Bianco worked as a designer in Italy until the late 1970s. From then until his death (24 October 1990), he began a new phase of his life, travelling throughout India while studying philosophy and religion.

THEODOR CRON (1921–1964): NEUES BAUEN AND PERUVIAN REGIONALISM

SWISS, EUROPEAN, AMERICAN EXPERIENCES

1921

Theodor Cron's birth (Basel, Switzerland)

1930

CZECH REPUBLIC Villa Tugendhat (Ludwig Mies van der Rohe, Brno, 1928–1930)

1933

SWITZERLAND Cron begins studies at the Humanistisches Gymnasium in Canton Basel

1940

Die Neue Architektur: Dargestellt an 20 Beispielen – 1930–1940 (Alfred Roth, Zürich-München)

1941

SWITZERLAND Cron begins studies at the Eidgenössische Technische Hochschule (ETH)

1943

USA *Brazil Builds: Architecture New and Old, 1652–1942* (MoMA, New York)

SWITZERLAND Cron works with Alfred Roth

1920s

1930s

1940s

PERUVIAN EXPERIENCES

1937

El Arquitecto Peruano's first issue

Establishment of the Sociedad de Arquitectos del Perú

1938

Establishment of the Consejo Nacional de Urbanismo

Swiss builder Carlo Galli moves to Peru

ETH engineer Ernst Frey moves to Peru

1940

Earthquake and tsunami in Lima and Callao

National Census

Establishment of the Peruvian construction company Flórez & Costa Ingenieros

1944

Establishment of the Instituto de Urbanismo del Perú

Paul Lester Wiener in Peru

1945

Espacio en el Tiempo. La arquitectura como fenómeno cultural (Luis Miró Quesada, Lima)

1945

SWITZERLAND Theodor Cron and colleague Adolf Bührer conclude their studies at the ETH

1946

VENEZUELA Adolf Bührer moves to Caracas

ITALY Cron's first stay

1947

UK CIAM VI (Bridgewater)

ITALY Cron's second stay

SWITZERLAND *Das italienische Zimmer* (Theodor Cron, Zurich)

1946

Italian engineer and builder Mario Vella moves to Peru

Reforma Universitaria

1946

Peruvian urban planning regulations: Ley de propiedad horizontal, Oficina Nacional de Planeamiento y Urbanismo, Corporación Nacional de Vivienda, Centros Climáticos de Esparcimiento

1947

Expresión de Principios de la Agrupación Espacio

VI Congreso Panamericano de Arquitectos (Lima, Cusco)

Plan Piloto de Lima (Oficina Nacional de Planeamiento y Urbanismo, with the advice of Ernesto Nathan Rogers, Josep Lluís Sert, 1947–1949)

1948

Cron moves to Peru

Casa Huiracocha (Luis Miró Quesada, Lima, 1947–1948)

1949

Apartments on Calle Roma (Theodor Cron, Lima, 1948–1949)

1949

ETH architect Adolf Bührer moves to Peru

Swiss builder Arturo Saredi moves to Peru

1951

SWITZERLAND *A decade of new architecture* (Sigfried Giedion, Zurich)

Walter Kern obtains his architecture degree at the ETH and moves to Peru

1952

FRANCE Unité d'Habitation (Le Corbusier, Marseille, 1947–1952)

SWITZERLAND Theodor Cron meets Roth

1953

SWITZERLAND Georg Rudolf obtains his architecture degree at the ETH and moves to Peru

1955

USA *Latin America Since 1945* (MoMA, New York)

1956

USA S. R. Town hall (Ludwig Mies van der Rohe, Chicago, Cook County, Illinois, 1950–1956)

1950s

1951

Casa Hochköppler (Theodor Cron, Lima, 1950–1951)

1952

Casa Oechsle (Adolf Bührer, Lima, 1952)

1953

Casa Schär (Theodor Cron, Lima, 1953)

ETH engineer Robert Steinegger moves to Peru

1956

Compañía de Seguros Peruano-Suiza (Theodor Cron, Lima, 1952–1956)

1958

SWITZERLAND Cron's stay

1962

USA Cron stays with Luisa Martinto and children in the US

SWITZERLAND Cron's stay

1963

SWITZERLAND Cron moves to Basel

1964

Theodor Cron dies (Klosters, Canton Grigioni, Switzerland)

1960s

1956

Cinema Roma (Theodor Cron, Lima, 1955–1956)

1959

Banco Continental (Theodor Cron, Lima, 1957–1959)

Residencial Peruano-Suiza (Christian Tgetgel, Lima, 1959)

1961

La Colmena Compañía de Seguros (Paolo Mariotta, Lima, 1958–1961)

1962

Fabrica d'Onofrio, Casa d'Onofrio and Casa Zuzunaga (Georg Rudolf, Lima, 1962)

1965

Edificio Nizzola (Georg Rudolf, Walter Kern, Lima, 1965)

1967

Planta industrial Volkswagen (Walter Kern, Lima, 1967)

Chapter IV
Theodor Cron (1921–1964), Neues Bauen and Peruvian Regionalism

IV.1. Architects trained at the Eidgenössische Technische Hochschule in Zurich and active in Peru in the mid-twentieth century (1937–1953)

In the mid-twentieth century, the modernist turn occurring in architectural practice was reinforced by the intense professional activity of Swiss architects who moved to Peru between the 1940s and 1960s. This phenomenon took place in a country that was not a historical destination for Swiss migration: it is estimated that of the approximately 300,000 Swiss who moved to the New World between 1820 and 1918, 260,000 arrived in the United States, 35,000 in Argentina and only 10,000 in other countries of the American continents.[1] The Swiss migration to Peru was therefore of minor numerical importance compared to other destinations; nevertheless, it left a remarkable architectural heritage, in terms of quantity and typological diversity, as well as the technical and spatial qualities of buildings.

The Bundesamt für Gewerbe, Industrie und Arbeit indicated in 1958 that the relocation of highly qualified Swiss figures to emerging countries, such as Peru, was in Switzerland's own best interests. These migratory phenomena facilitated the creation of Die Neue Helvetische Gesellschaft, 'The New Helvetian Society,' for the cultural cohesion of what the same body called the 'Fifth Switzerland.' This expression refers to the Swiss who moved abroad, representing a further cultural area: the fifth, if one considers the four distinct language areas present in Swiss territory.[2]

1 Baechler, Joseph, *Presencia suiza en el Peru* (Lima, 1991), p. 61.
2 See Purtschert, Patricia and Fischer-Tiné, Harald, *Colonial Switzerland: Rethinking Colonialism from the Margins* (Houndmills / Basingstoke / Hampshire, 2015).

Theodor Cron
Zurich
1944
ETH Zürich, gta Archives, Hans Hofmann Fund

Adolf Bührer
Zurich
1944

ETH Zürich, gta Archives,
Hans Hofmann Fund

This phenomenon is reflected in the consular register in Lima, which in 1952 recorded the presence of 10 Swiss architects practising in Peru,[3] a considerable number when one considers that only 20 graduated in Architecture from the Escuela Nacional de Ingenieros in Lima[4] that same year. Among the designers active at the time were professionals trained at the Eidgenössische Technische Hochschule (ETH) in Zurich, such as Ernst Frey, a civil engineer who moved to Peru in October 1937,[5] and the architect Fredéric Gautier,[6] who had been a resident there since 1941.

The activities of Swiss technicians, including professionals who had attended the ETH, increased in the second half of the twentieth century. Of the nine architects registered at the Swiss Consulate in Lima in 1961, five professionals trained at the ETH had emigrated to Lima after the war. In chronological order of arrival in Peru, they were Theodor Cron[7] (moved in 1948), Adolf Bührer[8] (1949), Walter Kern[9] (after 1951), Christian Martin Tgetgel[10] (1955) and Georg Rudolf[11] (1956).

In Cron's case, his departure for Peru was dictated neither by political nor professional reasons, as was the case for Paul Linder and Mario Bianco, but rather by cultural motivations. His interest in pre-Hispanic and viceregal societies is evident in the work of the young Swiss architect, who achieved a synthesis of modern civilisation and local culture while living and working in Peru.

3 Berger, Juan Adolfo, 'Revista de la Colonia Suiza en el Perú' (1952), p. 54.
4 See 'Graduación de veinte nuevos arquitectos', *El Comercio* (24 December 1952); 'Ayer se graduaron veinte Arquitectos egresados de la Escuela de Ingenieros', *La Crónica* (24 December 1952).
5 He worked until 1939 with the Polish architect Ricardo Jaxa Malachowski in the reconstruction of the *Palacio de Gobierno*. See Baechler, Joseph, *Presencia Suiza en el Peru* (Lima, 1991).
6 Architect, trained at the ETH between 1931 and 1935, active in Peru until the 1960s. Author of the *Suizo Club* headquarters and the cinemas *Le Paris* and *Le Biarritz*. Ibid.
7 Hans Theodor Cron Gröber (Basel, 9 September 1921 – 25 February 1964). Attended the ETH between 1941 and 1945. *ETH Zürich, Bibliothek Archiv*, EZ-PEK 1/1/25'355.
8 Stetten, Canton Schaffhausen, 1918 – Bargen, Canton Schaffhausen, 2003. Swiss architect and artist who spent time on the American continent between 1946 and 1975.
9 Born in Buchberg, Canton Schaffhausen, on 7 June 1925, he attended the ETH between 1946 and 1951. *ETH Zürich, Bibliothek Archiv*, EZ-PEK 1/1/31'013.
10 Born in Truns, Canton Graubünden, on 29 August 1928, he attended the ETH between 1948 and 1953. Ibid., EZ-REK 1/1/31'530.
11 Born in Ems, Canton Graubünden, on 6 May 1927, he attended the ETH between 1948 and 1953. Ibid., EZ-REK 1/1/31'515.

IV.2. Theodor Cron's training and departure for Peru (1921–1948)

Theodor Cron[12] was a Swiss architect, younger than both Paul Linder and Mario Bianco, whose projects were mainly realised in Peru. His Peruvian work can be divided into two phases: the first was characterised by a strong appreciation of local tradition; the second, an exaltation of the international trend. His architectural research was characterised by volumetric simplicity and imbued with the duelling natures of form and space, the latter taken from the Peruvian cultural tradition, although reformed in contemporary language. This interest in pre-Hispanic and viceregal heritage becomes evident in the work of the young Swiss architect, who achieved a cutting-edge synthesis between modern civilisation and local culture during his many years in Peru. In this regard, Fernando Belaúnde Terry recalled that '[Theodor Cron] Nos dejó ejemplos de una sobria, pero impactante arquitectura, para la zona árida.'[13]

Growing up in Basel in the inter-war period, Cron's childhood and adolescence were strongly influenced by his family environment. His mother Lina Gröber, who was very active in local cultural circles, passed on to her son an interest in artistic weaving.[14] However, it was his paternal family's business that determined the educational path of father Niklaus and sons Theodor and Leo, as their grandfather Jean[15] was the owner of the Jean Cron Construction Company, founded in 1936, a business taken over by Theodor's father. Cron's

12 Currently, a group of researchers coordinated by the Peruvian scholars Irene Arce and Johann Schweig are working on a publication and an exhibition on Theodor Cron's work, which is scheduled to open in 2023 at the Museo de Lima (we thank them for the shared material concerning the Theodor Cron Private Bequest).

13 '[Theodor Cron] left us some examples of essential but striking architecture for the arid zone.' Zapata, Antonio, *El joven Belaunde: historia de la revista El Arquitecto Peruano: 1937–1963* (Lima, 1995), p. 133.

14 See Pazos, Víctor, 'Theodor Cron: Ipséité et architecture', École d'Architecture de Paris-La-Villette/ Université Paris VIII (Paris, 2010).

15 Buschwiller, Alsace, 1884 – Basel, 1950. Jean Cron was a successful building contractor who built, among other things, St. Clare's Hospital in Basel.

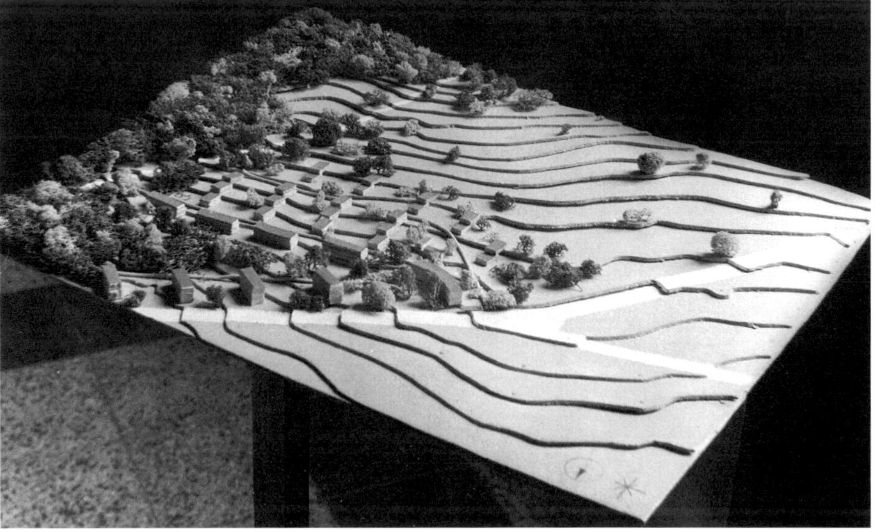

Wohnungsbau
Zurich
Theodor Cron
1944

ETH Zürich, gta Archives, Hans Hofmann Fund

personality, perhaps more introverted and sensitive than that of his family members, came to influence his interests in drawing and painting. In Basel, he studied at the Humanistiches Gymnasium. After graduating from high school in April 1941, he moved to Zurich to continue his studies.

Cron attended the ETH during the Second World War. His professors in architectural design and urban planning were William Dunkel[16] (1942 to 1944) and Hans Hofmann[17] (1944 to 1945) and he went on to receive his degree in architecture on 25 July 1945.[18] Hofmann's teachings, which focused on the themes of Neues Bauen and the rejection of the new architecture in traditional and regional models, as well as the reforms initiated by Karl Moser[19] after 1915, which gave constructive aspects a more prominent place in the curriculum, would have had a considerable influence on his education.

During his years of study, and through the ideas of Dunkel, Cron deepened his knowledge of the work of Bauhaus-related figures. Although no documents have been found to prove direct contact with Ludwig Mies van der Rohe,[20] it is possible to state that Cron was very familiar with the work of the German architect, who became a recurring design reference for him (see VI.5., VI.6.). In those years, he was known to have made the acquaintance of Alfred Roth,[21] a pupil of Karl Moser and a figure close to Le Corbusier and the CIAM. To be sure, Cron completed an apprenticeship in Roth's Zurich studio in 1943 and, over the same months, worked as part of the editorial staff of the magazine *Werk*, of which Roth was editor-in-chief.[22] The two remained in contact even after Cron's departure for Latin America.[23]

Cron's move to Peru can be ascribed to three key factors: the marked internationalisation of ETH; the considerable investment of foreign capital in the Latin American region; and the presence of Swiss figures in Peru. It is also probable that the experience on the American continent of Dunkel, who was born in the United States and had spent a period of his life in Argentina, influenced a few ETH students who then decided to stay for extended periods in their respective South American countries.

This hypothesis is confirmed by the experience of Adolf Bührer, who graduated in architecture, together with his colleague Cron, in July 1945.[24] As Dunkel's assistant, Bührer left Switzerland together with his wife Margrit in 1946, financed by a scholarship from the ETH to study in Venezuela.[25] Leaving Switzerland in August 1946 and embarking from the Swedish port of Gothenburg in the same year, they arrived in La Guaira, the port of Caracas, on board the ship Argentina.[26] As was the case with Bührer, Cron received funding from the ETH for a study trip to Italy. Two stays between 1946 and 1947 gave him the opportunity to immerse himself in that Mediterranean country,

16 New Jersey, USA, 1893 – Kilchberg, Canton Zurich, 1980. 'William Dunkel (1893–1980)', *ETH Zürich, Bibliothek Archiv* (2020).

17 Zurich, 1897–1957. Luchsinger, Christoph, *Hans Hofmann: vom neuen Bauen zur neuen Baukunst* (Zürich, 1985), pp. 141–154.

18 Minutes of the President of the Swiss School Board, awarding the Diploma of Architect to Theodor Cron. *ETH Zürich, Bibliothek Archiv, Hochschularchiv, Präsidialverfügungen 1945, Präsidialverfügung, Nr. 1022* (25 July 1945).

19 Baden, 1860 – Zürich, 1936.

20 Aachen, 1886 – Chicago, 1969.

21 Wangen an der Aare, 1903 – Zurich, 1998.

22 The Alfred Roth fund holds various documents, including Roth's account book (1942–1948) and diaries, as well as a letter from Cron to Roth dated 14 June 1943, which testify to the relationship established between both planners. *ETH Zürich, gta Archiv, Alfred Roth Fund*, 131-K-23.

23 Ibid.

24 He received the architect's diploma with a grade of 5.26, according to the provisions of the President of the Swiss Institute Council of 23 July 1945. *ETH Zürich, Bibliothek Archiv*, EZ-PEK 1/1/25›355.

25 Galerie Mera (ed.), 'Adolfo Bührer: 1918–2003 – Stetten – Südamerika – Bargen: ein malerisches Leben', *Galerie Mera* (Schaffhausen, 2011), p. 56.

26 'Schweizerisches Auswanderungsamt und Auswanderungsbüro. Überseeische Auswanderungen aus der Schweiz, 1910–1953', *Schweizerisches Bundesarchiv* (2011), E2175-2.

27 See Cron, Theodor, *Das italienische Zimmer*, Private Bequest Theodor Cron (Basel, s.d).

28 Galerie Mera (ed.), 'Adolfo Bührer: 1918–2003 – Stetten – Südamerika – Bargen: ein malerisches Leben', *Galerie Mera* (Schaffhausen, 2011), p. 56.

EIDGENÖSSISCHE TECHNISCHE HOCHSCHULE

PROTOKOLL DES PRÄSIDENTEN
DES SCHWEIZERISCHEN SCHULRATES 1022

ZÜRICH, den 25. Juli 1945.

Nach Entgegennahme eines Berichtes und Antrages der Diplomkonferenz der Abteilung für Architektur vom 23. Juli 1945 (3715/214.44),

in Ausführung des Art. 14 des Regulativs für die Diplomprüfungen vom 10. Mai 1924,

wird verfügt:

1. Folgenden Kandidaten der Abteilung für Architektur wird das Diplom als Architekt erteilt:

Bertrand, Jacques André, von Mülhausen (Elsass)
Bührer, Adolf, von Stetten (Schaffhausen)
Catella, Guido, von Oberrieden (Zürich)
Cron, Theodor, von Basel
Glaus, Otto, von Schänis (St. Gallen)
Lang, Peter, von Subingen (Solothurn)
Rüegger, Ernst, von Mauren (Thurgau)
von Seemann, Peter, von Schellenberg (Liechtenstein)
Siebenmann, Walter, von Aarau (Aargau)

2. Folgendem Kandidaten wird das Diplom wegen ungenügenden Prüfungsergebnisses nicht erteilt:

Gugelot, Johan, holländischer Staatsangehöriger

3. Die Namen der Diplomierten werden im schweiz. Bundesblatt veröffentlicht.

4. Mitteilung an die Genannten, das Rektorat, die Kasse und den Abteilungsvorstand zuhanden der Konferenz.

Alfred Roth
1958
Dräyer, Walter in ETH-Bibliothek, ETH Zürich

Protokoll des Präsidenten des Schweizerischen Schulrates
Minutes of the President of the Swiss School Council awarding the Diploma of Architect to Theodor Cron, Adolf Bührer and others
Zurich
25 July 1945
ETH-Bibliothek, ETH Zürich

the cradle of Latin culture (see IV.4.). In the report entitled *Das italienische Zimmer*,[27] Cron illustrates some of the characteristics of vernacular Sicilian and Calabrian architecture, which would later form part of his design lexicon: the square proportion; the use of double heights; the hermetic relationship between interior and exterior; and the counterpoint between white-plastered walls and ceilings and their brightly coloured floors.

In the same years, Bührer had been enquiring into professional possibilities in various Latin American countries.[28] The two colleagues had probably agreed to meet in Lima, an appointment to which Bührer arrived late, due to the unpredictable nature of his journey by automobile through South America on his way to reach the Peruvian capital. In 1948 Cron left Switzerland for Peru with the idea of staying there for a short time, but the period abroad lasted for over 15 years, until 1963.

IV.3. **The apartments on Calle Roma (1948–1949)**

The short time between his landing in the port of Callao, in August 1948, and the submission of the paperwork to San Isidro's municipal technical office for his first building permit, in December of the same year, testifies to Theodor Cron's rapid professional integration in Peru. Historical relations between Europe and the Andean country, which materialised in the presence of prosperous communities from the Old World, favoured his professional ascent in Lima. Moreover, his interest in artistic weaving, coupled with the knowledge inherited from his family business, not to mention his professional training in construction, facilitated the integration of Peruvian building systems into his projects, allowing him to closely follow all phases of design and construction: this catapulted him into the then unusual role of construction manager. In the end, his sojourns in Italy, alongside a keen sensitivity and intelligence, allowed Cron to employ elements of the traditional Peruvian coastal repertoire in his early works, mostly residential buildings for the Swiss who had settled in Peru. His architectural language, a mixture of Neues Bauen and Italian vernacular architecture, was enriched by using: courtyard distribution; the cubic composition of the dwellings built with mud bricks; the presence of Moorish-influenced windows; the use of *pasteleros* (brick tiles suitable for climates with little rainfall) as well as compact, coloured walls.

The relationships developed by Theodor Cron with some of the most important figures of the Peruvian bourgeoisie, including Pedro Weiss and Alejandro Ciurlizza, allowed the Swiss architect to settle in Lima for longer than originally planned. Alejandro Ciurlizza (see I.1.3.), an interior designer of great sensitivity, was responsible for the product lines of his family's furniture factory. He was a grandson of Louis Maurer, a Swiss from the canton of Berne, and Lorenzo Ciurlizza, a Croatian, both founding partners of the Peruvian Sociedad Maderera Ciurlizza Maurer, a wood extraction and processing company.[29] The presence of Weiss in Peru dates to the second half of the nineteenth century. His father, Robert, from Horgen, had been the first Swiss consul in Peru, a detail that underlined the position of this family within the Swiss community there.[30] Pedro Weiss, a renowned professional whom Cron met during his 1948 trip to Peru,[31] introduced him to the community of compatriots settled in Lima, in which the Ciurlizza-Maurer family were prominent.

Ciurlizza, a man of culture with a sociable character, had gathered around him a group of people from different geographical backgrounds with common interests, largely centred on the Andean world and its pre-Hispanic cultures. The acquaintance of Ciurlizza with some of these personalities represented

29 See Fistrovic, Branko, 'Presencia croata', *Boletín de Lima* (1998), p. 58; Baechler, Joseph, 'Presencia de Suiza en el Perú: Nomenclátor Biográfico', *Boletín de Lima* (2007), p. 282.

30 See Centurión Herrera, Enrique, *El Perú actual y las colonias extranjeras: la realidad actual y el extranjero en el Perú a través de cien años, 1821–1921* (Bergamo, 1924).

31 Theodor Cron arrived in Peru on 15 August 1948, as recorded in the Swiss consular register in Lima.

Theodor Cron
Lima
Second half of the 1950s

Theodor Cron Private Bequest

https://www.nzz.ch/feuilleton/hans-theodor-cron-ein-schweizer-praegt-die-baukunst-in-peru-ld.1513980?reduced=true

a considerable opportunity for Cron: for example, the work of the renowned archaeologist Arturo Jiménez Borja[32] had a considerable influence on his architecture, which immediately began incorporating references to pre-Hispanic and Peruvian viceregal cultures. In addition, participation in the cultural evenings organised in the Ciurlizza household enabled Cron to deepen his ties with Peruvian families, among them the Pardo Hereen and the Yzaga Martinto, who entrusted him with multiple assignments during the second part of his Peruvian career, between 1954 and 1962.[33]

The young Cron's first commissions came from families of Swiss origin who migrated to Peru between the nineteenth and twentieth centuries.[34] The existence of a well-established community of Swiss living in Lima meant not only the presence of a wealthy clientele, but also the availability of highly specialised technicians from back home who would collaborate with Cron in the realisation of his works.

In the mid-twentieth century, the architect's participation in the design and construction of a building followed a very different dynamic in Peru than in countries on the European continent. In a 1957 note, the Swiss magazine *Bauen + Wohnen* gave an overview of how buildings were constructed in Peru.[35] Whereas in Switzerland, a planner was usually in charge of the project from the preliminary to the execution phase, in Latin American countries, the construction phase was often entrusted to a single contractor, whose job was not only construction, but also the development of architectural details and construction management. The architect would therefore only carry out general supervision during construction after the final design had been drawn up and only then be called upon to sign off on the project's completion.

As far as the technical aspects were concerned, this process was facilitated by the characteristics of the climate. Specifically, on the Peruvian coast, the region with the greatest building activity, the absence of rainfall allowed the simplification of details related to insulation and waterproofing. Similarly, the presence of mild temperatures avoided the use of heating or cooling systems, which are used much more often in public buildings. Finally, the high seismic risk in Peruvian territory weighed heavily on structural considerations, discouraging the use of free-standing plans and large overhangs in all structures.

European designers who immigrated to Peru in the first half of the twentieth century were struck by these differences between professional practices in their countries of origin and those in their host's. Paul Linder, in a letter addressed to Walter Gropius in 1940, noted the disconnect that then existed between the conception and realisation of any work: the architect was either a mere executor of design drawings or a building contractor.[36] Similarly,

32 Tacna, 1908 – Lima, 2000. Arturo Jiménez Borja was a Peruvian doctor, writer, painter, museologist and ethnologist.

33 García Bryce, José, 'Arquitectos europeos en el Peru del siglo XX', *Interview* (24 September 2016).

34 Vella, Franco, 'Mario Vella Micocci, constructor de arquitectos europeos', *Interview* (22 February 2017).

35 Schuppisser, Santiago, 'Peruanische Notizen', *Bauen + Wohnen / Construction + Habitation / Building + Home: internationale Zeitschrift*, (1957), pp. 258–259.

36 Linder, Paul, Letter to Walter Gropius (14 January 1940), in Medina Warmburg, Joaquín (ed.), *Paul Linder, 1897–1968: de Weimar a Lima – antología de arquitectura y crítica* (Madrid, 2019), pp. 407–410.

in 1952, Mario Bianco confided to his colleague Giovanni Astengo regarding the construction of the pavilion of the Department of Architecture of the Escuela Nacional de Ingenieros: 'The Escuela also gives me its work; teaching, seminars on urban planning in its Institute, and finally the preliminary project and a bit of late management (because the executive project was developed by an office in charge of the works of the entire School, and they gave me a lot of crap).'[37] In this context, the figure of the builder became particularly important to the realisation of architectural projects, especially for Swiss architects, who were accustomed to direct control over their works.[38]

This lack of dialogue between the design and construction phases at first propelled Cron to take on the role of builder, as occurred in the apartments on Calle Roma (Lima, 1948–1949), exemplary for their unusual synthesis of Neues Bauen and Peruvian regionalism. The apartments on Calle Roma represent a milestone in twentieth century Peruvian architecture.[39] An early example of the horizontal property introduced by the 1946 town planning legislation (see I.2.2.), the building was first published in 1949 in the magazine *Bauen + Wohnen*.[40] The project envisioned the construction of four residential units for single persons (in this case, two brothers and two cousins, all Swiss origin), with parking and common services necessary for everyday life, in line with European housing standards.

An article published the following year in the magazine *El Arquitecto Peruano*[41] revealed details about the owners – Margarita Ciurlizza and Margarita Ciurlizza Maurer, both of Swiss-Croatian ancestry (see I.1.3.), as well as Charlotte Favre, a Swiss with roots in Peru – and its construction. Favre had moved to Lima to work as an official at the Swiss Embassy and lived there until the 1950s, having appeared in the Swiss Consular Register of 1957.[42] Margarita, Alejandro Ciurlizza's sister, belonged to the family that owned Sociedad Maderera Ciurlizza Maurer, a company engaged in the extraction and processing of wood for construction. This last characteristic would have been of great importance concerning construction details and fundamental in the creation of the wooden furniture and fixtures found in this dwelling.

In the realisation of the building, something akin to what Paul Linder and Mario Bianco experienced during their respective first Peruvian works had occurred: namely, the association with a technician already active in Lima. In this case, Cron took on the role of builder, together with the Moscow architect Waldermar Moser,[43] who had been a resident of Peru since 1939.

The project for the duplex on Calle Roma was realised in San Isidro, an expansion area of the city inhabited by Lima's upper-middle class. The building consisted of three floors containing four duplex-type dwellings. The proposal

37 Bianco, Mario, Letter to Giovanni Astengo, *Università Iuav di Venezia, Archivio Progetti, Giovanni Astengo Fund* (21 November 1952).

38 Ibid.

39 De la Torre Chaqui, Marco, 'Teodoro Cron, la poética del lugar', *Documentos de arquitectura y urbanismo* (1987), pp. 48–54.

40 The opportunity to publish this project in the magazine *Bauen + Wohnen* most likely came about through Otto Glaus, a colleague of Cron's during his formative years at the ETH, and since 1946 a partner of the editor of the Swiss magazine, Jacques Schader. 'Appartementhaus in Lima', *Bauen + Wohnen / Construction + Habitation / Building + Home: internationale Zeitschrift*, (1947–1949), pp. 10–11.

41 See 'Departamentos en la calle Roma', *El Arquitecto Peruano* (April 1950).

42 Ravines, Rogger, 'Presencia de Suiza en el Perú: nomenclátor biográfico', *Boletín de Lima* (1998), p. 180.

Apartments on Calle Roma
Main view
San Isidro, Lima
Theodor Cron
1948–1949

El Arquitecto Peruano (April 1950)

Apartments on Calle Roma
Ground, first and second floors; longitudinal section
San Isidro, Lima
Theodor Cron
1948–1949

Bauen + Wohnen (1947–1949)

https://www.e-periodica.ch/digbib/view?pid=buw-001%3A1947%3A1%3A%3A791#809

Apartments on Calle Roma
Living room view
San Isidro, Lima
Theodor Cron
1948–1949

Bauen + Wohnen (1947–1949)

https://www.e-periodica.ch/digbib/view?pid=buw-001%3A1947%3A1%3A%3A791#810

Apartments on Calle Roma
Façade detail
San Isidro, Lima
Theodor Cron
1948–1949

El Arquitecto Peruano (April 1950)

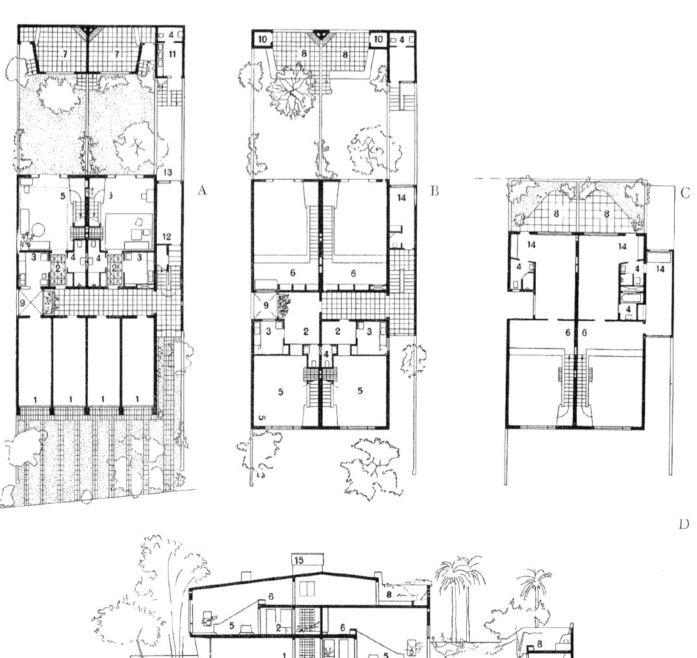

was completed by parking spaces facing the street, an internal garden and a basement structure, used for common services, with a terrace above. Cron's first work exhibited what would become a constant theme in his residential buildings: the introversion of spaces. The accepted use of large glass surfaces in international architecture, which allowed the extension of the building's rooms towards the outside, was shunned by the Swiss designer, as can be seen in the physical and visual connection between the house and its internal garden.

The main elevation on Calle Roma was composed of three elements that expressed a desire for clear separation from the street. The main entrance to the building was defined by the recessed volume of the condominium stairwell. The basement, containing a car park, had five exposed brick walls, as support and division of the parking spaces. The volume above, plastered and projecting, housed the living rooms of the upper duplex. The compactness of this volume was emphasised by the holes at the top, which were reminiscent of the earthen constructions found on the Peruvian coast. The inclusion of these architectural elements from the past, in keeping with the interests of the younger members of Agrupación Espacio,[44] found great acceptance among Peruvian architects.

The originality of the proposal lay in the mixture of Peruvian and European cultural references. The arrangement of the duplex, which in the longitudinal section of the building was reminiscent of the solution Le Corbusier had been promulgating, at least since 1947, in his Unité d'Habitation in Marseille, displayed the young Swiss architect's up-to-date architectural knowledge. The living quarters, arranged around a central corridor, presented the two-storey high living room as an articulating element of its interior space.

In addition to organising the internal distribution, the double-height living area connected the apartment with the outdoors: in the two duplexes on the lower levels, this space created a physical continuity between living room and inner garden; in the two duplexes on the upper levels facing the street, the visual connection was filtered using *moucharabies*, the wooden jalousies of colonial-Islamic origin. A third example highlighting the relationship between indoors and outdoors was found on the top level, where the bedrooms opened onto a terrace that replicated the extension of space felt on the ground floor rooms facing the garden.

The distinctive staircases inside each duplex, which had narrow passages of approximately 60 centimetres plus low and very wide parapets, approximately 40 centimetres high, were reminiscent of the circulations of Puruchuco, a pre-Columbian administrative complex restored by Arturo Jiménez Borja.[45] The parapet of the stairs, low and wide, extended towards the mezzanine, allowing it to be integrated with the double-height space. Later, as his circle of

43 Waldermar Moser Marc (Moscow, 1904 – Lima, 1988). Already fascinated by vernacular architecture during his studies at the Technische Universität in Graz, he moved to Barcelona the year after graduating in 1933. Married to a Peruvian woman, he settled in Lima from 1939. Attracted by the plasticity of Peruvian viceregal architecture, Moser devoted considerable efforts to the valorisation of this heritage, as can be seen in his collaboration with Cron for the apartments on Calle Roma. Author of several projects in the neo-colonial style, he collaborated with the Peruvian architect Emilio Harth-Terré on the project for the Municipal Palace in Lima's *Plaza Mayor*. Gutierrez, Ramón, 'Dizionario enciclopedico', in Dieste, Eladio et al. (eds.), *Architettura e società: l'America Latina nel XX secolo* (Milan, 1996), pp. 373–374.

44 Córdova, Adolfo, 'Los arquitectos europeos y la Agrupación Espacio', *Interview* (13 September 2016).

45 A human settlement from pre-Columbian times, with earthen construction, located east of Lima.

Puruchuco
Main view
Lima
2015
Mara Micaela Colletta

acquaintances widened and the number and importance of his commissions increased, Cron strictly limited his work to the design field, entrusting the realisation of much of his output to European-trained builders. Among them was Mario Vella,[46] an Italian civil engineer who trained in the 1930s at the Università di Roma and emigrated to Lima in 1946, where he took on small and medium-sized projects for private clients. Another European professional active in Peru at that time was Robert Steinegger,[47] a Swiss civil engineer trained at the ETH in Zurich who arrived in Lima in 1953. Steinegger founded a service and supply

46 Mario Vella Micocci (Rotella, Ascoli Piceno 1911 – Lima, 1961). Vella, Franco, 'Mario Vella Micocci, constructor de arquitectos europeos', Interview (22 February 2017).

47 Lachen, 1927 – ?. After attending the Swiss Federal Polytechnic between 1948 and 1952, he came to Peru in 1953, settling in Lima. He appears in the consular list of 1957. Ravines, Rogger, 'Presencia de Suiza en el Perú: nomenclátor biográfico', *Boletín de Lima* (1998), p. 229.

Puruchuco
Detail view
Lima
2015
Mara Micaela Colletta

company consisting of an architectural firm, a construction company and a furniture factory, which specialised in the design and construction of industrial complexes. Another of his builders was Carlos Costa[48] (of the company Flórez & Costa Ingenieros), a Peruvian of Italian origin who studied civil engineering at the Escuela Nacional de Ingenieros and the Regio Politecnico di Milano. All three, together with Swiss builders Carlo Galli and Arturo Saredi Ammann,[49] became Cron's collaborators in the construction of his most well-known work.

48 Carlos Costa Élice (Lima, 1912 – 1991). Costa, Germán, 'Carlos Costa Elice, constructor de arquitectos europeos Perù', *Interview* (22 February 2017).

49 Building contractors who appear in the 1939 consular list with the names Charles and Arthur respectively. Ravines, Rogger, 'Presencia de Suiza en el Perú: nomenclátor biográfico', *Boletín de Lima* (1998), pp. 184, 223.

IV.4. **Participation of European builders in early projects (1950–1953)**

Other examples of Cron's first phase in Peru can be found in the pages of *El Arquitecto Peruano*. One article was devoted to the Casa Hochköppler[50] (Lima, 1950–1951), built for the family of the same name by the Swiss builder Carlos Galli; another chronicled the Residencia del Señor Jean Schär[51] (Lima, 1953), built by the Italian engineer Mario Vella in partnership with the Swiss Arturo Saredi, manager of the Compañía de Seguros Peruano-Suiza. Both buildings, adhering to the courtyard typology, had similar characteristics to the duplex on Calle Roma. In addition to being built in San Isidro, a residential neighbourhood in Lima's expansion zone, these proposals featured: elevations which isolated the building from the outside; a real extension of the dwelling spaces towards the enclosed interiors; and the presence of architectural elements taken from the Peruvian cultural tradition.

In the Casa Hochköppler, Cron's use of a lexicon taken from Peru's past is highlighted didactically, such as its restrained use of holes in the volumes facing the street, not to mention the absence of sloping roofs, an architectural language reminiscent of the compactness of mudbrick. This courtyard dwelling, developed on a single level, was designed in 1950. As in the duplex on Calle Roma, here Cron favoured both a visual and physical relationship with the interior of the house: as such, all the rooms are organised around a central space, the fulcrum of the proposal, which also acts as a filter with the outside, giving great intimacy to the residence. This spatial sequence, which obliged the visitor to pass through the patio to enter the building, created a transition between the street and the house. The atrium, arranged on one side of the courtyard, provided access to the living and sleeping area.

50 See Velarde, Héctor, 'Una casa peruana... Hecha por un suizo', *El Arquitecto Peruano* (November–December 1951).

51 See 'Residencia del Señor Jean Schaer', *El Arquitecto Peruano* (January–February–March 1958).

Casa Hochköppler
Main view
Lima
Theodor Cron
1950–1951

El Arquitecto Peruano (November–December 1951)

Casa Hochköppler
Patio
Lima
Theodor Cron
1950–1951
El Arquitecto Peruano
(November–December 1951)

Ernesto Hochköppler, who commissioned the house, was a gynaecologist living in Lima. As such, Cron proposed the inclusion of a bas-relief inspired to his work, designed by the American artist Ronald Joseph.[52] In the pages of *El Arquitecto Peruano*, Héctor Velarde wrote that the subject of the artist's work, alluding to the owner's profession, was changed from European storks to Peruvian pelicans, a species found in South America which, besides being a symbol of fertility and prosperity, can also be traced back to the decorations of archaeological sites dating from the pre-Hispanic Mochica culture.[53]

The design for Residencia Schär, on the other hand, envisaged three bodies, developed on a single level, delimiting the inner garden. From the outside, two horizontally oriented volumes are set back from the limits of the plot. Their mass was emphasised by the solution he found for the openings which, by incorporating the wall cupboards along the hallway of the sleeping area, reached thicknesses comparable to the walls made of *adobe*, the mud bricks widely used in the Peruvian coastal strip. The presence of a low shutter gave these volumes the appearance of floating on the ground, imbuing them with an absence of gravity. The meeting of the two prisms at the corner defined the main entrance, accentuated by the presence of the chimney along the pathway provided for the living room. At the same time, it was reminiscent of Mies van der Rohe's solution to the entrance of Villa Tugendhat (Brno, 1928–1930).

As in the Casa Hochköppler, all the spaces of this dwelling were organised around the central interior space; however, unlike the previous case, in which the house was accessed via the patio, in the Schär project visitors had to first enter the building to discover the inner courtyard. The rooms in the dwellings designed by Cron were characterised by a number of design details he absorbed during his 1947 study trip to southern Italy and later summarised in the text *Das italienische Zimmer* (see IV.2.): the proportion of the spaces; the play of natural light on the surfaces of the rooms; the use of plaster for walls and ceilings; the arrangement of the joints in the flooring (which emphasised the depth of the spaces); the presence of low parapets without railings (to accentuate the spatial continuity between the living room and mezzanine); and but a few pieces of furniture, freely placed in the space, like sculptures bathed in light.[54]

The prestige achieved by Cron as a reknowned architect, as well as the departure in 1953 of his colleague and friend Adolf Bührer for his first stay in the United States, induced him to leave his duplex on Calle Roma and build himself a studio-house in the pre-Andean area of Lima known as Monterrico. The Italian engineer Mario Vella (see IV.5.), with whom Cron established an esteemed professional relationship as well as a personal friendship,[55] was responsible for the realisation of many projects by the Swiss architect.

52 St. Kitts, 1910 – Brussels, 1992.
53 See Velarde, Héctor, 'Una casa peruana… Hecha por un suizo', *El Arquitecto Peruano* (November–December 1951).
54 See Cron, Theodor, 'Das italienische Zimmer', *Private Bequest Theodor Cron* (Basel, s.d.).
55 Vella, Franco, 'Mario Vella Micocci, constructor de arquitectos europeos', *Interview* (22 February 2017).

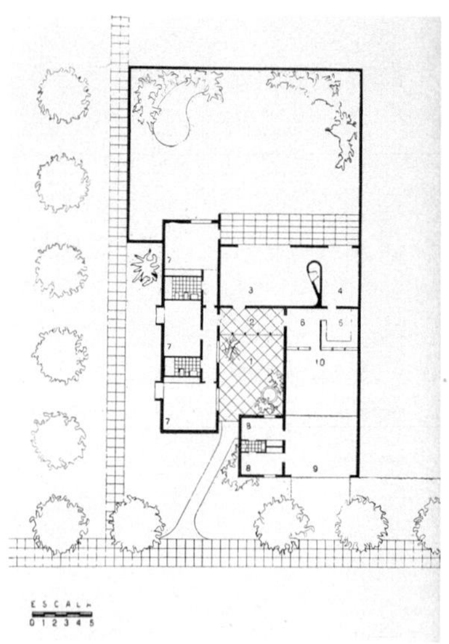

Casa Hochköppler
Ground floor
Lima
Theodor Cron
1950–1951

El Arquitecto Peruano
(November–December 1951)

Casa Hochköppler
Detail of the American artist
Ronald Joseph bas-relief
Lima
Theodor Cron
1950–1951

El Arquitecto Peruano
(November–December 1951)

Residencia Schär
Main view
Lima
Theodor Cron
1953

El Arquitecto Peruano
(January–February 1958)

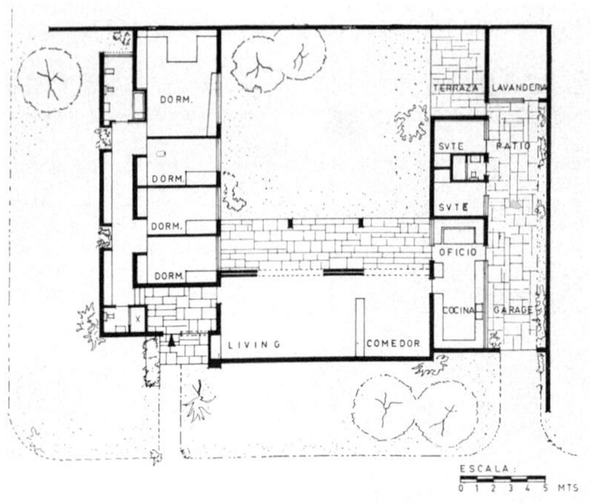

Residencia Schär
Ground floor
Lima
Theodor Cron
1953

El Arquitecto Peruano
(January–February 1958)

IV.5. European commissioning and construction of the Compañía de Seguros Peruano-Suiza (1952–1956)

As was the case with Paul Linder's repertoire, an architectural language more in keeping with the modern movement were to be found in Theodor Cron's non-residential projects, built between the second half of the 1950s and his definitive return to Switzerland. Most of these works saw the participation of the engineers Robert Steinegger and Mario Vella. This second design moment was also characterised by a clientele that was no longer exclusively Swiss. Cron had a keen sense of space and a remarkable mastery of drawing. These gifts, combined with his circle of acquaintances established through Alejandro Ciurlizza, earned him numerous commissions from Peruvians, which ended up convincing him to extend his stay in the Andean country.

The main clients for commercial projects, however, remained European. These works, which displayed accuracy in construction details alongside an awareness of the use of materials that were favoured by the International Style (reinforced concrete, steel, aluminium and glass) were published in *El Arquitecto Peruano*: the Cinema Roma[56] and the Edificio Compañía de Seguros Peruano Suiza[57] (both built by the company Mario Vella Ingenieros), as well as a report dedicated to the Banco Continental[58] (built by Enrique de la Piedra Ingenieros).

The European presence in Lima was ever-present in the construction of offices for the service sector. Several Swiss insurance companies, including the Schweizerische Rückversicherungs-Gesellschaft and Basler Versicherungen, both of which had been actively involved in the Peruvian market since the 1930s, facilitated the creation of new entities by allocating capital, providing consultants and promoting the transfer of management personnel. In this way, from the 1940s, with the interest of the Swiss diplomat in Peru, Juan Adolfo Berger, a group of Swiss-Peruvian entrepreneurs started several business associations with the aim of creating banking, financial and insurance companies. Most notable among them: the Compañía de Seguros y Reaseguros Peruano-Suiza and La Colmena Compañía de Seguros y Reaseguros. The strong support of these foreign partners favoured the creation and rapid development of new entities, as well as the demand for architects capable of designing their headquarters and executive residences.

The Peruvian experience of the ETH architect Paolo Mariotta[59] is here worth noting. Based on plans drawn up in his Locarno studio, the headquarters of La Colmena Compañía de Seguros y Reaseguros was eventually realised (1958–1961). The construction of this multi-storey building in the historical

56 See 'Moderno Cine en Lima', *El Arquitecto Peruano* (October–November 1957).

57 Cruchaga Belaunde, Miguel, '25 Años de Arquitectura Comercial', *El Arquitecto Peruano* (October–November–December 1963), pp. 7–13.

58 'El Banco Continental Inaugura su Nuevo Local en Miraflores', *El Arquitecto Peruano* (July–August–September 1959), pp. 26–28.

59 Riverso Ortelli, Angela (ed), *Paolo Mariotta: architetto 1905–1972: AAT, Fondazione Archivi Architetti Ticinesi, Documenti del fondo Paolo Mariotta* (Bellinzona, 2013), pp. 29–32.

centre of Lima, designed and built between 1958 and 1961, was an example of collaboration between a Peruvian insurance company and a Swiss designer's studio in his country of origin.

Neither the contacts nor the way the Locarnese designer was commissioned to draw up the design for the administrative headquarters of La Colmena in Lima are known. It is possible, however, to speculate that his experiences on the Iberian Peninsula represented an important influence. These collaborations,

La Colmena Compañía de Seguros y Reaseguros
Main view
Lima
Paolo Mariotta
1958–1961
Fondazione Archivi Architetti Ticinesi, Paolo Mariotta Fund

La Colmena Compañía de Seguros y Reaseguros
Solución D – Perspective of the building proposal
Locarno
Paolo Mariotta
10 December 1958

Fondazione Archivi Architetti Ticinesi, Paolo Mariotta Fund

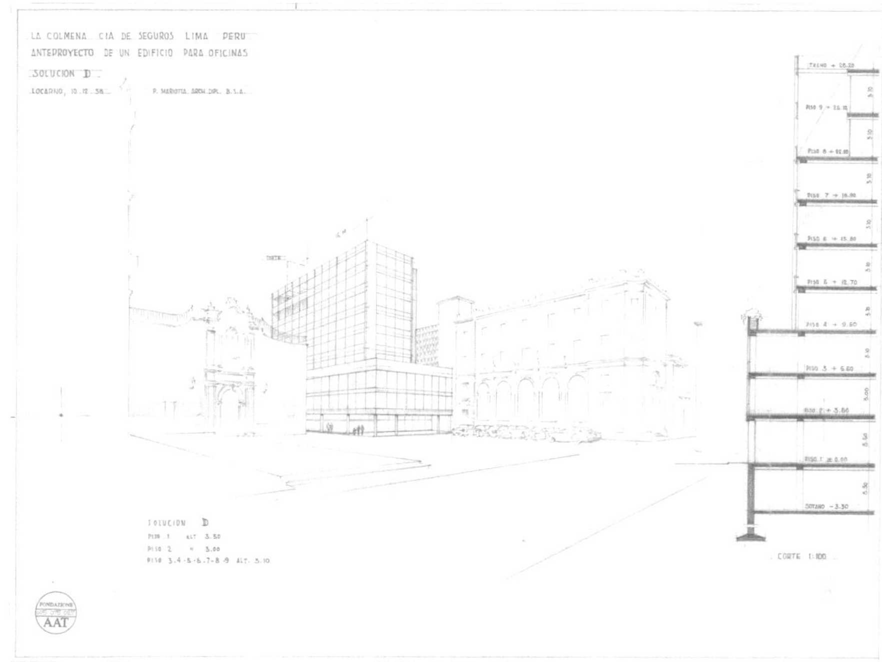

which most likely arose from the architect's Swiss knowledge, began in 1950 when Mariotta developed the first renovation project for the Sociedad Española de Precios Unicos department store in Madrid. Furthermore, the managers of Swiss Re, whose capital had been present in La Colmena's assets since 1951, might very well have been part of Mariotta's Zurich circle of acquaintances in the 1940s. Undoubtedly, the presence in Lima of colleagues from the ETH facilitated his participation during the project's design phase.

In the early 1950s, Cron designed the headquarters of the Compañía de Seguros Peruano-Suiza (Lima, 1952–1956), a Peruvian insurance company founded with Swiss capital. This represented one of the first and most important collaborations with Vella. Three of the characteristic elements of Cron's work can be found in his design: the use of the section in the planning phase to establish the height of the building and to define the proportions of the urban space in front; the use of greenery in the latter to reduce the impact of the new edifice on the San Agustín church; and his acute attention to construction details.

This multi-storey building, consisting of nine above-ground levels and a basement level dedicated to garages, incorporated the premises of the *Plan Piloto de Lima* of 1949 (see I.3.3.), which was concerned with the reinforcement

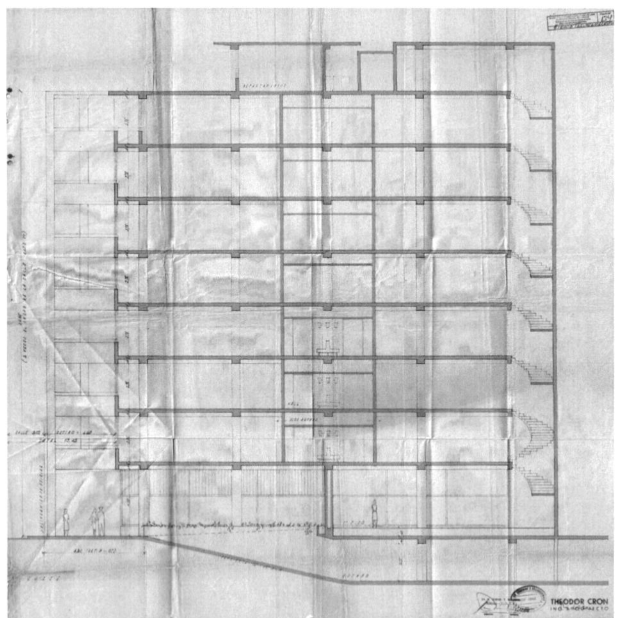

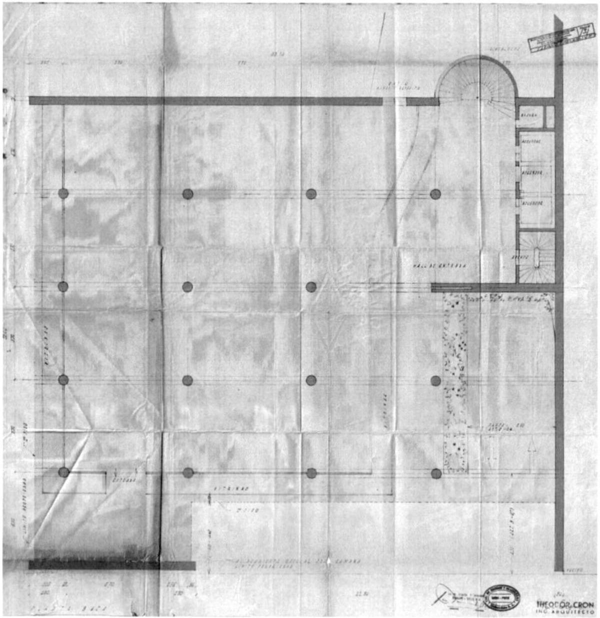

Compañía de Seguros Peruano-Suiza
Section along the parking entrance and ground floor
Lima
Theodor Cron
1952–1956
Municipalidad Metropolitana de Lima, Archivo Central

of the administrative function of the Peruvian capital's historic centre. The pre-existing building, a two-storey Art Nouveau palace, had been renovated and extended in the first half of the twentieth century,[60] probably after the 1940 earthquake. The Plaza San Agustín, located two blocks from the Plaza Mayor (a square of colonial foundation, see I.1.1.), was much frequented by the cultural and bohemian circles of the time[61] and named after the convent from the seventeenth century which overlooks the square.

The elevation of the Peruano-Suiza towards the square had a classical composition of basement, elevation and crowning, and was finished with a distinctive green mosaic cladding in small rectangular tiles. The horizontal course of the ribbon windows was emphasised using aluminium window frames, a system that allowed the windows to form a continuous line set back from the main elevations. The proposal included the partial setback of the factory, five metres towards Jirón Camaná, to create a transitional space between the street and the square. The ground floor of the building, open to the public, was conceived as an extension of the urban space in front. A large glass wall allowed visual and physical continuity between the square and the interior lobby. A café, located within this space, reinforced the urban character envisioned by the Swiss designer.[62]

60 García Bryce, José, 'Arquitectos europeos en el Peru del siglo XX', *Interview* (24 September 2016).

61 Córdova, Adolfo, 'Los arquitectos europeos y la Agrupación Espacio', *Interview* (13 September 2016).

Compañía de Seguros Peruano-Suiza
Main view
Lima
Theodor Cron
1952–1956

Theodor Cron Private Bequest

http://www.miradalibre.org/en/projects/th-cron

Compañía de Seguros Peruano-Suiza
Helicoidal staircase detail view
Lima
Theodor Cron
1952–1956

Theodor Cron Private Bequest

https://www.nzz.ch/feuilleton/hans-theodor-cron-ein-schweizer-praegt-die-baukunst-in-peru-ld.1513980?reduced=true

Office building
Prague
Josef Havlicek and Karel Honzik
1932–1934

Die Neue Architektur: Dargestellt an 20 Beispielen – 1930–1940

Two more multi-storey buildings – the Edificio Peicher and the Edificio Chavín, designed by the Peruvian architect Enrique Seoane in the late 1950s and 1960s respectively – later completed the remaining elevations of the square. This public space comprised four evergreen trees encircling a sculpture by the Spanish artist Jorge de Oteiza of the Peruvian poet César Vallejo in its centre, itself one of the earliest examples of an abstract public art installation.[63]

Inside the building, vertical circulation was formed by a group of three lifts, the service stairs and an elegant helicoidal staircase finished in mosaic. This architectural element, which served all levels above ground, was built as an addition to the building. This feature allowed natural lighting from above, which highlighted the small square tile cladding. The office floors were designed as open plan with half-height partitions. The large format of the interior flooring, made of vinyl material, accentuated the spatial continuity throughout the floor.

The use of the open floor plan and ribbon windows, the corner solution between the bodies of the building, and the ground connection, all reflected the new architecture publicised by Alfred Roth, an architect with whom Cron maintained contact after his many years at the ETH.[64] These design choices find several points of contact with the proposal of the architects Josef Havlicek and Karel Honzik for an office building in Prague (1932–1934), a project included among the 20 examples published by Roth in 1940 in the trilingual edition *Die Neue Architektur: Dargestellt an 20 Beispielen – 1930–1940*.[65] With its use of an international language, publicised in Roth's catalogue, and of local building materials and techniques, the Peruano-Suiza was an important example of the new Latin American architecture.

62 Vella, Franco, 'Mario Vella Micocci, constructor de arquitectos europeos', *Interview* (22 February 2017).

63 Bonilla di Tolla, Enrique, and Fuentes Huerta, María del Carmen (eds.), *Lima y el Callao: guía de arquitectura y paisaje – an architectural and landscape guide* (Lima / Seville, 2009), p. 210.

64 In October 1952, Roth answered Adolf Bührer's letter informing him of Cron's visit to Switzerland. Roth, Alfred, Letter to Adolf Bührer (28 October 1952), *ETH Zürich, gta Archiv, Alfred Roth Fund*, 131-K-23.

65 Roth, Alfred, *La Nouvelle architecture / Die neue Architektur / The new architecture – 1930–1940: Présentée en 20 exemples* (Zurich / Munich, 1940), pp. 205–250.

IV.6. Other commercial projects and return to Switzerland (1956–1963)

The Peruano-Suiza was completed in 1956, the same year in which another example of collaboration between Theodor Cron and Mario Vella, the Cinema Roma (Lima, 1955–1956), was built.[66] The name of the cinema alluded to the geographical origin of its managers, among whom was the Italian engineer.[67] The building was constructed in an area of twentieth-century expansion, south of the city, where other important locations for the Italian diaspora in Lima were located, among them the Colegio Italiano Antonio Raimondi (see I.3.1.).

The proposal aimed to isolate the building from the street and to extend the interior towards an open space, however sheltered from the outside, echoing two recurring themes in Cron's work. The volume, a parallelepiped with a horizontal orientation, was set back to create a space in front. A canopy (sheltering the entrance, curved upwards at both ends), a powerful central pillar (tapering downwards) and two tall planters (placed on either side of the lot) delimited the space created between the building and the street. Behind the monumental façade was housed the main vestibule with the projection room above. Access to the public was through two openings in the middle of the main elevation.

66 See 'Moderno cine en Lima', *El Arquitecto Peruano* (October–November 1957).

67 Vella, Franco, 'Mario Vella Micocci, constructor de arquitectos europeos', *Interview* (22 February 2017).

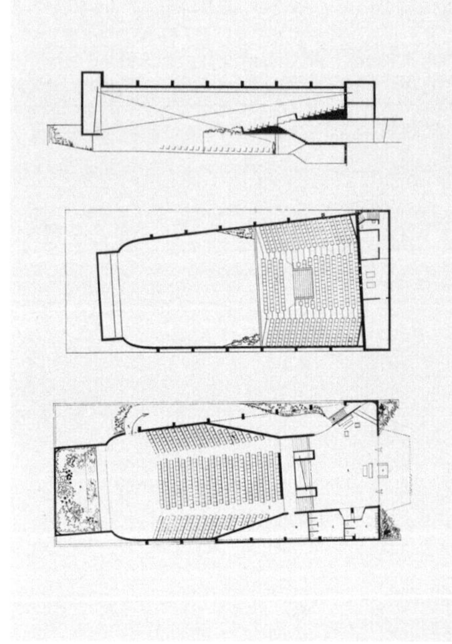

The foyer was located at an intermediate height between the stalls and the mezzanine. The longitudinal section made it possible to appreciate the Cinema Roma's characteristic feature: a large glass window, situated below the projection screen, connecting the hall with the inner garden, located at the end of the lot. During the interval between performances and at the end of the projection, the thick curtains that covered this window would slide open to let the spectators see the green space outside.

Experimentation with the relationship between exterior and interior spaces can also be seen in the Banco Continental headquarters[68] (1957–1959), built in the coastal area of Miraflores. Whereas for the Cinema Roma Cron developed a clear separation between the building and the street, for the Continental he found a solution already proposed for the Peruano-Suiza headquarters. The corner building, consisting of a basement level (dedicated to the vault, archive, and exhibition spaces) and a double-height mezzanine level for the bank's public reception, had full-height glazing on both main façades (one of the first examples in Peru), which allowed the visual continuation of the surrounding streets towards the reception area inside.

The decomposition of the building into clearly distinguishable architectural elements – such as the structure and the roof; the large glass surfaces and the monumental staircase; the suspension of the roof slab by an extrados structure – all allude to the Miesian language. A sequence of exposed reinforced concrete porticoes supported the large roof tapering outwards. The structural scheme used, with its powerful partitions accompanying the space, gave great flexibility to the interior. The lighting system, likewise, scanned the intrados of the roof. The interior was characterised by the staircase-mezzanine system for which, as he had already experimented with in the duplex on Calle Roma, he designed a planter that acted as a low and very deep parapet, allowing spatial integration between the upper and lower levels.

Cinema Roma
Main view
Lima
Theodor Cron
1955–1956
El Arquitecto Peruano (October–November 1957)

Despite the professional success that Theodor Cron achieved while living in Peru, in the early 1960s problems in his personal and professional life led him to consider returning to Switzerland. Mario Vella, with whom Cron had established an association resulting in works of great technical quality, died suddenly in a car accident in 1961. It was probably for this reason that Cron considered living together with Luisa Martinto on Lake Geneva.[69] The collapse of their romantic relationship caused this plan to be shelved.

Adolf Bührer, a Swiss colleague with whom he had shared his early years in Lima, moved to the Peruvian Amazon in 1962.[70] Cron had never established contacts with other European architects in Lima, neither Paul Linder nor Mario Bianco, nor had he taught at the Escuela Nacional de Ingenieros; and

68 See 'El Banco Continental inaugura su nuevo local en Miraflores', *El Arquitecto Peruano* (July–August–September 1959).

69 The 1961 correspondence between Theodor and Leo Cron indicates the younger brother's intentions to build a house on Lake Geneva in the canton of Vaud. *Theodor Cron Private bequest.*

70 See Galerie Mera (ed.), 'Adolfo Bührer: 1918–2003 – Stetten – Südamerika – Bargen: ein malerisches Leben', *Galerie Mera* (Schaffhausen, 2011).

not having participated in cultural collectives such as Agrupación Espacio, he decided to return to his homeland. In January 1963, he returned definitively to Switzerland.[71] He died shortly afterwards, prematurely, in Klosters, Canton Graubünden, in 1964.

71 Theodor Cron returned definitively to Basel on 9 January 1963, as recorded in the Swiss consular register in Lima.

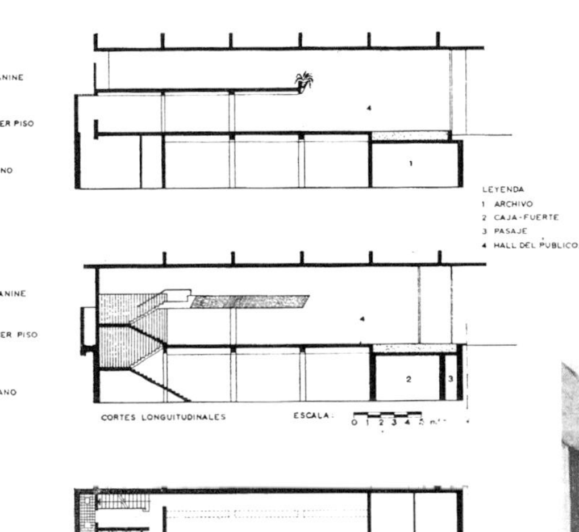

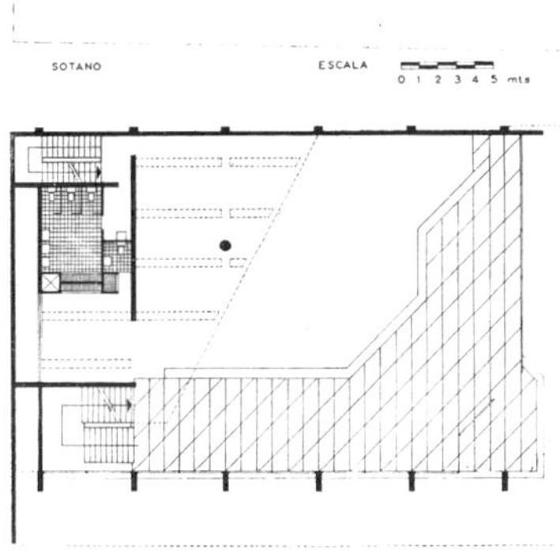

Banco Continental
From left to right:
Main view,
Sections, basement and ground levels
Double-height mezzanine level
Lima
Theodor Cron
1957–1959

El Arquitecto Peruano
(July–August–September 1959)

MULTI-STOREY BUILDINGS IN LIMA: GENEALOGY OF A MODERN TYPE (1939–1970)

BUILDINGS BY EUROPEAN DESIGNERS

Edificio Gildemeister (Werner Benno Lange, Lima, 1928–1930)

Edificio Irma (Gianfelice Fogliani, Lima, 1946–1948)

1930s

1940s — **Earthquake in Lima (1940)** — **Urban Planning Regulations (1946)**

BUILDINGS BY PERUVIAN DESIGNERS

Edificio Rizo Patrón (Enrique Seoane, Luis Solimano, Lima, 1939–1940)

Tacna-Nazarenas (Enrique Seoane, Lima, 1945–1946)

Edificio Ferrand (Fernando Belaúnde, modifications by Alejandro Alva, Lima, 1945–1947)

Edificio de la Compañía de Seguros La Fénix (Enrique Seoane, Lima, 1945–1948)

Edificio La Nacional (Enrique Seoane, Lima, 1947–1948)

Edificio Arnodi
(Paul Linder, Lima, 1950)

Plan Piloto de Lima (1947–1949)

1950s

Edificio y Cine Tacna (Alejandro Alva, Lima, 1949)

Edificio Guzmán Blanco (Manuel Villarán, Lima, 1952)

Edificio Ambassador (Miguel Alvariño, Lima, 1952)

Ministerio de Hacienda y Comercio (Guillermo Payet, Lima, 1952–1953)

Edificio Ostolaza (Enrique Seoane, Lima, 1952–1954)

Edificio Radio El Sol (Luis Miró Quesada Garland, Lima, 1953–1954)

MULTI-STOREY BUILDINGS IN LIMA: GENEALOGY OF A MODERN TYPE (1939–1970)

BUILDINGS BY EUROPEAN DESIGNERS

Edificio de la Compañía de Seguros Peruano-Suiza (Theodor Cron, Lima, 1952–1956)

Hotel Savoy (Mario Bianco, Lima, 1954–1957)

1950s

BUILDINGS BY PERUVIAN DESIGNERS

Compañía de Seguros Atlas (José Alvarez Calderón, Walter Weberhofer, Lima, 1953–1955)

Edificio Málaga Santolla (Alfredo Málaga, Lima, 1955)

Ministerio de Educación Pública (Enrique Seoane, Lima, 1951–1956)

Edificio San Reynaldo (Enrique Seoane, Lima, 1954–1956)

Edificio Nyci (Inversiones Inmobiliarias Republica, Enrique Seoane, Lima, 1956)

Edificio Seguros El Sol (Enrique Seoane, Lima, 1956–1958)

Edificio La Colmena Compañía de Seguros (Paolo Mariotta, Lima, 1958–1961)

1960s

1970s

Galerías Comerciales Mogollón (Raúl Morey, Lima, 1958)

Edificio La Fénix Peruana (Fernando de Osma, Lima, 1959)

CONACO (Fernando Bryce, Benjamín Doig, Eduardo Irigoyen, Lima, 1960s)

Banco Comercial (Enrique Seoane, Lima, 1962–1963)

Mercado Central de Lima – Gran Mariscal Castilla (Alfredo Dammert, Lima, 1967)

Centro Cívico y Comercial de Lima (Adolfo Córdova et al., Lima, 1966–1970)

Chapter V
Multi-storey buildings in Lima: genealogy of a modern type (1939–1970)

V.1. **Foreign references and the import of a type (1928–1943)**

The work of Paul Linder, Mario Bianco and Theodor Cron is representative of the evolution of Peruvian architecture during the mid-twentieth century, from the valorisation of local traditions to the exaltation of an international modernism and, finally, to the search for a synthesis of both. Within this heterogeneity, their architectural repertoire finds in the examples of multi-storey buildings the most influential works of local architecture: for reasons related to the historical moment in which they were realised, the innovation they brought to their craft and the great publicity given to them in the mainstream and specialised press.

The dissemination of the multi-storey typology was favoured by a group of articles included in the first years of publication of *El Arquitecto Peruano*, also illustrating the main European and American precedents. Among the paradigmatic models, both in terms of development in height and dialectical relationship with the historical context, is certainly the Ministerio da Educação e Saúde Pública (Affonso Reidy et al., with the advice of Le Corbusier, Rio de Janeiro, 1937–1943), a work widely publicised in the Peruvian media. The Brazilian work had first been published in *El Arquitecto Peruano* (March 1944), then in Luis Miro Quesada's written work (1945); in the end, it was included in the VI Exposición Panamericana de Arquitectura y Urbanismo, obtaining the Premio de Honor y Diploma (October 1947).[1]

In the Ministerio da Educação e Saúde Pública, the structural potential of reinforced concrete was exploited: the volumes on the ground floor were used for public exhibition spaces and covered by a roof-garden; the tower above rested on these volumes and on pilotis in the central part; the main north and south elevations were characterised by a full-height curtain wall; the northern façade, a front to be screened (as Brazil lies below the equator), was protected by fibre cement sunshades; finally, curved reinforced concrete elements contained the technical compartments of the lifts and water tank.

It is therefore not surprising that the Brazilian building was among the foreign realisations published by Fernando Belaúnde Terry in the Peruvian magazine. Other examples are the Longfellow Building (Washington, DC, 1941), by William Lescaze[2] the Swiss architect who had migrated to the United States in 1920 and the project for the first Unité d'Habitation (Marseille, 1947–1952), in which the Peruvian magazine detailed urban planning and construction aspects which Le Corbusier was developing.[3]

But it was not only the foreign projects published in the specialised press and promoted by CIAM members in the American continent that favoured the spread of the multi-storey type (see I.2.2., I.3.3.). The work of European

1 See 'Modernismo Brasileño', *El Arquitecto Peruano* (March 1944); Miró Quesada, Luis, *Espacio en el tiempo. La arquitectura moderna como fenómeno cultural* (Lima, 1945), pp. 72–73; *Actas del VI Congreso Panamericano de Arquitectos: Lima, 15 de octubre de 1947, Cuzco 25 de octubre de 1947* (Lima, 1953), p. 207.

2 Geneva, 1896 – New York, 1969.

3 See 'Arquitectura moderna en los Estados Unidos', *El Arquitecto Peruano* (December 1944); 'La audaz Ciudad Vertical de Le Corbusier en Marsella', *El Arquitecto Peruano* (December 1949).

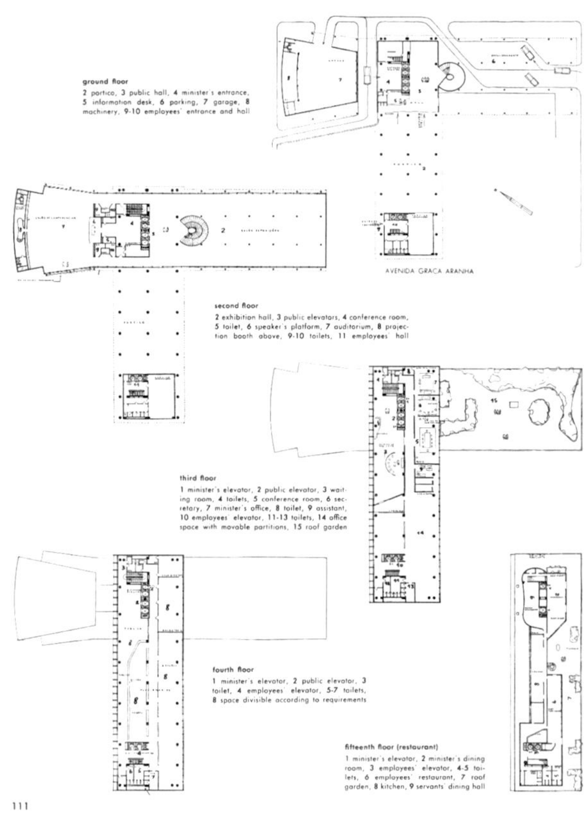

Ministerio da Educação e Saúde Pública
South façade of the Ministry of Education,
Ground, first, second, third, fourth and fifteenth floors,
North façade
Rio de Janeiro
Affonso Reidy et al., with the advice of Le Corbusier
1937–1943

Museum of Modern Art

https://www.moma.org/documents/moma_catalogue_2304_300061982.pdf

designers active in Peru in the twentieth century – Linder, Bianco and Cron – together with Werner Benno Lange, Gianfelice Fogliani and Paolo Mariotta, played a decisive role in the introduction of these constructions in the Peruvian capital. In the wake of such examples, foreign and local, the Lima buildings not only gradually freed themselves from historical references, but at the same time moved away from viceregal influences.

V.2. **Evolution of the Peruvian multi-storey building (1939–1970)**

According to Argentine historian Jorge Francisco Liernur, twentieth century relations between the United States and Latin American countries were characterised by three phases: first came the rejection of the American model through the exaltation of local culture and traditions; this was followed by imitation as a means of competition and overcoming foreign influences; and finally, the search for a new synthesis.[4] These three phases are visible in the conspicuous number of multi-storey buildings constructed in Lima between the end of the 1930s and the 1960s, regulated since 1949 by the *Plan Piloto de Lima* (see I.3.3.).

To better understand the introduction of the multi-storey typology, it is worth dwelling on projects by Europeans in the Peruvian capital. The Casa Gildemeister (Werner Benno Lange, 1928–1930, see II.5.) is an early example of a Peruvian multi-storey building in the Art Deco style, intended for the headquarters of a trading company founded by a family of German origin. The then unusual height of this building, at six storeys, anticipated by about a decade the change of scale that new constructions in Lima would undergo. The Edificio Irma (Gianfelice Fogliani, 1946–1948, see III.6.) constitutes one of the first multi-storey constructions erected following the enactment of the 1946 town planning regulations (see I.2.2.) concerning housing. And the Edificio Arnodi (Paul Linder, 1950, see II.5.) is a clear example of the coexistence of a language linked to tradition in a vertically developed building, consisting of flats in the then unusual formula of horizontal ownership.

The exaltation of local culture and traditions in architecture, the first phase in the relationship between North and South America, can be seen in many Peruvian buildings constructed in the mid-twentieth century. The tensions generated by the culture-civilisation dichotomy, reflected in an architectural language rich in references to tradition, can be seen in the Edificio Rizo Patrón[5] (Enrique Seoane, Luis Solimano, Lima, 1939–1940), a work in which Peru's most prolific architect in multi-storey buildings, Enrique Seoane, participated.[6] Eclectic in style due to its neo-colonial declination, this eight-storey work presents a symmetrical composition formed by the base, body and crowning. Access to the commercial premises is emphasised by the insertion of a triple-height neo-Baroque doorway. The reinforced concrete frame is masked by the adoption of a compact volumetry, characterised by the presence of vertically oriented windows, behind which the load-bearing structure is concealed. The construction system used can only be read in the planimetry, where the open plan can be seen.

4 Liernur, Jorge Francisco, *Escritos de arquitectura del siglo XX en América Latina* (Madrid / Seville, 2002), p. 69.

5 See 'El Edificio Rizo Patrón, por la firma Gramonvel', *El Arquitecto Peruano* (August 1940).

6 Enrique Seoane Ros (Lima 1915 – 1980) attended the Escuela Nacional de Ingenieros, completing his studies in 1938. In 1944, after obtaining the title of engineer with a specialisation in architecture, he created the Enrique Seoane Ros Arquitectos studio, with which he won the Chavín Prize in 1950 and 1953. A lecturer in the Department of Architecture between 1946 and 1957, he spent part of his professional career in Panama, where a portion of his built work remains. See Bentín Diez Canseco, José, *Enrique Seoane Ros: una búsqueda de raíces peruanas* (Lima 2014), p. 11.

Edificio Rizo Patrón
Avenida Wilson in 1944, formerly known as Avenida El Sol, with the Edificio Rizo Patrón (left)
Lima
Enrique Seoane Ros, Luis Solimano
1939–1940
Plaza Francia Antiques

The first phase, representative of this exaltation of local culture and traditions, is divided into three subgroups of multi-storey buildings. A first subgroup, constructed between 1945 and 1948, which can be traced back to the Art Deco style, uses a reinforced concrete frame structure, a language more in keeping with construction techniques and materials employed, as well as a simplification of decorative devices. Among the examples with classical-style tripartition of the façade are: the Edificio Tacna-Nazarenas[7] (Enrique Seoane, 1945–1946), which is of particular interest, seeing as it constitutes the first example in Lima of a cantilever structure in reinforced concrete; and the Edificio Ferrand[8] (Fernando Belaúnde Terry, with modifications by Alejandro Alva, 1945–1947), whose elevations are characterised by the coexistence of ribbon windows, cornices and pilasters – the result of a request for contextualisation by the client.

In front of the Edificio Ferrand was the Edificio de la Compañía de Seguros La Fénix (Enrique Seoane, 1945–1948), a work that earned Seoane the Chavín Prize 1950[9] (see VI.1.1.). The building, whose concave volumetry towards the Plaza de la Salud resembles that of the Edificio Ferrand, has a convex base (with full-height glazing), a central body with a horizontal orientation (with ribbon windows) and two vertical side bodies crowned by canopies. At the rear, the glazing that accompanies the helicoidal staircase is one of the earliest examples of the use of curtain wall.

A second subgroup, which presents the characteristics of the rationalism that was being consolidated in local architectural production, is formed by the Edificio de la Compañía de Seguros La Nacional[10] (Enrique Seoane, 1947–1948),

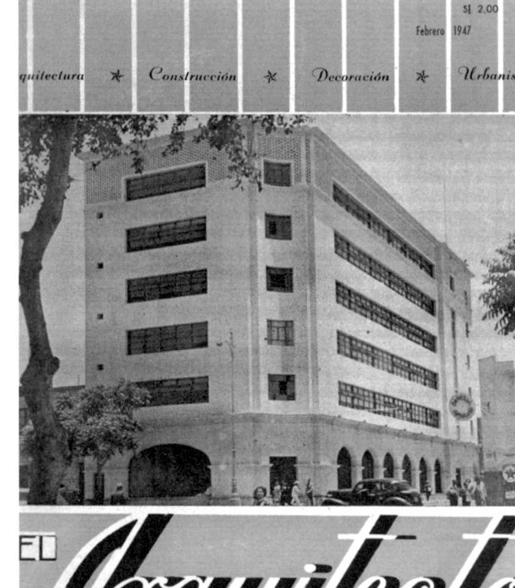

Edificio Tacna-Nazarenas
Magazine cover
Lima
Enrique Seoane Ros
1945–1946
El Arquitecto Peruano (February 1947)

Edificio Ferrand
Main view
Lima
Fernando Belaúnde Terry, with modifications by Alejandro Alva
1945–1947
El Arquitecto Peruano (March 1948)

7 See 'Edificio Tacna-Nazarenas, en Lima', *El Arquitecto Peruano* (February 1947).

8 See 'Edificio que construye la firma Flórez y Costa, Ingenieros, para la casa Ferrand', *El Arquitecto Peruano* (April 1947); 'El nuevo Edificio Ferrand', *El Arquitecto Peruano* (March 1948).

9 See 'Adjudicación del premio Chavín de 1950 al Arquitecto Enrique Seoane Ros', *El Arquitecto Peruano* (September 1950).

Edificio Ferrand
Magazine cover
Lima
Fernando Belaúnde Terry, with modifications by Alejandro Alva
1945–1947

El Arquitecto Peruano (March 1948)

one of the first examples of the separation of volumetry in the basement and the body above, and the Edificio y Cine Tacna[11] (Alejandro Alva, 1949), in which reinforced concrete and metal trusses were used for the roof of the cinema hall.

A third and final subgroup, attributable to monumentalism, consists of buildings constructed during the military regime of Manuel A. Odría (1950–1956). These include the Ministerio de Hacienda y Comercio[12] (Guillermo Payet, 1952–1953), a peculiar mixture of marble-clad façades with floor-to-ceiling

10 'Edificio de la Compañía de Seguros "La Nacional"', *El Arquitecto Peruano* (April 1949).

11 See 'El Edificio Tacna y el Cine Paramount Tacna', *El Arquitecto Peruano* (July 1949).

Edificio de la Compañía de Seguros La Fénix
Lima
Enrique Seoane Ros
1945–1948
Javier Atoche Intili (2018)

Abril 1949
S/o. 4.00

Edificio de la Compañía de Seguros La Nacional
Magazine cover
Lima
Enrique Seoane Ros
1947–1948
El Arquitecto Peruano (April 1949)

Edificio y Cine Tacna
Magazine cover
Lima
Alejandro Alva
1949
El Arquitecto Peruano (July 1949)

windows, ribbon windows and a large central atrium, and the Ministerio de Educación Pública[13] (Enrique Seoane, 1951–1956), whose scale is monumental, with large portions of its façade clad in curtain wall.

Imitation as a means of competition and overcoming foreign references, characteristic of the second phase in relations between the United States and Latin America, was facilitated in Peru by activities aimed at the dissemination of modern culture. These activities, carried out by architecture students (between 1945 and 1946, see I.3.1.) and members of Agrupación Espacio (between 1947

12 See 'Ministerio de Hacienda y Comercio', *El Arquitecto Peruano* (March–April 1953).

13 See 'Ministerio de Educación Pública', *El Arquitecto Peruano* (July–August–September 1956).

Edificio y Cine Tacna
Cinema's entrance detail view and longitudinal section, hall detail view, main view from Avenida Abancay
Lima
Alejandro Alva
1949

El Arquitecto Peruano
(July 1949)

Entrada al Cine

Ingenieros Constructores:
FLOREZ Y COSTA

★

Arquitecto del Edificio:
ALEJANDRO ALVA M.

★

Instalaciones Eléctricas:
Salvador Payet.

Arquitectos Consultores
para el Cine Tacna:
SCHLANGER, HOFFBEY,
REISNER Y URBHAN.

★

Cálculos Estructurales:
Ingº ALBERTO URQUIAGA

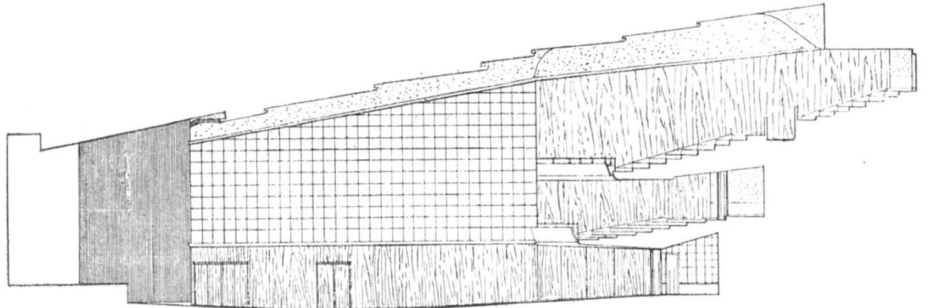

SECCION LONGITUDINAL DEL CINEMA

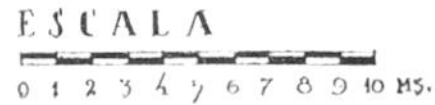

and 1955, see I.3.2.), achieved an important result when the Edificio Guzmán Blanco[14] (Manuel Villarán, 1952) was recognised with the Chavín Prize. The building, which rested on pilotis, displayed a reinforced concrete structure. The presence of balcony-frames, full-height glazing and the overcoming of the classical tripartition in its elevations were architectural elements that would later be found in buildings constructed in Lima, as documented in the *Latin American Architecture Since 1945* catalogue.[15]

The final part of the MoMA catalogue, entitled *Urban Façades,* included two Peruvian multi-storey buildings which would become the progenitors of many future projects.[16] The first was the Edificio Ostolaza[17] (Enrique Seoane, 1951–1953), which earned the Peruvian architect Seoane the Chavín Prize in 1953 – the second of his career. The corner solution features a two-storey plinth, which echoes the scale of the neighbouring buildings, and two blocks of flats and offices that follow the course of the streets.

The division of the volumes into planes, the absence of symmetry, the expression of the structure in its façade and the use of *moucharabies* in the main elevations are all elements of Ostolaza found in later examples: in the

14 See 'Edificio de Departamentos', *El Arquitecto Peruano* (October–November 1952).
15 Hitchcock, Henry-Russell, *Latin American Architecture Since 1945* (New York, 1955), pp. 195, 197.
16 Ibid., pp. 191–197.
17 See 'Edificio Tacna-Nazarenas', *El Arquitecto Peruano* (July–August–September 1955).

Ministerio de Educación Pública
Main view from Avenida Abancay, Magazine cover (left and bottom, respectively)
Lima
Enrique Seoane Ros
1951–1956

El Arquitecto Peruano
(July–August–September 1956)

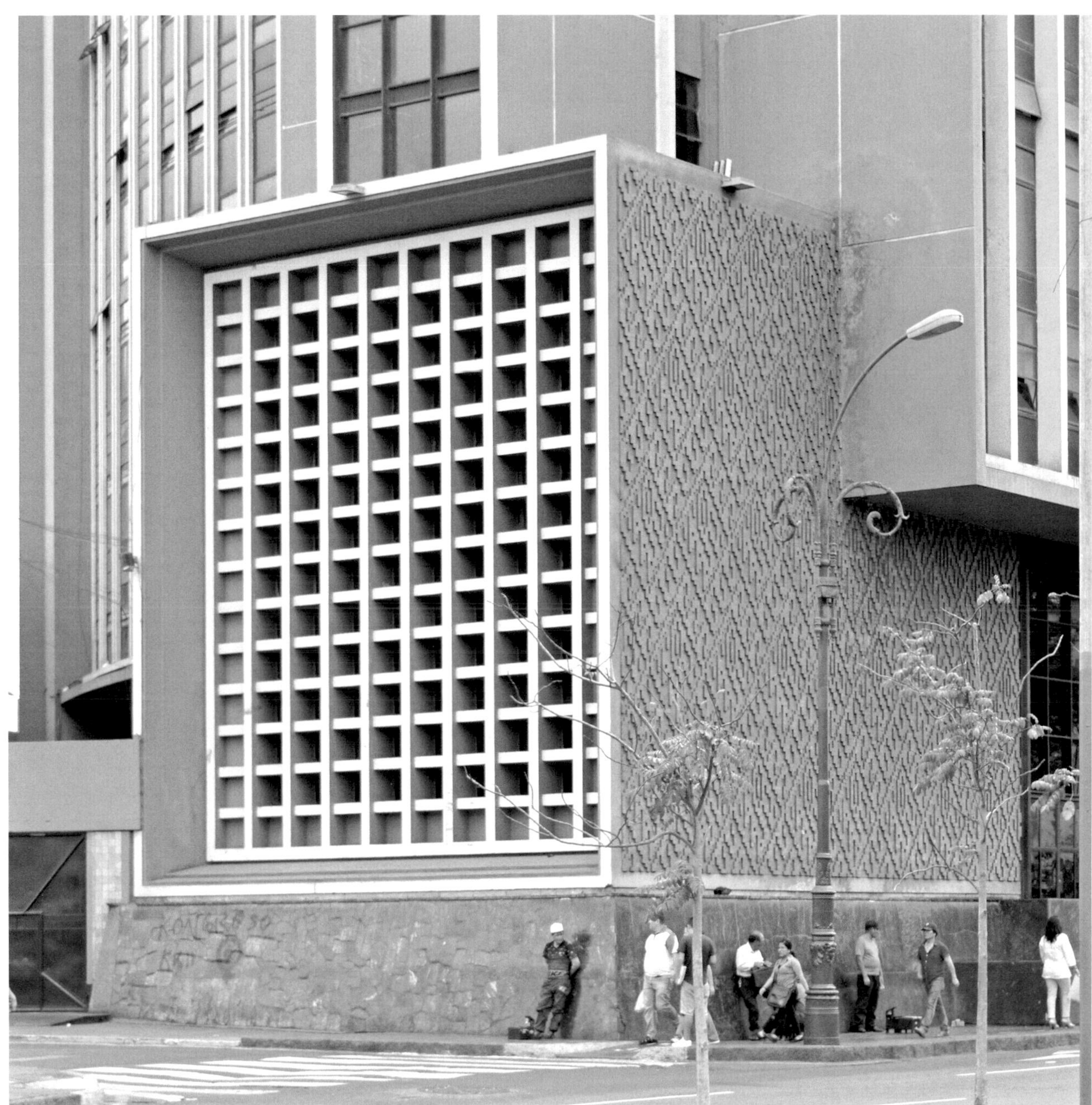

Ministerio de Educación Pública
Detail view
Lima
Enrique Seoane Ros
1951–1956
Javier Atoche Intili (2018)

Edificio Guzmán Blanco
Main view and ground and first floors
Lima
Manuel Villarán
1952

El Arquitecto Peruano (October–November 1952)

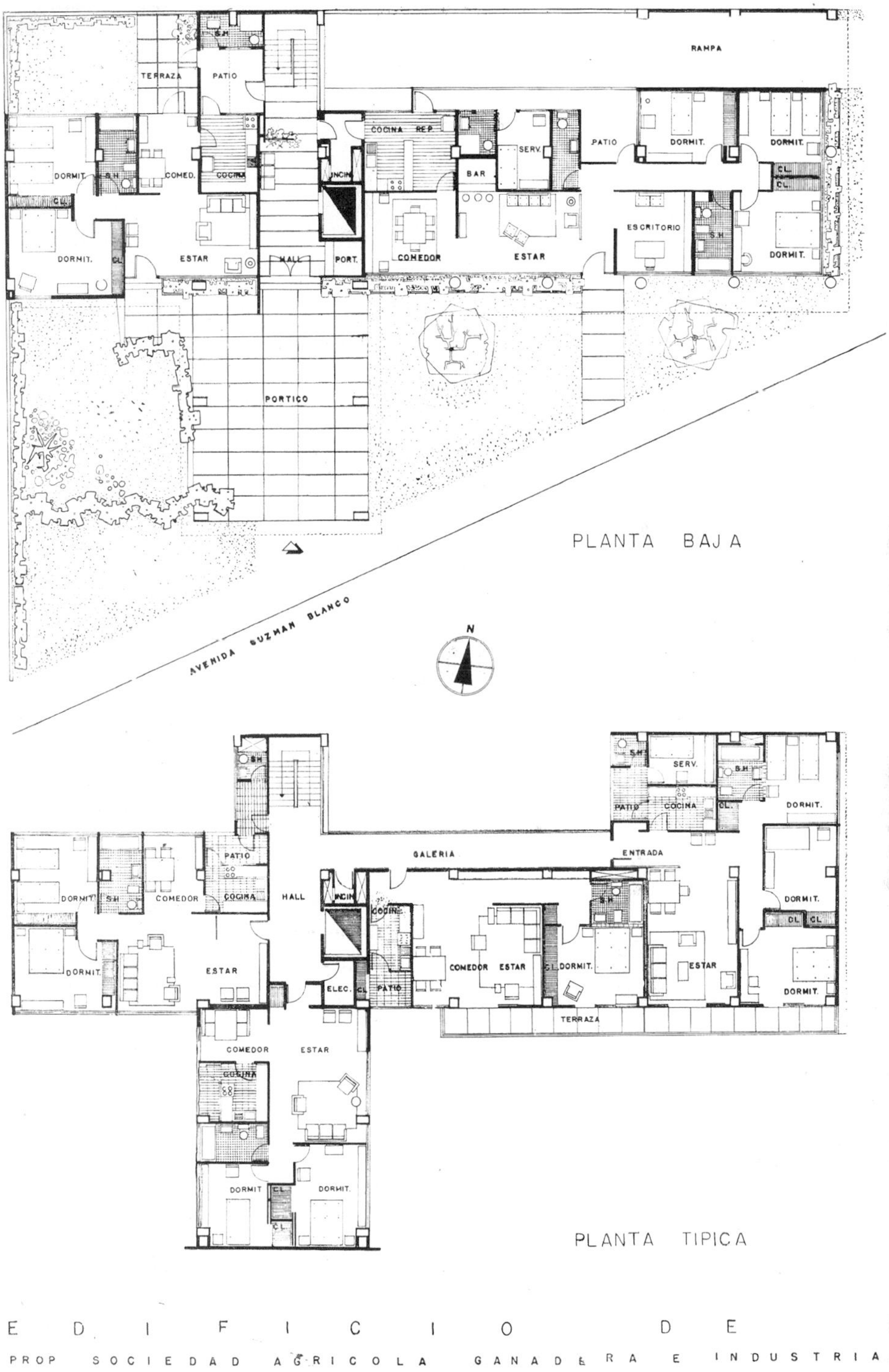

PLANTA BAJA

AVENIDA GUZMAN BLANCO

PLANTA TIPICA

E D I F I C I O D E

PROP SOCIEDAD AGRICOLA GANADERA E INDUSTRIA

Edificio Ostolaza
Main view from Avenida Tacna
Lima
Enrique Seoane Ros
1951–1953

El Arquitecto Peruano
(July–August–September 1955)

Edificio San Reynaldo[18] (Enrique Seoane, 1954–1956), with a basement and tower characterised by a reinforced concrete grid; in the Galerías Comerciales Mogollón[19] (Raúl Morey, 1958), an ambitious project consisting of four towers and a commercial gallery crossing the entire block and joining two streets; and in the Edificio de la Compañía de Seguros Atlas[20] (José Alvarez Calderón, Walter Weberhofer, 1953–1955). The latter has a volumetry composed of a two-storey

Edificio Ostolaza
Detail view of the stairs
Lima
Enrique Seoane Ros
1951–1953

El Arquitecto Peruano
(July–August–September 1955)

Edificio San Reynaldo
Main view
Lima
Enrique Seoane Ros
1954–1956

El Arquitecto Peruano
(April–May–June 1958)

basement and a tower above resting on pilotis, a roof treated as a garden and a reinforced concrete canopy, its north-facing elevations sheltered by aluminium sunshades. The Municipalidad de Lima recognised the architectural value of the Edificio de la Compañía de Seguros Atlas, on 28 July 1955, as well as the Edificio San Reynaldo, on 28 July 1958, both with the prestigious Municipalidad de Lima Award[21] (see VI.1.1.).

The Edificio Radio El Sol (Luis Miró Quesada, 1953–1954) is the second Peruvian example included in the MoMA catalogue. As with the Ostoloza, Radio El Sol earned its architect the Chavín Prize in 1954.[22] The corner solution, a reinforced concrete frame structure with an overhang towards both streets, represents one of the first local examples of a fully curtain-walled façade. This technological solution gives it the appearance of a glazed parallelepiped resting

18 See 'Edificio San Reynaldo', *El Arquitecto Peruano* (April–May–June 1958).
19 See 'Galerías Comerciales Mogollón', *El Arquitecto Peruano* (January–February–March 1958).
20 See 'Nuevo Edificio "Atlas"', *El Arquitecto Peruano* (May–June 1955).

Galerías Comerciales Mogollón
From left to right:
View from Jirón Moquegua
View from the hall
Longitudinal section, ground and first floors
Lima
Raúl Morey
1958

El Arquitecto Peruano (January–February–March 1958)

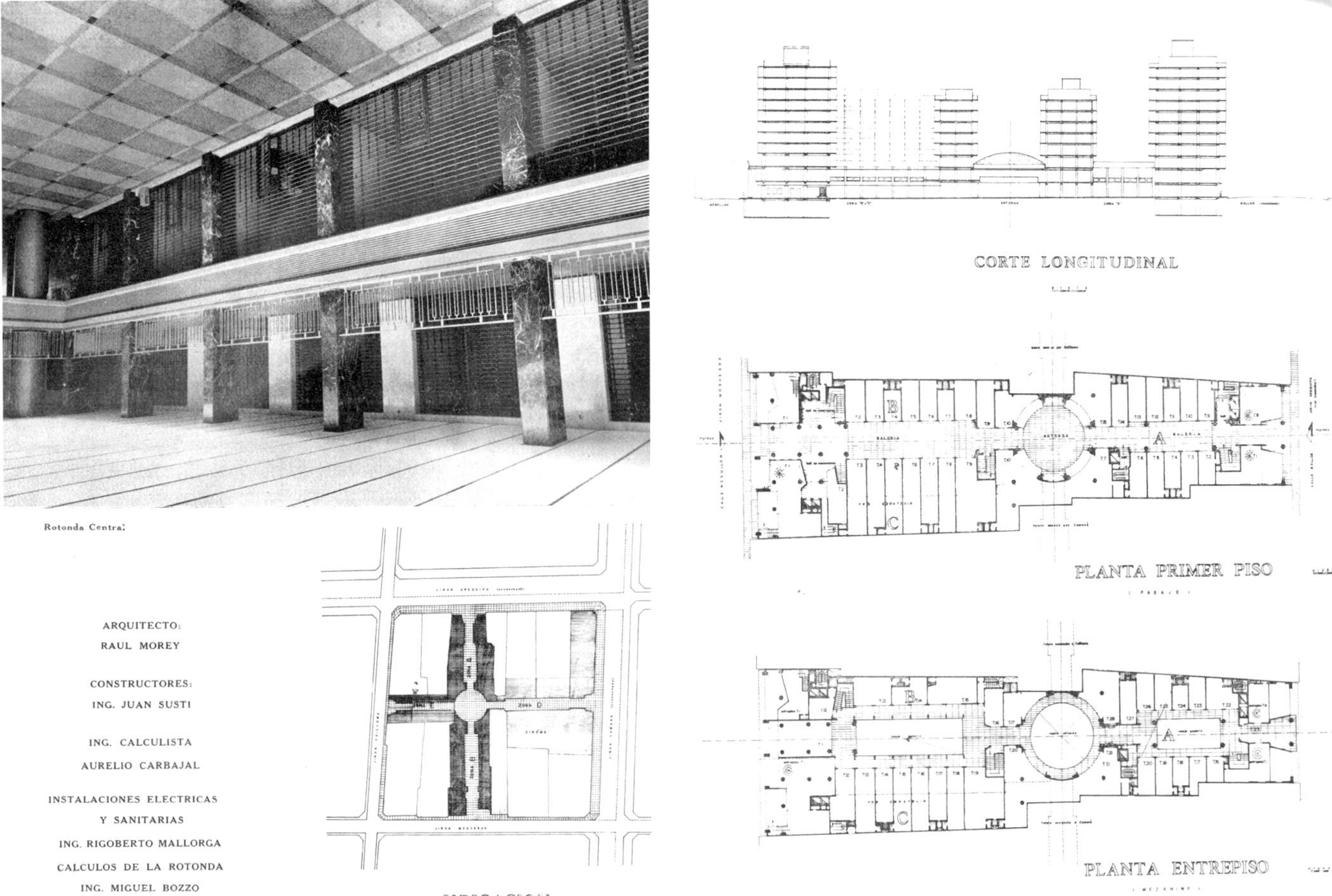

on pilotis. Also belonging to this family, characterised by the extensive use of glass in their façades, are: the Edificio Nyci[23] (Enrique Seoane, 1956), in which the volumetry is formed by the base, tower and an opaque prism containing the vertical circulation; and the Edificio Seguros El Sol[24] (Enrique Seoane, 1956–1958), a tower on a plinth whose cladding alternates between the use of traditional (brick) and industrial (glass, plastic, aluminium) materials.

The spread of new construction technologies and industrial materials was facilitated by the realisation of multi-storey buildings designed by Europeans in the 1950s. Such was the case with the Compañía de Seguros Peruano-Suiza (Theodor Cron, 1952–1956, see IV.5.), in its use of open plan and aluminium

21 See 'Premio de Arquitectura Chavín: Espíritu y Realidad', *Dimensión Arquitectónica* (1958).

22 See 'Luis Miro Quesada Garland: Premio Chavín de La Arquitectura', *El Arquitecto Peruano* (May–June 1955).

23 See 'Edificio para Inversiones Inmobiliarias SA', *El Arquitecto Peruano* (April–May–June 1958).

Edificio de la Compañía de Seguros Atlas
Proposal perspectives
Lima
José Alvarez Calderón,
Walter Weberhofer
1953–1955

El Arquitecto Peruano
(May–June 1955)

La Compañía de Seguros "Atlas" construye un gran edificio

Edificio de la Compañía de Seguros Atlas
Main view
Lima
José Alvarez Calderón, Walter Weberhofer
1953–1955

El Arquitecto Peruano (May–June 1955)

Edificio Radio El Sol
Main view
Lima
Luis Miró Quesada
1953–1954

El Arquitecto Peruano
(May–June 1955)

Edificio Nyci
Opposite page, from left to right:
View from Paseo de la República
View from Jirón Antonio Raimondi
Lima
Enrique Seoane Ros
1956

El Arquitecto Peruano
(April–May–June 1958)

frames; the Hotel Savoy (Mario Bianco, 1954–1957, see III.6.), in the insertion of parking spaces in the level between the basement and the hotel tower; and the Compañía de Seguros La Colmena (Paolo Mariotta, 1958–1961, see IV.5.), in its unusual use of steel structure with aluminium cladding. These characteristics would often be found in multi-storey buildings constructed in the years to come.

A synthesis between internal culture and external civilisation, characterising the third phase in American relations, finds its first examples in two multi-storey buildings in the historic centre of Lima. Experimentation with the aesthetic potential of this approach – through a structural presence in the façade, as seen in the Edificio Ostolaza, and through the widespread use of curtain walls in the façade, as in the Edificio Radio El Sol – reached its apogee in the proposals for the Banco Comercial and the Centro Cívico y Comercial de Lima, both realised in the Peruvian capital in the 1960s.

24 'Nuevo Edificio "El Sol"', *El Arquitecto Peruano* (July–August–September 1959), pp. 23–25.

The Banco Comercial[25] (Enrique Seoane, 1962–1963) was a private investment proposal for the administrative headquarters of a local bank. The base, whose ceramic cladding recalls the geometry found in pre-Hispanic textiles, consisted of two volumes occupying the entire plot, with different heights echoing those of neighbouring buildings. Above, a fully glazed monolith marked the bank's presence in Lima's urban skyline. The contrasts between the materials used, the progression of the volumes, the hermeticity of the base and the transparency of the tower: all were part of a dialogue between culture (internal – linked to tradition) and civilisation (external – based on technology). As stated in the article dedicated to this building in *El Arquitecto Peruano*, the Banco Comercial represented 'the new expression of an ancient language.'[26]

The Centro Cívico y Comercial de Lima[27] (Adolfo Córdova et al., Lima, 1966–1970), built on the land formerly occupied by an old penitentiary, was the result of a competition announced during the first term of Fernando Belaúnde Terry, President of the Republic (1963–1968). As had been hypothesised by Josep Lluís Sert and subsequently taken up by the Oficina Nacional de Planeamiento y Urbanismo in their proposal for the 1949 *Plan Piloto de Lima* (see I.3.3.), the chosen lot allowed the Centro Cívico to act as a union between the consolidated urban centre and those areas of twentieth-century expansion. The proposal, chosen from a range of variations on brutalism, exploits the structural and expressive potential of reinforced concrete, emphasised by exposed material, the considerable spans and their overhanging structures. The monumental complex resembles a contemporary archaeological site (Puruchuco is an eloquent example, see IV.3.), the scale of which was calibrated to the metropolitan area of influence: the volumes are organised around a 33-storey high tower, the tallest at the time it was built, which housed offices, an auditorium and complimentary services. Its construction can be seen as the epilogue to the *Plan Piloto de Lima* and, with the start of Juan Velasco Alvarado's revolutionary regime, marks the closure of Peru to foreign capital and, with it, the end of an era rich in the construction of multi-storey buildings.

Edificio Seguros El Sol
Magazine cover
Lima
Enrique Seoane Ros
1956–1958
El Arquitecto Peruano
(July–August–September 1959)

Edificio Seguros El Sol
Detail view
Lima
Enrique Seoane Ros
1956–1958
Javier Atoche Intili (2018)

V.3. **Multi-storey buildings: Lima's modern vocation**

Multi-storey buildings were widely used in Lima from the 1930s to the end of the 1960s. Until the 1940s, their construction was facilitated by the need for many foreign and local companies to erect their headquarters, along with the desire of wealthy individuals to emphasise their social status by building income housing at a time of rapid economic growth. In the following decade, these

25 'El Banco Comercial', *El Arquitecto Peruano* (September–October 1965), pp. 33–40.
26 Ibid.
27 'El Centro Cívico Concurso de Época', *El Arquitecto Peruano* (August 1966), pp. 20–21.

Banco Comercial
Magazine cover (left)
Ground and tower floors (top right)
View of the hall (bottom right)
Lima
Enrique Seoane Ros
1962–1963

El Arquitecto Peruano
(September–October 1965)

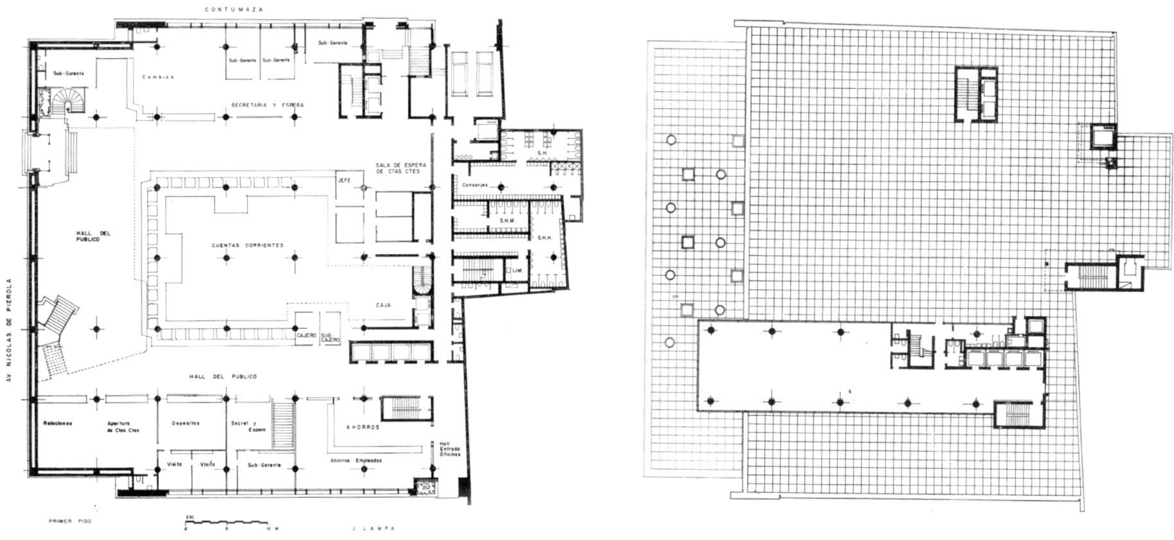

CONTUMAZA
Sub-Gerente
Cambios
SECRETARIA Y ESPERA
SALA DE ESPERA DE CTAS CTES
JEFE
Conserjes
S.H.
S.H.M.
S.H.H.
HALL DEL PUBLICO
CUENTAS CORRIENTES
CAJA
CAJERO
AV NICOLAS DE PIEROLA
HALL DEL PUBLICO
Relaciones
Apertura de Ctas Ctes
Depositos
Secret y Espera
AHORROS
Visita
Sub-Gerente
Ahorros Empleados
Hall Entrada Oficinas
PRIMER PISO

Centro Cívico y Comercial de Lima
Magazine cover (left)
Fernando Belaúnde Terry points to the model of the proposal (below)
Lima
Adolfo Córdova et al.
1966–1970

El Arquitecto Peruano (August 1966)

Centro Cívico y Comercial de Lima
Main view
Lima
Adolfo Córdova et al.
1966–1970
Archivo de Arquitectura PUCP,
José García Bryce Fund

Centro Cívico y Comercial de Lima
View of the tower from Jirón Carabaya
Lima
Adolfo Córdova et al.
1966–1970

Javier Atoche Intili (2018)

reasons were compounded by the need to reconstruct buildings destroyed by the earthquake (see I.2.1.), as well as by Peruvian town planning regulations (see I.2.2.), which encouraged the spread of multi-storey buildings in the historic centre of the Peruvian capital after the war. A fundamental role in introducing these constructions was played by European designers active in Peru in the last century, among whose records many early examples can be found (see I.3.3.).

As mentioned above, the Peruvian press documented the reception of these buildings at home. Likewise, bodies such as the Municipalidad de Lima and the Ministerio de Educación recognised their qualities. In the first editions of the Chavín Prize, between 1949 and 1955, five of the seven works awarded this distinction were multi-storey buildings. In chronological order, the award-winning projects were: the Edificio de la Compañía de Seguros La Fénix (Enrique Seoane, Lima, 1945–1948, Chavín Prize 1950); the Edificio Guzmán Blanco (Manuel Villarán, Lima, 1952, Chavín Prize 1952); the Edificio Ostolaza (Enrique Seoane, Lima, 1951–1953, Chavín Prize 1953); the Edificio Radio El Sol (Luis Miró Quesada, Lima, 1953–1954, Chavín Prize 1954); and the Edificio Málaga Santolla (Alfredo Málaga, Lima, 1955, Chavín Prize 1955, renounced).[28]

Peruvian examples of this type were also featured in the New York exhibitions of the Museum of Modern Art, *Latin American Architecture Since 1945* and *Latin American in Construction: Architecture, 1955–1980*. Henry-Russell Hitchcock highlighted the fine quality and great variety found in these Latin American examples.[29] *El Arquitecto Peruano* and the Swiss trade magazine *Bauen + Wohnen* also dedicated an article in 1960 to the Edificio El Pacifico[30] (Fernando de Osma, 1958), a complex consisting of a two-storey basement, a one-storey roofed car park and two seven-storey towers, the layout of which is reminiscent of Mario Bianco's design for the Hotel Savoy.

Lima's multi-storey buildings are thus the manifestation of the government's economic and political project developed for the centre of the Peruvian capital. As such, they represent 'manifesto buildings,' deserving of preservation for future generations.

28 See 'Premio de Arquitectura Chavín: espíritu y realidad', *Dimensión Arquitectónica* (1958).

29 Hitchcock, Henry-Russell, *Latin American Architecture Since 1945* (New York, 1955), p. 29.

30 See 'Nuevo Edificio El Pacífico', El Arquitecto Peruano (July–August–September 1964); 'Wohn-und Geschäftsgebäude in Lima', *Bauen + Wohnen / Construction + habitation / Building + home: internationale Zeitschrift* (1960).

Edificio El Pacifico
Magazine cover
Miraflores, Lima
Fernando de Osma
1958

El Arquitecto Peruano
(July–August–September 1964)

Edificio El Pacifico
Magazine article
Miraflores, Lima
Fernando de Osma
1958

Bauen + Wohnen (1960)

S. de Osma

Wohn- und Geschäftsgebäude in Lima

Das Gebäude steht auf einem Grundstück neben dem Park von Millaflores. Im Sockelgeschoß befinden sich Läden und ein Restaurant, im Kern des Sockelgeschosses ein Kino. Ein Teil der Terrasse des Sockelgeschosses dient als Parkplatz. Im achtgeschossigen Hochhaus, das vom Sockelgeschoß abgehoben ist, sind eine Vierzimmer- und je zwei Dreizimmerwohnungen. Das Pfeilersystem und die Grundrisse stimmen miteinander nicht überein, die Anordnung der Wohnungsgrundrisse ist ungewohnt, und ihre Qualität entspricht nicht jener der Fassade. g

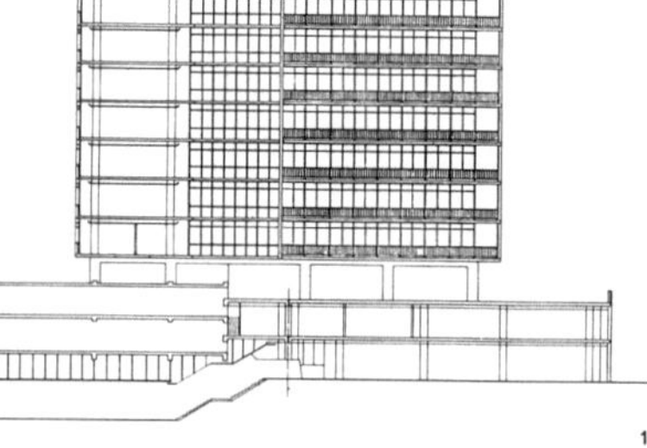

1

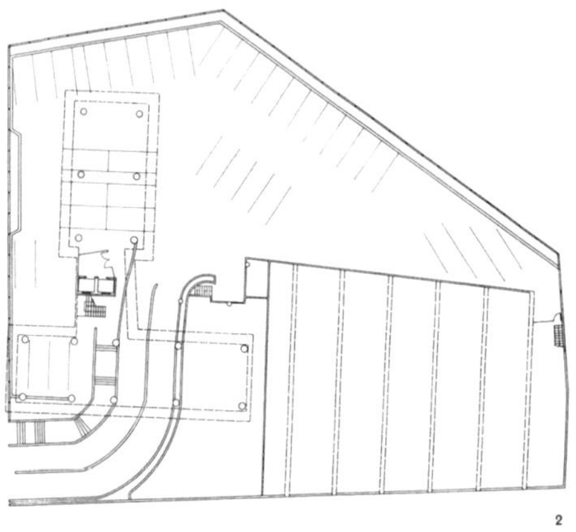

2

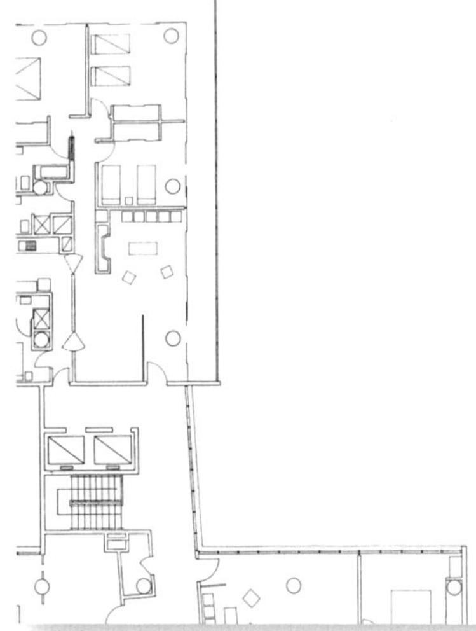

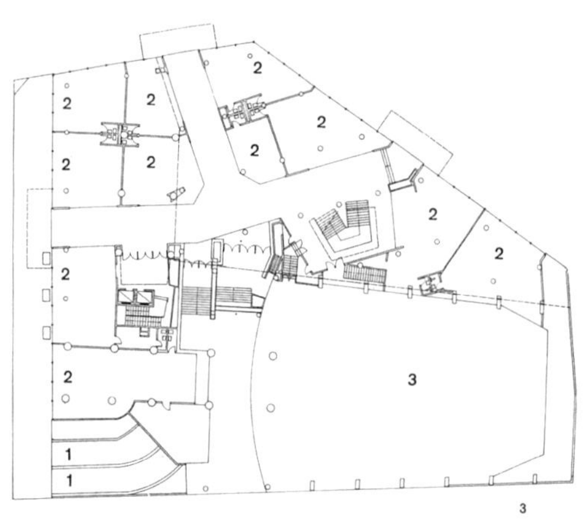

3

Overlay of Spanish foundation grid on historical map
Lima
1954

Oficina Nacional de Planeamiento y Urbanismo

DIPROVE

PART III

On the recognition of the values of twentieth century Peruvian architecture

MULTI-STOREY BUILDINGS IN LIMA: A HERITAGE 'UNDER CONSTRUCTION' (1964–2020)

1960

ITALY Peruvian architect Víctor Pimentel Gurmendi returns to Peru after a period of study in Italy (1955–1960)

1964

ITALY Pimentel participates in the Secondo congresso internazionale degli architetti e tecnici dei monumenti, Venice

Carta di Venezia

1968

USA The deposed president Fernando Belaúnde Terry moves to the US after the military coup led by Juan Velasco Alvarado

1960s

1970s

1963

Junta Deliberante Metropolitana de Monumentos Históricos Artísticos y Lugares Arqueológicos de Lima (1961–1963)

Fernando Belaúnde Terry is elected president of Peru

1965

Carta di Venezia (Universidad Nacional de Ingeniería, Lima, 1965)

Ley de Fomento de la Cultura

1970

First architecture biennial of the Colegio de Arquitectos del Perú

Peruvian building regulations. Title IV – Architectural Heritage

1972

FRANCE World Cultural and Natural Heritage (UNESCO)

ITALY *Carta del Restauro* (Alfredo Barbacci, Cesare Brandi, Pietro Romanelli)

1976

EL SALVADOR Convention of San Salvador

1987

ITALY *Carta della Conservazione e del Restauro degli Oggetti d'Arte e di Cultura* (Consiglio Nazionale delle Ricerche)

1988

THE NETHERLANDS DoCoMoMo International

1980s

1990s

1971

Creation of the Instituto Nacional de Cultura

1975

Centro Cívico y Comercial de Lima (Adolfo Córdova et al., Lima, 1966–1970) fire

1979

Constitution of the Republic of Peru includes the term 'cultural heritage' in the Title on Cultural Assets

1980

Fernando Belaúnde Terry is elected president of Peru (second term)

1985

Ley General de Amparo al Patrimonio Cultural de la Nación

Instituto Nacional de Cultura responsible for the 'Inventario general de los bienes inmuebles'

1986

Instituto de Investigación y Conservación del Patrimonio Histórico-Artístico (Universidad Nacional de Ingeniería, Lima)

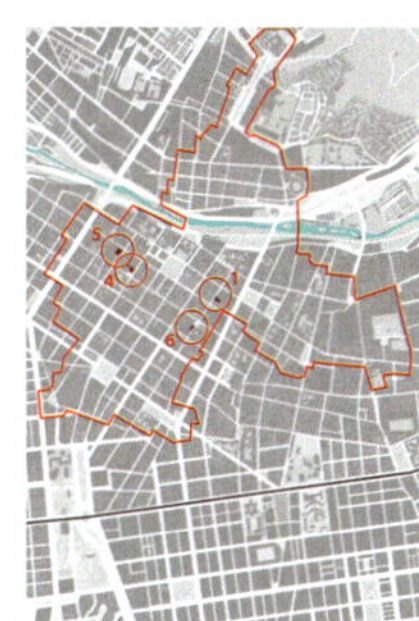

1991

Historic centre of Lima World Heritage (UNESCO, 1988–1991)

1993

Constitution of the Republic of Peru. Elimination of the Title on Cultural Assets

2000

POLAND *Charter of Cracow*

1990s

2000s

1994

Inventario del Patrimonio Monumental Inmueble de Lima – Valles de Chillón, Rímac y Lurín (UNI, Ford Foundation, Lima, 1986–1994)

1994

Hotel Savoy (Mario Bianco, Lima, 1954–1957). Removal of original furnishings. Modification of the spatial distribution of the plinth planes and the colours of the main façades

1996

The Instituto Nacional de Cultura recognises the Casa Huiracocha (Luis Miró Quesada, Lima, 1947–1948) as a site of cultural interest

2000

Fire and demolition of the Banco Comercial (Seoane, Lima, 1962–1963)

2002

Modification of the spatial distribution of the Edificio de la Compañía de Seguros Peruano-Suiza (Theodor Cron, Lima, 1952–1956)

2004

Ley General del Patrimonio Cultural de la Nación

Modification of the building's entrance hall of the Edificio Irma (G. Fogliani, Lima, 1946–1948)

2010s

2010

Establishment of DoCoMoMo Perú

Instituto Nacional de Cultura becomes Ministero de Cultura

2010

Modification of the main façade of the Edificio Arnodi (Paul Linder, Lima, 1950)

2013

The 'Inventario general de los bienes inmuebles' recognises 5,174 monumental properties (Ministerio de Cultura)

2014

Peruvian architectural heritage in the *DoCoMoMo Virtual Exhibition* (DoCoMoMo Perú, Lima, 2014)

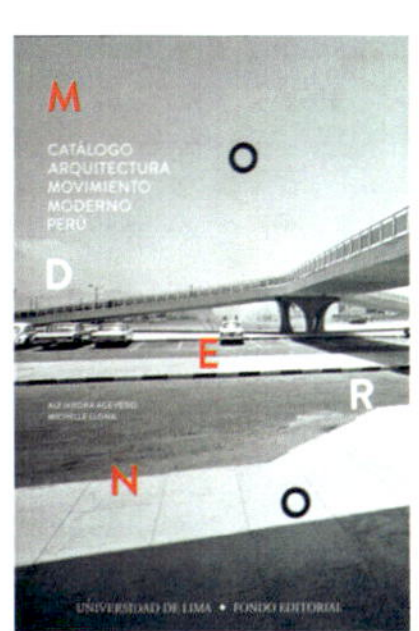

2016

Catalogo Arquitectura Movimiento Moderno Perù (Universidad de Lima, Lima, 2014–2016)

2020s

2020

The Ministerio de Cultura recognises the cultural value of the Ministerio de Educación Pública (Enrique Seoane, Lima, 1951–1956)

Chapter VI
Multi-storey buildings in Lima: a heritage 'under construction' (1964–2020)

VI.1. Protection of Peruvian architecture, from the origins of the problem to the institutionalisation of the twentieth-century's heritage concept

Among Peru's greatest challenges in the field of cultural rights is the protection and enhancement of its vast built heritage. This Andean country is not only the repository of millenary cultures but also the custodian of a registry spanning diverse historical periods, including pre-Columbian civilisations, the viceregal phase and the republican period. Consulting UNESCO data provides an overview of the richness and complexity of this legacy: the country boasts 13 World Heritage Sites, nine of which are cultural, two natural and two mixed, plus 23 awaiting recognition.[1] The historic centre of Lima itself has been on the UNESCO World Heritage List since 1988.

Peru's centuries-old legislation on the preservation of monuments exists due to the presence on its territory of traces of some of the most important pre-Hispanic cultures to be found on the American continent. The first notions of Peruvian heritage can be traced back to the regulations issued in the sixteenth century by the Spanish Crown, intended for the inventorying of huge ceremonial areas in the conquered territories.[2] Although these first listings of pre-Hispanic sites had different intentions from those of protection, fundamental rules were, nevertheless, laid down regarding the patrimonial sphere,[3] which delineated the relationship between a central administration and private individuals.

At the same time as the founding phase of the viceroyalty of Peru (between the sixteenth and seventeenth centuries), the first recorded interest in the preservation of the vestiges of the Inca Empire was noted. In his work *Comentarios Reales de los Incas*, Inca Garcilaso de la Vega recognised the documentary value of the complexes built before the arrival of the Spaniards that were subsequently destroyed.[4]

VI.1.1. Precedents in the Peruvian architectural heritage census (1542–1963)

At the dawn of the republican period (see I.1.2.), a new collective memory was emerging, as Peru moved away from its recent viceregal past.[5] Although the first preservation regulations of the young Peruvian Republic were aimed at protecting only the pre-Hispanic heritage, the aims were not exclusively economic.

The legislation enacted after the declaration of independence from the Spanish Court on 28 July 1821, while confirming the priority of pre-Columbian artefacts in state cultural policies,[6] was conditioned by the sheer brevity of

1 UNESCO, 'Peru: Properties Inscribed on the World Heritage List', *World Heritage Convention* (2 January 2023).

2 Córdova, Rodrigo and Soria, Judith, 'Peru', in Carughi, Ugo and Visone, Massimo (eds.), *Time Frames: Conservation Policies for Twentieth-Century Architectural Heritage* (London / New York, 2017), p. 107.

3 Instituto Nacional de Cultura, *Política cultural del Perú* (Paris, 1977).

4 See de la Vega, Garcilaso, *Primera parte de los Comentarios reales, que tratan del origen de los yncas, y de todo lo que fue aquel imperio y su republica, antes que los españoles passaran a el* (Lisbon, 1609).

5 See Hernández Asensio, Raúl, *Señores del pasado: Arqueólogos, museos y huaqueros en el Perú* (Lima, 2018).

Sacred city of Caral-Supe
UNESCO World Heritage Site
since 2009
Supe
Javier Atoche Intili (2016)

Historic centre of Lima
UNESCO World Heritage
Site since 1988
Lima
Javier Atoche Intili (2018)

262

INSTITUTO NACIONAL DE CULTURA
MUSEO DE ARTE ITALIANO

Museo de Arte Italiano
Lima
Gaetano Moretti
1921–1923
Javier Atoche Intili (2018)

Peruvian governments. This, combined with subsequent changes in political orientation, hindered the development of actions to protect pre-Hispanic legacy. Shortcomings in public cultural policies were initially compensated for by the efforts of individuals, who nevertheless had limited influence in the public and economic spheres. As a result, in the first century of the Peruvian Republic, a considerable number of private collections were sold abroad to enrich the collections of European and American museums.[7]

The loss of a conspicuous part of its archaeological heritage, due to the discontinuity in the Peruvian Republic's preservation actions, prompted the State to take measures to halt this cultural devastation. As evidenced by the legal provisions issued in 1929, the legislation included (in the definition of a historical monument, for the first time in the history of the Republic and limited to the territory of Cusco) assets dating back to the viceregal period.[8]

Although this change was begun in Cusco, it was extended to a national level in the 1930s, as the State recognised the need to safeguard artefacts built after the establishment of the viceroyalty of Peru.[9] At the end of the decade, the first public body for the protection of monuments was created, establishing itself as the main organ for their conservation. In 1939, Law no. 8853 established the Consejo Nacional de Conservación y Restauración de Monumentos Históricos y Artísticos,[10] declaring in its text the State's role in the conservation of the country's historical and artistic heritage, differentiating between the protection of pre-Hispanic assets and those of the viceregal period.[11]

The first steps taken by the Peruvian government towards the promotion and dissemination of different forms of cultural expression can be seen in the various regulations issued during the 1940s. The laws of 1942 and 1947 recognised the diverse scientific and humanistic disciplines as contributors to the country's development, and consequently began to promote their production, especially with the creation of an architectural prize, called the Chavín Prize (Premio Nacional de Fomento a la Cultura, see V.2.), which awarded the winning authors monetarily.[12] Before that, the Premio Municipalidad de Lima, created in 1939, had been the most prestigious award for architecture in Peru.[13]

Between the 1940s and early 1960s, particularly during the first and second terms of Manuel Prado y Ugarteche's government, the Consejo Nacional de Conservación's functions were strengthened; it established regulations for interventions on buildings from the viceregal era.[14] This period also saw the recognition of the historical value of artefacts from the republican period.[15]

Although the Comisión Nacional de Cultura (1962–1963) and its executive body, the Casa de la Cultura,[16] were created in the 1960s, a true turning point in Peru's cultural protection policies came about only following

6 See Congreso de la República del Perú, 'Decreto Supremo', *Archivo Digital de la Legislación Peruana* (11 June 1921); Hayakawa Casas, José Carlos, *Restauración en Lima: pasos y contrapasos* (Lima, 2010).

7 See Hernández Asensio, Raúl, *Señores del pasado: Arqueólogos, museos y huaqueros en el Perú* (Lima, 2018).

8 Congreso de la República del Perú, 'Ley N° 6523', *Archivo Digital de la Legislación Peruana* (9 February 1929).

9 'Constitución Política del Perú, Capitolo II Garantías individuales, Titolo III Educación, art. 82', Ibid. (29 September 1933).

10 'Ley N° 8853', Ibid. (9 March 1939).

11 Ibid.

12 See Congreso de la República del Perú, 'Ley N° 9614', *Archivo Digital de la Legislación Peruana* (30 September 1942); 'Ley N° 10869', Ibid. (31 March 1947); 'Premio de Arquitectura Chavín: espíritu y realidad', *Dimensión Arquitectónica* (1958).

13 See Belaúnde Terry, Fernando, 'Puntos de vista... Premios municipales para las "mejores" construcciones', *El Arquitecto Peruano* (August 1939).

14 *See* Congreso de la República del Perú, 'Ley N° 9630', *Archivo Digital de la Legislación Peruana* (13 October 1942); 'Reglamentación para las Comisiones Departamentales y Provinciales', Ibid. (24 October 1942).

15 See Hayakawa Casas, José Carlos, *Restauración en Lima: pasos y contrapasos* (Lima, 2010).

16 See Congreso de la República del Perú, 'Decreto Supremo N° 48', *Archivo Digital de la Legislación Peruana* (24 August 1962); 'Decreto Ley N° 14479', Ibid. (9 May 1963).

the participation of the country's delegation in the Second International Congress of Architects and Monumental Technicians, held in Venice in May 1964.

VI.1.2. The Second International Congress of Restoration in Venice and its repercussions on Peruvian cultural policies (1964–2010)

The mid-1960s saw some important precedents concerning the cultural policies of the Peruvian state, due in part to the considerable influence of the *Carta di Venezia* (1964). On the one hand, the need to rebuild historic centres damaged by natural disasters (namely, the earthquakes recorded in Lima, in 1940, in Cusco, in 1950; and in Arequipa, in 1960) made it a necessary instrument for local preservation policies. On the other hand, the participation of Peruvian architect Víctor Pimentel Gurmendi in Italy facilitated the dissemination of the Charter's contents in Peru.[17]

Pimentel was among the most active figures in the research, conservation and dissemination of Peru's historical and artistic heritage in the second half of the twentieth century. Together with José García Bryce, he was part of

17 Pimentel Gurmendi, Víctor, *Víctor Pimentel Gurmendi y el patrimonio monumental: textos escogidos*, in Beingolea, José Luis (ed.) (Lima, 2015), pp. 19–25.

Víctor Pimentel Gurmendi in Milan
About 1957
Víctor Pimentel Gurmendi y el patrimonio monumental: textos escogidos

Fernando Belaúnde Terry, President of the Republic of Peru, and Víctor Pimentel Gurmendi
Lima
1964
Víctor Pimentel Gurmendi y el patrimonio monumental: textos escogidos

a group of students trained at the Department of Architecture at the Escuela Nacional de Ingenieros who carried out specialisation studies in post-war Italy. Mario Bianco, at the time a teacher of the fifth-year design workshop, put them in contact with various Italian intellectuals, such as Bruno Zevi and Giovanni Astengo, enriching their training experiences in Europe (see III.4.). After five-years abroad, Pimentel helped organise in 1960 a course on the restoration of monuments at the former Escuela Nacional de Ingenieros, before leaving for Venice.

The participation of the Peruvian delegation in the Second International Congress of Restoration (1964) stimulated the timely diffusion of the *Carta di Venezia* in the Andean country. Upon returning home, Pimentel made its dissemination his priority, with the first printed edition of the Charter – published in the Universidad Nacional de Ingeniería (formerly Escuela Nacional de Ingenieros) – dating to 1965, the year after its drafting. Participation in the 1964 Venetian congress was fundamental to the creation of the censuses that have been carried out since the last quarter of the twentieth century, as demonstrated by the experience of the Instituto de Investigación y Conservación del Patrimonio Histórico-Artístico. Pimentel recalled that: 'mi presencia en Venecia en 1964, cuando se produjo la redacción de la famosa Carta, sería un hecho importantísimo para mí y creo también para la conservación del patrimonio monumental en el país.'[18]

18 'my presence in Venice in 1964, in conjunction with the drafting of the well-known Charter, would have been a very important event for me and I believe also for the preservation of the monumental heritage in the country [Peru]'. Pimentel Gurmendi, Víctor, *Víctor Pimentel Gurmendi y el patrimonio monumental: textos escogidos*, Beingolea, José Luis (ed.) (Lima, 2015), p. 22.

The influence of the *Carta di Venezia* in the Peruvian legislative framework continued during the decade following its drafting. In 1970, the *Reglamento Nacional de Construcciones* was published, the first Peruvian building regulation to include a paragraph dedicated to 'patrimonio arquitectónico.'[19] This document would subsequently serve as the main regulatory framework for the bodies in charge of safeguarding monuments, such as the Instituto Nacional de Cultura.

The Instituto Nacional de Cultura, a decentralised public body forming part of the organisational structure of the Peruvian Ministry of Education, was created on 9 March 1971.[20] Along with its activities of conservation and protection was added the valorisation of monumental heritage. Toward this end, it was decided to identify and appoint a group of specialists in the field, organised in 1973 into the Centro de Investigación y Restauración de Bienes Monumentales, responsible for the cataloguing of monumental heritage in the pre-Hispanic, viceregal and republican periods.[21]

Despite the various measures enacted, the lack of effective decision-making power prevented the Instituto Nacional de Cultura from performing its tasks in a timely manner. The relationship of political and economic dependence on the central education department,[22] the meagreness of the funds allocated, as well as a notable inefficiency in terms of organisation related to personnel and resources, rendered it feeble, a body with limited capacity for intervention in the field of monuments protection. This institution would remain in operation for nearly four decades, until 2010, when the Ministerio de la Cultura was created: the current public body responsible for the conservation, protection and valorisation of Peru's cultural heritage.

VI.1.3. **Peruvian architectural heritage: from cultural heritage to economic and social rights (1979–2020)**

The first half of the 1980s was marked by political turbulence in Peru – the first activities of the extreme left-wing Peruvian terrorist groups Sendero Luminoso and Movimiento Revolucionario Túpac Amaru date back to 1980 and 1984 respectively – which led to a severe economic recession in the last quarter of the twentieth century. As far as Peru's architectural heritage of the twentieth century is concerned, this period entailed risks, relatively small compared to the twenty-first century, which mainly affected multi-storey buildings as representative seats of political (public buildings) and economic (predominantly private buildings) power.

19 See Congreso de la República del Perú, 'Decreto Supremo N° 039-70-VI, Título IV – Patrimonio Arquitectónico', *Archivo Digital de la Legislación Peruana* (5 May 1970).

20 *Decreto Ley N° 18799, Art. 49, Ley Orgánica del Sector Educación* (9 March 1971). See Instituto Nacional de Cultura, *Política cultural del Perú* (Paris, 1977), p. 26.

21 Ibid., pp. 59-63.

22 Decreto Ley N° 19268, Art. 27–28 (11 November 1972), Ibid., p. 26.

The Constitutional Charter of 1979[23] (1979–1993), which included the term 'patrimonio cultural' for the first time and delegated the conservation and enjoyment of archaeological and architectural legacy to provincial administrations, became a document of great importance for the protection and enhancement of monuments in Peru.

Peruvian cultural heritage was protected by the State, which was responsible for its preservation and transmission to future generations.[24] Furthermore, the recognition of supranational agreements in the Peruvian legal system, enshrined in this Charter, would be a fundamental step towards adherence to international conventions as pertains to the protection of cultural and natural legacy.[25] Finally, the Constitution identified local governments as the bodies in charge of the conservation and valorisation of archaeological and historical monuments in their territories.[26]

In 1985, with the 1979 Charter in force, the Ley General de Amparo al Patrimonio Cultural de la Nación[27] was enacted, the first Peruvian reference law on the protection of cultural heritage, remaining in force for 19 years. There were three main provisions concerning the protection of architectural heritage: the ratification of international treaties such as the Convention for the Protection of the World Cultural and Natural Heritage UNESCO (1972) and the Convention of San Salvador (1976); the inclusion of landscape assets in the definition of cultural assets; and the creation of the Consejo del Patrimonio Cultural de la Nación, a coordinating body for Peruvian cultural institutions. The Consejo del Patrimonio Cultural de la Nación was thus called upon to approve the rules for the inventorying of immovable property.

The activities of recognition, regulation, conservation, protection, research, and dissemination were entrusted to the Biblioteca Nacional,[28] the Archivo General de la Nación[29] and the Instituto Nacional de Cultura, while the actions of supervision, regulatory compliance and study were assigned to central ministries, local governments, and universities. The Instituto Nacional de Cultura was designated as the body responsible for the organisation and management of the 'Inventario general de los bienes inmuebles,' which was carried out through the drawing up of special sheets, one for each property. The Peruvian provincial administrations were identified as cooperating in the activities of collecting and classifying data concerning this heritage.[30]

The legal framework summarised in the above paragraph became a precedent in the survey of recent Peruvian architecture, initiated in 1986 by the Universidad Nacional de Ingeniería in collaboration with the Ford Foundation (see VI. 2.1.). The enactment of these regulatory laws took place in a period, the last quarter of the last century, which saw important modifications and

23 Congreso de la República del Perú, 'Constitución política para la República del Perú', *Archivo Digital de la Legislación Peruana* (12 July 1979).
24 Art. 36. Ibid.
25 Art. 101. Ibid.
26 Art. 255. Ibid.
27 'Ley N° 24047', Ibid. (3 January 1985).
28 Instituto Nacional de Cultura, Política cultural del Perú (Paris, 1977), p. 43.
29 Ibid., p. 47.
30 Ley N° 24193, Ibid. (June 1985).

demolitions of emblematic buildings of the multi-storey type built in the historical centre of Lima: these include the Centro Cívico y Comercial de Lima (damaged in the riots of 5 February 1975 that preceded the ousting of the military regime of Juan Velasco Alvarado); the La Colmena Compañía de Seguros (affected by a fire on 26 October 1977); and the Banco Comercial (burnt down during the protests on 28 July 2000 and later demolished).

This period, characterised by political turbulence linked to extreme left-wing movements, was succeeded by a phase marked by liberal Peruvian policies and a booming economy. As far as Peruvian cultural heritage is concerned, this change in the political-economic framework was documented in the 1993 Political Constitution (currently in force), which represented a regression in the definition of protection. The new Charter, in fact, removed the title *Cultural Heritage* from the text and included it in the chapter *Economic and Social Rights*.

In 2004, a new law was enacted, the Ley General del Patrimonio Cultural de la Nación, which remains the current legislation on cultural heritage. However, it still has the 1993 Charter as a reference, including among the immovable assets 'los edificios, obras de infraestructura, ambientes y conjuntos monumentales, centros históricos y demás construcciones.'[31] This law provides for the preservation of the legacy of the pre-Hispanic, viceregal and republican eras, but leaves the protection of the considerable number of buildings of the first half of the last century – including buildings constructed for the commemoration of the centenary of Peru's Independence (held on 28 July 1921) and the second half of the twentieth century – without a specific legal framework.[32]

The twenty-first century saw the separation of cultural and educational policies, along with the transformation of the Instituto Nacional de Cultura (formerly dependent on the Ministero de Educación) into the Ministerio de Cultura,[33] the main public institution for the preservation, protection, and valorisation of tangible and intangible cultural assets. Currently, the strategies of the Peruvian Ministerio de Cultura include campaigns aimed at disseminating the historical and artistic values of monuments, focusing mainly on older cultural works built before the last century. Nevertheless, the situation seems to be evolving. As illustrated below, research carried out over the last 35 years by Peruvian architecture and art scholars is beginning to bear fruit: it is largely contributing to the construction of Peru's twentieth-century heritage.

31 Ley N° 28296 (21 June 2004) reads: 'buildings, infrastructural works, environments and monumental complexes, historical centres and other constructions'. Ministerio de Cultura (ed.), *Marco legal de protección del patrimonio cultural* (Lima 2018), pp. 5–29.

32 Decreto Supremo N° 011-2006ED (1 June 2006). Ibid., pp. 31–60.

33 Córdova, Rodrigo and Soria, Judith, 'Peru', in Carughi, Ugo and Visone, Massimo (eds.), *Time Frames: Conservation Policies for Twentieth-Century Architectural Heritage* (London / New York, 2017), p. 107.

VI.2. The multi-storey building in inventories and research on twentieth century Peruvian architecture

The first documentation and inventorying activities of the architecture of the second half of the twentieth century in Peru dates to the 1980s, to the surveys of the Universidad Nacional de Ingeniería through the Instituto de Investigación y Conservación del Patrimonio Histórico-Artístico. The Instituto was created in 1986 on the initiative of the Peruvian professor Víctor Pimentel with the aim of training professionals in the discipline of conservation and restoration of monumental heritage, through degree and specialisation courses at the Universidad Nacional de Ingeniería (formerly the Escuela Nacional de Ingenieros). The main contribution of this university institution was its desire to involve civil society in the research, conservation, and dissemination of the country's historical and artistic heritage.[34]

VI.2.1. *Inventario del Patrimonio Monumental Inmueble de Lima – Valles de Chillón, Rímac y Lurín*, Universidad Nacional de Ingenieria, Ford Foundation (Lima, 1986–1994)

The work of the Peruvian university began at a time when a community-wide awareness was emerging that architectural heritage, for multiple reasons, was undergoing a process of progressive and irreversible degradation, primarily due to the lack of recognition of its cultural dimension. The Universidad Nacional de Ingeniería, through the Instituto de Investigación y Conservación del Patrimonio Histórico-Artístico and in agreement with the Ford Foundation,[35] carried out a census between 1986 and 1989 in three Peruvian localities (Lima, Callao and Cusco) and drew up the *Inventario del Patrimonio Monumental Inmueble de Lima – Valles de Chillón, Rímac y Lurín.*

The Instituto de Investigación, using computers, carried out pioneering university research on the continent, concerning the collection of information and the monitoring of architectural legacy.[36] The census activities, aided by students, recent graduates and teachers from the Faculty of Architecture, Urbanism and Arts at the Universidad Nacional de Ingeniería, were carried out in two phases (1986–1988 and 1989). Víctor Pimentel coordinated the survey campaign, fresh from his experience with the lists of the Junta Deliberante Metropolitana de Monumentos Históricos Artísticos y Lugares Arqueológicos de Lima[37] (completed in 1963), the first systematic register of monuments in the Peruvian capital.[38]

34 Pimentel Gurmendi, Víctor, *Víctor Pimentel Gurmendi y el patrimonio monumental: textos escogidos*, Beingolea, José Luis (ed.) (Lima, 2015), p. 126.

35 US non-profit foundation with social and humanitarian aims, including the development of scientific and cultural knowledge in emerging countries.

36 See Universidad Nacional de Ingeniería, *Inventario del patrimonio monumental inmueble – Lima* (Lima, 1994).

37 Created during the municipal administration of Héctor García Ribeyro as an instrument to safeguard the archaeological and architectural heritage threatened by the accelerated and uncontrolled growth of Lima in the first half of the last century.

38 Pimentel Gurmendi, Víctor, *Víctor Pimentel Gurmendi y el patrimonio monumental: textos escogidos*, Beingolea, José Luis (ed.) (Lima, 2015), pp. 22–35.

Office of the Junta Deliberante Metropolitana de Monumentos históricos, artísticos y lugares arqueológicos de Lima
Lima
1961–1963
Víctor Pimentel Gurmendi y el patrimonio monumental: textos escogidos

The working group recorded 1,061 real estate properties in Lima, classified by periods: pre-Hispanic (up to 1531); viceregal (1532–1821); republican (1822–1920); and contemporary (from 1921 – which coincided with the centenary of independence – onwards). The census included 16 multi-storey buildings constructed in the historic centre of Lima between 1937 and 1969, of which 3 were designed by European architects: the Hotel Savoy (Mario Bianco, see III.6.); the Compañía de Seguros Peruano-Suiza (Theodor Cron, see IV.6.); and the Edificio Irma (Gianfelice Fogliani, Lima, 1946–1948, see III.6.). The material was catalogued and organised in a series consisting of five volumes, one for each historical period, with the fifth dedicated to statistical data extrapolated from the collected information.

Published in 1994, the UNI-Ford inventory was delivered to official institutions and had an immediate impact, since examples of modern architecture were for the first time considered worthy of preservation. Listed buildings that were not considered monuments at the time, such as the Casa Huiracocha[39] by Luis Miró Quesada (see I.3.2.), were later declared 'Patrimonio cultural inmueble de la Nación' (see VI.1.2.).

39 See Congreso de la República del Perú, 'Resolución Directoral Nacional N° 298-96/INC', *Archivo Digital de la Legislación Peruana* (22 August 1996).

VI.2.2. The Peruvian list in the *DoCoMoMo Virtual Exhibition,* DoCoMoMo Perú (Lima, 2014)

The twenty-first century has seen a significant increase in survey campaigns of architecture of the second half of the twentieth century. Although it does not reach a level of comprehensiveness, either in terms of the quantity of the selected assets or the documentary depth of those surveyed, the *Guía de arquitectura y paisaje – Lima y el Callao*[40] (2009) represents an important contribution to the dissemination of twentieth century architectural values. Still, it is important to note that an attempt at an inventory devoted entirely to the Peruvian architectural heritage of the last century was carried out by DoCoMoMo Perú[41] twenty years after the Universidad Nacional de Ingeniería began its surveys.

DoCoMoMo International is a non-profit organisation that has had, since 1988, the documentation and preservation of twentieth century architecture as one of its main objectives, considering the ever-increasing distortion of this heritage. Since then, it has been coordinating activities of surveillance in case of danger of loss through demolition or transformation of its characterising elements. It also encourages the exchange of ideas on conservation methodologies, history and education. And perhaps most importantly, it creates interest in this built heritage, promoting the ideas that made its construction possible.

With considerable delay compared to other delegations in the Latin American region,[42] the Peruvian section of the association has been campaigning since 2010 for the dissemination of the cultural values of last century's architecture, in a period – that of the present millennium – characterised by a high risk of loss of these assets. The delayed response by Peruvian actors has been conditioned by: periods of strong economic contraction; the political unrest that occurred in the last quarter century; and then, accelerated economic growth, supported by the liberal policies adopted since 1993 until today[43] (see VI.1.3.).

One of the most important initiatives of DoCoMoMo Perú for this purpose was the compilation of a list in 2014 by a group coordinated by Pedro Belaúnde, a Professor at the Department of Architecture of the Pontificia Universidad Católica del Perú and director of the delegation, which consisted of architectural examples built in different Peruvian cities in the second half of the twentieth century. The information gathered during the documentation campaign was published in the *DoCoMoMo Virtual Exhibition – MoMove,* a website dedicated to keeping the built heritage of the modern movement alive, by identifying buildings, places and itineraries in different countries, as well as giving international visibility to Peruvian architecture.[44]

Compañía de Seguros Peruano-Suiza
View from Plaza San Agustín (right)
View from the hall (left)
Aluminium window frames detail (bottom)
Lima
Theodor Cron
1952–1953
Javier Atoche Intili (2018)

The work of the Peruvian delegation focused extensively on the period of local affirmation of the modern movement in Peru, between the 1940s and 1960s, recording 105 buildings and architectural complexes, of which 97 are in Lima, three in Callao and five in other Peruvian cities.[45] If we consider the time span covered by this research, between 1937 and 1969, the multi-storey type is represented by 16 examples built in the historic centre of Lima,[46] one of which is the work of Theodor Cron (the Compañía de Seguros Peruano-Suiza, see IV.6.) and another by Mario Bianco (the Hotel Savoy, see III.6.).

VI.2.3. ***Catálogo Arquitectura Movimiento Moderno Perú*, Universidad de Lima (Lima, 2014–2016)**

A third survey of twentieth-century architecture was carried out between 2014 and 2016 by the Instituto de Investigación Científica of the Universidad de Lima. Edited by Alejandra Acevedo and Michelle Llona, the work was published in the *Catálogo Arquitectura Movimiento Moderno Perú*. Unlike previous assessments carried out for the UNI-Ford inventory (see VI.2.1.) and DoCoMoMo Perú (see VI.2.2.), the research for the Peruvian catalogue is largely based on the consultation of archival sources. This documentation and cataloguing work stemmed from the patronage of the Colegio de Arquitectos del Perú (formerly Sociedad de Arquitectos, see I.2.1.), not to mention the desire of the Peruvian historian José García Bryce to inform the local Ministerio de Cultura (see VI.1.3.) about the current state of modern heritage, with a view to its preservation, as well as conducting an in-depth study of the recent history of Peruvian architecture.[47]

Between 2009 and 2013, the Comisión Nacional de Defensa del Patrimonio Arquitectónico, Urbanístico, Histórico y Natural (National Commission for the Defence of the Architectural, Urban, Historical and Natural Heritage) of the CAP drew up a list of buildings considered part of the twentieth century heritage, with the aim of proclaiming the value of these works and making their protection possible.[48] Starting from the work carried out within the Architects' Association, the investigations for the catalogue resulted in a registry of works, including information collected from scientific literature and surveys, plus a systematic organisation of the data found. The examination of the bibliography made it possible to identify a large group of architects and their ample architectural production, built largely during the 1940s and 1960s, corresponding to the democratically elected governments of José Luis Bustamante y Rivero (1945–1948) and Fernando Belaúnde Terry (1963–1968).

40 See Bonilla, Enrique and Fuentes, María del Carmen (eds.), *Lima y el Callao: guía de arquitectura y paisaje – an architectural and landscape guide* (Lima / Seville, 2009).

41 'About', *DOCOMOMO International* (2 January 2023).

42 For instance, the Brazilian delegation was created in 1992 and the Mexican one in 2003. The formalisation of DoCoMo Peru took place on 26 August 2010, in the context of the Conference of DoCoMo International in Mexico City. Belaúnde, Pedro, 'Editorial', *DOCOMOMO Perú: Boletín Informativo* (2011), p. 1.

43 Ibid.

44 'Find Modern Movement Architecture on the Map!', *DOCOMOMO Virtual Exhibition* (2 January 2023).

45 Ibid.

46 A further 14 multi-storey buildings were selected, designed between 1945 and 1970 and built in the historic centre of Lima. Ibid.

47 See Acevedo, Alejandra and Llona, Michelle (eds.), *Catálogo Arquitectura Movimiento Moderno Perú* (Lima, 2018).

48 Córdova, Rodrigo and Soria, Judith, 'Peru', in Carughi, Ugo and Visone, Massimo (eds.), *Time Frames: Conservation Policies for Twentieth-Century Architectural Heritage* (London / New York, 2017), p. 107.

As was demonstrated previously in the UNI-Ford inventory, the stated aim of the editors was to publish a four-volume series containing all the material found for each building, organised by files, to be handed over to the Ministerio de Cultura as a vital contribution to the protection of the country's modern architectural heritage. This work of cataloguing resulted in a list of 448 works, covering a time span between 1934 and 1978, 60 of which were included in the 2016 publication. The published projects were selected by a scientific commission composed of two leading architects of the period, García Bryce himself and the architect Adolfo Córdova (a founding member of Agrupación Espacio, see I.3.2.); two professors and researchers from Peruvian universities, Elio Martuccelli and Enrique Santillana; along with the curators Alejandra Acevedo y Michelle Llona.

This census of twentieth-century Peruvian works, the aim of which was the publicising of their value while raising awareness of the risks of their loss, has begun to yield results: the Ministerio de Cultura recognised the cultural value of the former headquarters of the Ministerio de Educación Pública[49] (Enrique Seoane, 1951–1956, see V.2.) in 2020. This building is part of a large group of multi-storey edifices built in the historic centre of Lima, 25 of a total of 60 catalogued buildings – including two by Italian designers, the Hotel Savoy (Mario Bianco, see III.6.) and the Edificio Irma (Gianfelice Fogliani, 1948, see III.6.) – that are awaiting recognition by the Peruvian government.[50]

49 See Congreso de la República del Perú, 'Resolución Viceministerial N° 034-2020-VMPCIC-MC del 2020', *Archivo Digital de la Legislación Peruana* (10 February 2020).

50 See Acevedo, Alejandra and Llona, Michelle (eds.), *Catálogo Arquitectura Movimiento Moderno Perú* (Lima, 2018).

Hotel Savoy
Detail of the façade
Lima
Mario Bianco
1954–1957
Javier Atoche Intili (2018)

Hotel Savoy
View from Jirón Cailloma
Lima
Mario Bianco
1954–1957

Javier Atoche Intili (2018)

VI.3. Considerations for the role of research in the protection of Peruvian architectural heritage in the twentieth century

Peruvian architecture of the twentieth century is currently undergoing a long but unstoppable process of heritagisation, having begun with the research undertaken by the Universidad Nacional de Ingeniería in 1986. Since then, growing interest in the architecture of the last century, documented by the abundance of university and other institutes' research in recent years, has changed both the objectives and ways that public cultural institutions act. The 2010s saw important attempts by public administrations to recognise the aesthetic and documentary values of twentieth century Peruvian architecture, which were then manifested in several architecture exhibitions, not to mention a plethora of publications.

In 2012, the Gerencia de Cultura – the main governing body for cultural policies of the municipality of Lima – promoted the Call for Curators and Artists,[51] awarding its first classification to the project entitled *Parecía Inquebrantable*. In the art and architecture exhibition of the same name in 2013, a varied casuistry of multi-storey buildings, constructed in the historical centre of Lima in the second half of the twentieth century, was presented.[52] This type, which considerably transformed the morphology of Lima's urban fabric, is illustrated in several examples of horizontal ownership (or institutional representation), widely present in the Old World, a style European architects who moved to Peru helped to spread.

Another opportunity for research and insight into the diffusion of the multi-storey type in the history of Peruvian architecture was provided in 2014 by the 14th International Architecture Exhibition, La Biennale di Venezia, entitled *Fundamentals*.[53] In *Absorbing Modernity: 1914–2014*, one of the three sections of the Biennale, 66 national delegations identified and studied the most important moments and events in the modernisation of their countries over the last 100 years. In the proposal for the Peruvian exhibition space in the Arsenale[54] – entitled *In/formal: Urban encounters for the next 100* – several examples of multi-storey buildings were included as milestones in twentieth century Peruvian architecture.

As part of the growing process of heritagisation in our time, the MoMA in New York produced an exhibition entitled *Latin America in Construction: Architecture, 1955–1980*[55] (2015), illustrating the rich architectural production in the second half of the twentieth century in Latin America. This exhibition showed how modern architectural culture is far less homogenous than Hitchcock

51 The Gerencia de Cultura is responsible for promoting the production, dissemination and enjoyment of the Peruvian capital's cultural assets through the development of projects aimed at integrating the city's multiple identities, while at the same time strengthening a sense of community. See Municipalidad Metropolitana de Lima, *Gerencia de Cultura* (2 January 2023).

52 Title of the exhibition held between 8 August and 15 September 2013 in the Galería Municipal de Arte Pancho Fierro, exhibition space of the municipality of Lima. See Abugattas, Sebastián, Aramburú, Iosu and Llona, Michelle (eds.), *Guía Arquitectura Moderna en el Centro Histórico* (Lima, 2013).

53 *Fundamentals*, 14th International Architecture Exhibition, La Biennale di Venezia, held from 7 June to 23 November 2014, with Rem Koolhaas as artistic director. See International Architecture Exhibition, *Fundamentals – La Biennale di Venezia*, Marsilio (Venice, 2014).

54 In this edition of the Biennale, Peru participated for the first time with its own exhibition space thanks to the agreement signed between the Biennale, and Peruvian public and private institutions: Ministerio de Comercio Exterior y Turismo; Ministerio de Cultura, Ministerio de Relaciones Exteriores del Perú; Wiese Foundation; and the newspaper *El Comercio*. The commissioner was José Orrego Herrera and the curator was Sharif S. Kahatt.

55 Review of Latin American Architecture of the Second Twentieth Century, held in New York from 29 March to 19 July 2015. See Bergdoll, Barry et al. (eds.), *Latin America in Construction: Architecture 1955–1980* (New York, 2015).

illustrated in the 1955 catalogue. The construction of numerous buildings with predominantly vertical development, such as the Mario Bianco's Hotel Savoy, is mentioned in the catalogue of the same name: 'Latin America saw a dramatic increase in the number of skyscrapers, a type of building and real estate instrument rarely used before then.'[56]

The Hotel Savoy has received great interest from scholars in recent years, as documented in the research carried out by the Department of Architecture of the Universidad de Lima and the Triennale di Milano, in the respective exhibitions *Mario Bianco: El Espacio Moderno en el Perú*[57] and *Comunità Italia*,[58] from 2015.

In 2019, to coincide with the centenary of the Bauhaus, the Archivo de Arquitectura of the Pontificia Universidad Católica del Perú organised a critical theory seminar (Taller de producción crítica e teórica), with the aim of staging a temporary exhibition entitled *Paul Linder. Arquitecto: Modernidad universal / Sincretismo local.*[59] An overview of Linder's *Edificio Arnodi* (see II.5.) and other experiments with the multi-storey type, on both the European and American continents, was proposed the same year in the book *Paul Linder, 1897–1968: De Weimar a Lima, antología de arquitectura y crítica.*[60]

56 Ibid., p. 72.
57 *Mario Bianco y el Espacio Moderno en el Perú* (an exhibition held from 6 November to 2 December 2015 at the Universidad de Lima and the publication of the same name in 2018) was a result of the work of students from the architecture course, coordinated by Prof. Martin Fabbri and Prof. Octavio Montestruque, with the collaboration of the Bianco heirs and the Istituto Italiano di Cultura in Lima, not to mention other professors and researchers at the Peruvian university.
58 Review of Italian architecture of the second half of the twentieth century, held between 28 November 2015 and 6 March 2016. See Ferlenga, Alberto, and Biraghi, Marco, *Comunità Italia: architettura, città, paesaggio. Exhibition catalogue, Milan, Triennale* (Cinisello Balsamo, 2015).
59 Monographic exhibition on Paul Linder, held from 18 March to 28 April 2019. See Llona, Michelle and Mejía, Víctor, *Paul Linder, Arquitecto – modernidad universal / sincretismo local* (Lima, 2019).
60 Atoche Intili, Javier, 'Tres cartas desde Lima. Paul Linder y los arquitectos europeos', in Medina Warmburg, Joaquín (ed.), *Paul Linder, 1897–1968: de Weimar a Lima – antología de arquitectura y crítica* (Madrid, 2019), pp. 80–91.

Edificio Arnodi
View from Alfonso
Avenida Ugarte
Breña, Lima
Paul Linder
1950

Javier Atoche Intili (2018)

Edificio Arnodi
Detail of the façade
Breña Lima
Paul Linder
1950
Javier Atoche Intili (2018)

The investigations into twentieth-century Peruvian architecture, carried out over the last thirty-five years, allow for a critical evaluation of this heritage and, at the same time, represent concrete actions for the dissemination of their principles and values, with the aim of coordinating the strategies of supervisory bodies, technicians, owners, and users towards their preservation.[61] They also lead to the rediscovery of authors and works relegated to the margins of official culture, which are not protected by public bodies.

As illustrated above, in the last quarter of the twentieth century, multi-storey buildings were often the target of social and political turbulence. In the current century, due to strong economic growth underpinned by liberal economic policies, many of these structures in the historic centre of Lima have been renovated, either by public bodies or private individuals, without considering the distinctive elements that warrant preservation. Other buildings have been abandoned, either totally or partially, due to the shift of investment from the historic centre to the limiting districts of twentieth-century expansion.

The loss of a conspicuous part of the architectural legacy took place, until recent years, with total indifference on the part of state protection agencies. To be sure, between 1949 and 1971, none of the multi-storey buildings recognised by the Chavín Prize (see VI.1.1.) was declared a monument by the relevant bodies (neither the Instituto Nacional de la Cultura, see VI.1.2., nor the Ministerio de Cultura, see VI.1.3.). This lack of interest was prevalent even though Peru has a long tradition of protecting its national historical heritage, considering the richness of its centuries-old past. As a response to the inertia of the central government, there has been an increase in research into twentieth century Peruvian architecture since the 1980s. The gradual return of the results of these investigations to the Peruvian state bodies has become one of the most effective and concrete operations in the protection of the architecture of the period under examination. The censuses of twentieth-century architectural heritage and, more generally, the research carried out by professionals and experts grouped around local or international institutions, illustrate how, for a considerable part of the architecture built in the second half of the twentieth century, these initiatives are a first step towards the recognition of their values and their belonging to Peru's cultural legacy.

'Heritagisation' – understood as the process of recognising, understanding and appreciating the historical, aesthetic, artistic and documented values of a given cultural expression – allows a different dimension of value to be attributed to a building than its original one. It marks a shift from a predominantly economic value (which in market logic tends to keep an artefact alive only insofar as it produces income, employment and/or profit) to a cultural one. Thus, structures

61 Carughi, Ugo, *Maledetti vincoli: la tutela dell'architettura contemporanea* (Turin, 2012), p. 14.

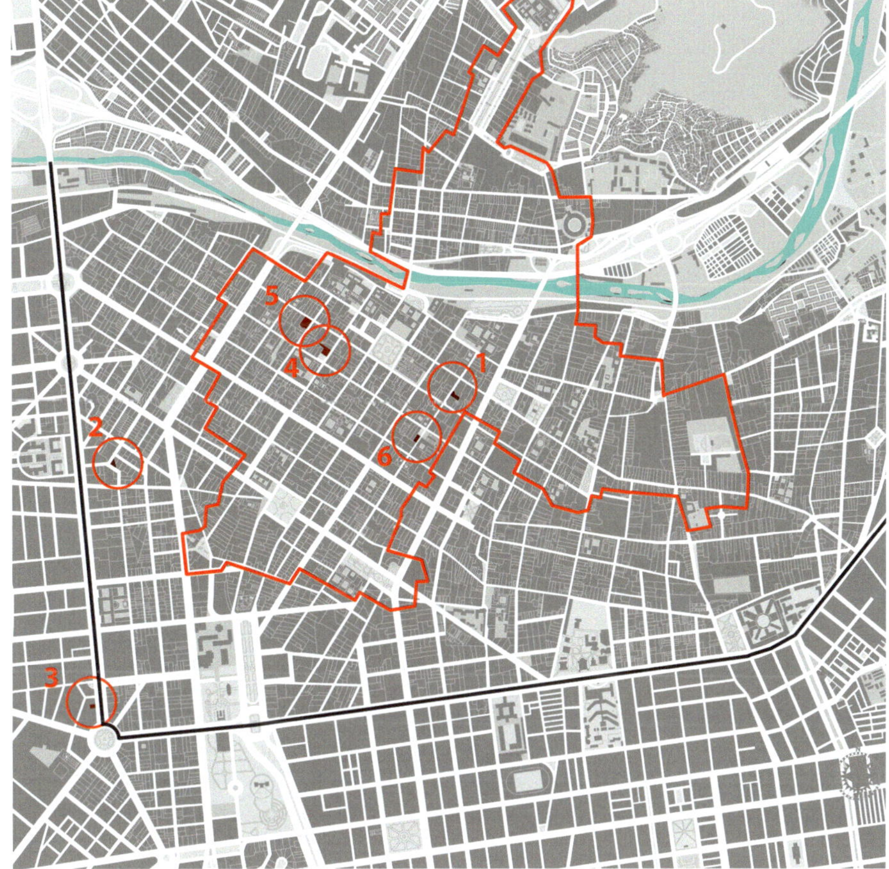

Historic centre of Lima
1. Casa Gildemeister
2. Edificio Irma
3. Edificio Arnodi
4. Compañía de Seguros Peruano-Suiza
5. Hotel Savoy
6. La Colmena Compañía de Seguros y Reaseguros

Javier Atoche Intili (2021)

may be seen as heritage to be safeguarded as an expression of collective identity, of relevance and importance not only for a small group of people, but for a whole community.[62]

While waiting for an update of the current Peruvian legislation on architectural heritage, which provides for specific preservation of that from the twentieth century, research dedicated to the most representative designers of the last century are a fundamental step towards the recognition of their works and the enrichment of Peruvian cultural heritage.

62 Tamma, Michele, *Cultural Rights, Heritage, Sustainability, Citizens of Europe – culture and rights* (Venice, 2015), p. 485.

Plaza Mayor
Lima
Javier Atoche Intili (2018)

Bibliography

1924
Centurión, Enrique, *El Perú actual y las colonias extranjeras: la realidad actual y el extranjero en el Perú a través de cien años, 1821–1921* (Bergamo: Instituto italiano d'arti grafiche, 1924).
Lacasa, Luis, 'Un interior expresionista', *Arquitectura: órgano oficial de la Sociedad Central de Arquitectos*, no. 61, 1924, pp. 174–176.
Linder, Paul, 'La construcción de rascacielos en Alemania', *Arquitectura: órgano oficial de la Sociedad Central de Arquitectos*, no. 67, 1924, pp. 310–313.

1926
Linder, Paul, 'Tres ensayos sobre la nueva arquitectura alemana. Primer ensayo. A manera de introducción', *Arquitectura: órgano oficial de la Sociedad Central de Arquitectos*, no. 81, 1926, pp. 20–22.
Linder, Paul, 'Tres ensayos sobre la nueva arquitectura alemana. Segundo ensayo. Los tectónicos', *Arquitectura: órgano oficial de la Sociedad Central de Arquitectos*, no. 86, 1926, pp. 235–241.

1927
Linder, Paul, 'El nuevo Bauhaus en Dessau', *Arquitectura: órgano oficial de la Sociedad Central de Arquitectos*, no. 95, 1927, pp. 110–112.
Linder, Paul, 'La exposición "Werkbund Ausstellung" en Stuttgart', *Arquitectura: órgano oficial de la Sociedad Central de Arquitectos*, no. 103, 1927.

1929
Linder, Paul, 'Arquitectos, pensad y construid con sentido social!', *Arquitectura: órgano oficial de la Sociedad Central de Arquitectos*, no. 117, 1929, pp. 12–22.
Linder, Paul, 'El arquitecto Max Taut', *Arquitectura: órgano oficial de la Sociedad Central de Arquitectos*, no. 127, 1929, pp. 422–430.
Linder, Paul, 'El arquitecto Wilhelm Riphahn', *Arquitectura: órgano oficial de la Sociedad Central de Arquitectos*, no. 131, 1930, pp. 75–81.
Linder, Paul, 'Sobre especialistas, sobre arquitectura universal y sobre el arquitecto hamburgés Karl Schneider', *Arquitectura: órgano oficial de la Sociedad Central de Arquitectos*, no. 139, 1930, pp. 333–339.
Linder, Paul, 'Walter Gropius', *Arquitectura: órgano oficial de la Sociedad Central de Arquitectos*, no. 136, 1930, pp. 245–254.

1931
Linder, Paul, 'Exposición berlinesa de la construcción', *Arquitectura: órgano oficial de la Sociedad Central de Arquitectos*, no. 149, 1931, pp. 287–295.
Linder, Paul, 'Umwandlung von Altwohnungen', *Bauwelt*, a. 22, no. 43, 1931, pp. 1370–1372.

1932
Museum of Modern Art, *Modern Architecture: International Exhibition* (New York: Museum of Modern Art, 1932).

1933
'Die St. Thomaskirche in Berlin-Charlottenburg. Architekt Paul Linder, Berlin', *Bauwelt*, no. 46, 1933.
'Die St. Thomaskirche in Berlin-Charlottenburg', *Wasmuths Monatshefte Für Baukunst*, no. 12, 1933, pp. 553–556.
Linder, Paul, 'Acerca de la plástica en arquitectura. Obras de Georg Kolbe', *Arquitectura: órgano oficial de la Sociedad Central de Arquitectos*, no. 167, 1933, pp. 80–84.

1939
'La Vivienda Obrera en el Perú', *El Arquitecto Peruano*, a. III, no. 26, 1939.
Belaúnde Terry, Fernando, 'Puntos de vista… El Plano Regulador de Lima'. *El Arquitecto Peruano*, no. 22, 1939, pp. 12.
Linder, Paul and Velarde, Héctor, 'Proyecto para la Cía. Edificadora de Colegios SA', *El Arquitecto Peruano*, a. III, no. 22, 1939.
Belaúnde Terry, Fernando, 'Puntos de vista… Premios municipales para las "mejores" construcciones', *El Arquitecto Peruano*, a. III, no. 25, 1939.

1940
'El Edificio Rizo Patrón, por la firma Gramonvel', *El Arquitecto Peruano*, a. IV, no. 37, 1940.
'El sismo en Perú ha originado consternación en Argentina y Chile', *La Prensa. Edición extraordinaria*, 25 May 1940.
'El terremoto de ayer en Lima, Callao y balnearios', *El Comercio*, 25 May 1940.
'Lima después del sismo', *La Crónica. Diario de la mañana*, 25 May 1940.
Belaúnde Terry, Fernando, 'Puntos de vista... El sentido de la reconstrucción', *El Arquitecto Peruano*, a. IV, no. 35, 1940.
Linder, Paul and Velarde, Héctor, 'Proyecto para la Nunciatura Apostólica', *El Arquitecto Peruano*, a. IV, no. 39, 1940.
Roth, Alfred, *La Nouvelle architecture / Die neue Architektur / The new architecture – 1930–1940: Présentée en 20 exemples* (Zurich / Munich: Verlag für Architektur Artemis, 1940), pp. 205–250.

1941
Ortiz de Zevallos, Luis. 'El Concepto de La Ciudad'. *El Arquitecto Peruano*, a. V, no. 47, 1941.

1942
'La nueva residencia de la Nunciatura Apostólica', *El Arquitecto Peruano*, a. VI, no. 61, 1942.

1943
Goodwin, Philip Lippincot, *Brazil builds: architecture new and old, 1652–1942* (New York: Museum of Modern Art, 1943).

1944
'Modernismo Brasileño', *El Arquitecto Peruano*, a. VIII, no. 80, 1944.
'El barrio-unidad, elemento de descentralización urbana', *El Arquitecto Peruano*, a. VIII, no. 83, 1944.
'Arquitectura moderna en los Estados Unidos', *El Arquitecto Peruano*, a. VIII, no. 89, 1944.
Bromley, Juan, and Barbagelata, José, *Evolución urbana de la ciudad de Lima* (Lima: Consejo Provincial de Lima, 1944).
Museum of Modern Art, *Built in USA: 1932–1944* (New York: Museum of Modern Art, 1944)
Renard, Carmen, 'Los pueblos Greenbelt en los Estados Unidos', *El Arquitecto Peruano*, a. VIII, no. 82, 1944.

1945
'El Pensamiento creador en arquitectura y urbanismo', *El Arquitecto Peruano*, a. IX, no. 93, 1945.
Astengo, Giovanni, and Bianco, Mario, *Agricoltura e urbanistica: analisi e rappresentazione della situazione agricola dal punto di vista urbanistico*, Biblioteca moderna di cultura 4 (Turin: A. Viglongo e C., 1945).
Astengo, Giovanni and Bianco, Mario, 'Case componibili ad elementi unificati in lamiera stampata', *Metron: rivista internazionale d'architettura*, no. 4–5, 1945, pp. 74–83.
Miró Quesada, Luis, *Espacio en el tiempo. La arquitectura moderna como fenómeno cultural* (Lima: Compañía de impresiones y publicidad, 1945), pp. 72–73.

1946
'Algunos principios de urbanismo aprobados por el IV Congreso de Arquitectura Moderna (CIAM) celebrado en Atenas en 1933, con participación de notables personalidades de la arquitectura y urbanismo', *El Arquitecto Peruano*, a. VII, no. 76, 1946.
Astengo, Giovanni, 'Sul soleggiamento degli edifici di abitazione', *Metron: Rivista Internazionale d'architettura*, no. 9, 1946.
Belaúnde Terry, Fernando, 'Puntos de vista… La oficina del Plan Regulador de Lima', *El Arquitecto Peruano*, no. 106, 1946.
Belaúnde Terry, Fernando, 'Puntos de vista… Una ley que inicia una era', *El Arquitecto Peruano*, no. 111, 1946.
Córdova, Adolfo and Williams, Carlos, 'El Cuzco monumental e intangible', *El Sol*, 30 September 1946.

1947
'Centro Climático de Esparcimiento, Perú'. *El Arquitecto Peruano*, a. XI, no. 125, 1947.
'Edificio que construye la firma Flórez y Costa, Ingenieros, para la casa Ferrand', *El Arquitecto Peruano*, a. XI, no. 117, 1947.
'Edificio Tacna-Nazarenas, en Lima', *El Arquitecto Peruano*, a. XI, no. 115, 1947.
'Expresión de principios de la Agrupación Espacio', *El Arquitecto Peruano*, a. XI, no. 119, 1947.
'Expresión de principios de la Agrupación Espacio', *El Comercio*, 15 May 1947.
'Iglesia San Felipe Apóstol', *El Arquitecto Peruano*, a. XI, no. 118, 1947.
ABRR, 'Arteria di attraversamento Nord-Sud di Torino', Atti e rassegna tecnica della società degli Ingegneri e degli Architetti in Torino, no. 8, 1947, pp. 236–241.
Astengo, Giovanni, 'La sistemazione ferroviaria di Torino', Cronache economiche, no. 14, 1947, pp. 12–14.
Astengo, Giovanni, Bianco, Mario, Renacco, Nello and Rizzotti, Aldo, 'Cenni sul Piano Regionale Piemontese. Origine e cronaca della compilazione del piano', *Metron: Rivista Internazionale d'architettura*, no. 14, 1947, pp. 3–6.
Becker, Gino. 'Mostra internazionale di edilizia a Torino', *Metron: Rivista Internazionale d'architettura*, no. 13, 1947, pp. 61–66.
Belaúnde Terry, Fernando, 'Puntos de vista… Un gran paso adelante', *El Arquitecto Peruano*, a. XI, no. 119, 1947.
Belaúnde Terry, Fernando, 'Discurso del arquitecto Fernando Belaúnde Terry en la inauguración de la VI Exposición Panamericana de Arquitectura y Urbanismo'. *El Arquitecto Peruano*, a. XI, no. 123, 1947.
Le Corbusier (Charles-Édouard Jeanneret-Gris), 'La Morada Del Hombre'. *El Arquitecto Peruano*, a. XI, no. 119, 1947.
Letourneau, Jean, 'L'exposition internationale de l'urbanisme et de l'habitation', *L'architecture d'aujourd'hui*, no. 13–14, 1947, pp. 120–135.
Department of Architecture, *Two cities: planning in North and South America* (New York: Museum of Modern Art, 1947).

1948
'Edificio Irma, en Lima, propiedad de la Compañía de Seguros "La Colmena"', *El Arquitecto Peruano*, a. XII, no. 134, 1948.
'El nuevo Edificio Ferrand', *El Arquitecto Peruano*, a. XII, no. 128, 1948.

'Proyecto para el Club Internacional de Tiro al Blanco en Arequipa', *El Arquitecto Peruano*, a. XII, no. 131, 1948.
Astengo, Giovanni, *I piani urbanistici*, in Istituto nazionale di urbanistica (ed), *Urbanistica e edilizia in Italia* (Rome: Istituto nazionale di urbanistica, 1948), pp. 37–83.
Bianco, Mario, 'La remodelación del centro de Lima', *El Comercio*, 10 February 1948.
Bianco, Mario, 'Prefabricación', *El Comercio*, 3 June 1948.

1949
'Agrupación Espacio 1947–1949'. *El Comercio*, 19 May 1949.
'Appartementhaus in Lima,' *Bauen + Wohnen / Construction + Habitation / Building + Home: internationale Zeitschrift*, aa. 1–5, no. 8, 1947–1949, pp. 10–11.
'Edificio de la Compañía de Seguros "La Nacional"', *El Arquitecto Peruano*, a. XIII, no. 141, 1949.
'El Edificio Tacna y el Cine Paramount Tacna', *El Arquitecto Peruano*, a. XIII, no. 144, 1949.
'La audaz Ciudad Vertical de Le Corbusier en Marsella', *El Arquitecto Peruano*, a. XIII, no. 149, 1949.
'Plan Nacional de La Corporación de La Vivienda', *El Arquitecto Peruano*, a. XIII, no. 145, 1949.
Belaúnde Terry, Fernando, '¡Y hay en Lima quienes fingen no verla!' *El Arquitecto Peruano*, no. 146, 1949.
Bianco, Mario, 'La arquitectura y el medio. La caña como elemento estructural', *El Arquitecto Peruano*, a. XIII, no. 141, 1949.
Bianco, Mario, 'Il dimensionamento nell'urbanistica regionale', *Urbanistica*, no. 2, 1949, pp. 11–14.
Bianco, Mario, 'Valores eternos y valores perecederos', *El Comercio*, 12 May 1949.
Bianco, Mario, 'Carta Abierta a Ernesto Nathan Rogers', *El Comercio*, 24 March 1949.
Bianco, Mario, 'El Tamaño de Lima', *El Comercio*, 19 May 1949.
Bianco, Mario, 'La Arquitectura y El Medio. La Caña Como Elemento Estructural', *El Arquitecto Peruano*, no. 141, 1949.
Bianco, Mario, 'Urbanismo y Tradición', *El Comercio*, 17 March 1949.
Le Corbusier (Charles-Édouard Jeanneret-Gris), '¡Cuando Las Catedrales Eran Blancas!' *Espacio*, no. 1, 1949, p. 1.
Le Corbusier (Charles-Édouard Jeanneret-Gris), 'La morada del hombre', *Espacio*, no. 3, 1949, p. 1.
Linder, Paul, 'Reconocimiento a la Arquitectura Peruana', *El Arquitecto Peruano*, a. XIII, no. 142, 1949.
Oficina Nacional de Planeamiento y Urbanismo, 'La Hoja de Urbanismo', *El Arquitecto Peruano*, a. XIII, no. 144, 1949.
Oficina Nacional de Planeamiento y Urbanismo, *Plan Piloto de Lima* (Lima, Empresa Gráfica T. Scheuch SA, 1949).

1950
'Residencia del Señor Luis D'Onofrio en Orrantia del Mar, por el Arqto. Mario Bianco y el Constructor José de Bona', *El Arquitecto Peruano*, a. XIV, no. 150–151, 1950, pp. 38–44.
'Departamentos en la calle Roma', *El Arquitecto Peruano*, a. XIV, no. 153, 1950.
'Adjudicación del premio Chavín de 1950 al Arquitecto Enrique Seoane Ros', *El Arquitecto Peruano*, a. XIV, no. 158, 1950.
'Iglesia de Santa Ursula', *El Arquitecto Peruano*, a. XIV, no. 161, 1950.
Belaunde Terry, Fernando, 'La Vacación Familiar, Nueva Conquista Social', *El Arquitecto Peruano*, no. 161, 1950.
Belaunde Terry, Fernando, 'Puntos de vista… El Plan Piloto de Lima', *El Arquitecto Peruano*, no. 150–151, 1950.
Bianco, Mario, 'La Ricostruzione del Callao, Porto di Lima', *Urbanistica*, no. 4, 1950, pp. 61–62
Bianco, Mario, 'Nuovi Quartieri Organici al Callao', *Urbanistica*, no. 6, 1950, pp. 49–52.
Bianco, Mario, 'Respetemos La Zonificación Urbana', *Espacio*, no. 4, 1950.
Le Corbusier (Charles-Édouard Jeanneret-Gris, 'Foro sobre el Cusco', *Espacio*, no. 6, 1950, p. 2.
Linder, Paul, 'Encuentros con Antonio Gaudí', *Mar del sur: Revista peruana de cultura*, no. 4, 1950, pp. 1–11.
Miro Quesada, Luis, 'Residencia en San Felipe', *Espacio*, no. 5, 1950, p. 5.
Wiener, Paul Lester, and Sert, Josep Lluís 'Quatre Plans Directeurs pour des villes sud-américaines: Medellin, Tumaco, Chimbote and Lima', *Architecture d'aujourd'hui*, no. 33, 1950, pp. 10–55.

1951
'Construcción del Edificio para el Departamento de Arquitectura', *El Arquitecto Peruano*, a. XV, no. 170–171, 1951.
'Departamentos modernos en Lima', *El Arquitecto Peruano*, a. XV, no. 166–167, 1951.
Bianco, Mario, 'Plan Regulador Del Callao', *Espacio*, no. 9–10, 1951.
Giedion, Sigfried (ed.), *A Decade of New Architecture* (Zurich: Girsberger, 1951).
Velarde, Héctor, 'Una casa peruana... Hecha por un suizo', *El Arquitecto Peruano*, a. XV, no. 172–173, 1951.
Wiener, Paul Lester, and Josep Lluís Sert. 'Conditions Générales de l'urbanisme En Amérique Latine'. *Architecture d'aujourd'hui*, no. 33, 1951, pp. 46–55.

1952
'Ayer se graduaron veinte Arquitectos egresados de la Escuela de Ingenieros', *La Crónica*, 24 December 1952.
'Casa Matriz MSC y Clínica Stella Maris', *El Arquitecto Peruano*, a. XVI, no. 175–176, 1952, p. 38.
'Clínica Stella Maris'. *El Arquitecto Peruano*, a. XVI, no. 175–176, 1952.
'Edificio de Departamentos', *El Arquitecto Peruano*, a. XVI, no. 183–184, 1952.
'Graduación de veinte nuevos arquitectos', *El Comercio*, 24 December 1952.
Berger, Juan Adolfo, 'Revista de la Colonia Suiza en el Perú', no. 54, 1952, p. 54.
Bianco, Mario, 'Posibilidades Plásticas de La Arquitectura'. *El Arquitecto Peruano*, a. XVI, no. 177–178, 1952.
Ministero dei lavori pubblici (ed), *I piani regionali. 1* (Rome: Ministero dei lavori pubblici, 1952).
Tyrwhitt, Jaqueline, Sert, Josep Lluís and Rogers, Ernesto Nathan (eds.), *CIAM [8]: The Heart of the City: Towards the Humanisation of Urban Life* (London: L. Humphries, 1952).

1953
'Ministerio de Hacienda y Comercio', *El Arquitecto Peruano*, a. XVII, a. XVII, no. 188–189, 1953.
'Sert y Gropius Profesores Honorarios de La Escuela', *El Arquitecto Peruano*, a. XVII, no. 196–197, 1953.
'Visita de Enrico Tedeschi', *El Arquitecto Peruano*, a. XVII, no. 186–187, 1953.
Belaúnde Terry, Fernando, 'Aspiración lograda', *El Arquitecto Peruano*, a. XVII, no. 190–191, 1953, pp. 17–18.
Bianco, Mario, 'Urbanismo Integral'. *El Arquitecto Peruano*, a. XVII, no. 183–184, 1953.
Congreso panamericano de arquitectos, *Actas del VI. Congreso Panamericano de Arquitectos: Lima, 15 de octubre de 1947, Cuzco 25 de octubre de 1947* (Lima: Imprenta Santa Maria, 1953).
Gropius, Walter, 'Walter Gropius Se Dirige a La Promoción 1953', *El Arquitecto Peruano*, a. XVII, no. 196–197, 1953.
Linder, Paul, 'Homenaje a Walter Gropius', *El Arquitecto Peruano*, a. XVII, no. 188–189, 1953.
Linder, Paul, 'Josef Albers, artista y educador', *El Comercio, Suplemento Dominical*, July 1953.
Linder, Paul, 'Discurso de Orden Con Ocasión de La Graduación de Arquitectos', *El Arquitecto Peruano*, a. XVII, no. 186–187, 1953.
Lodi, Carlos, 'Considerações sobre pontos fundamentais do Planejamento Urbanistico', *Acrópole*, 1953, pp. 378–382.
Ministero dei lavori pubblici (ed.), *I piani regionali. 2* (Rome: Istituto poligrafico dello Stato, 1953).
Wiener, Paul Lester, 'Five Civic Centers in South America', *Architectural Record*, no. 114, 1953, pp. 121–136.

1954
Oficina Nacional de Planeamiento y Urbanismo, *Lima metropolitana. Algunos aspectos de su expediente urbano y soluciones parciales varias* (Lima: Oficina Nacional de Planeamiento y Urbanismo, 1954).
Linder, Paul, 'La arquitectura en la Alemania de hoy', *El Arquitecto Peruano*, a. XVIII, no. 200–201, 1954.

1955
'El Departamento de Arquitectura de la Escuela Nacional de Ingenieros', *El Arquitecto Peruano*, a. XIX, no. 210–211, 1955.
'Luis Miro Quesada Garland: Premio Chavín de La Arquitectura', *El Arquitecto Peruano*, a. XIX, no. 214–215, 1955.
'Nuevo Edificio "Atlas"', *El Arquitecto Peruano*, a. XIX, no. 214–215, 1955.
Hitchcock, Henry-Russell, *Latin American Architecture Since 1945* (New York: Museum of Modern Art, 1955).
Linder, Paul, 'Arquitectura y Cristianismo', *El Arquitecto Peruano*, no. 219–220–221, 1955.

1956
'Arequipa construye el moderno Club Internacional', *El Arquitecto Peruano*, a. XX, no. 226–227, 1956.
'Ministerio de Educación Pública', *El Arquitecto Peruano*, a. XX, 1956, no. 228–229–230, 1956.

1957
'Moderno Cine en Lima', *El Arquitecto Peruano*, no. 243–244, 1957.
'Hotel Savoy', *El Arquitecto Peruano*, no. 245, 1957.
Schuppisser, Santiago, 'Peruanische Notizen', *Bauen + Wohnen / Construction + Habitation / Building + Home: internationale Zeitschrift*, a. 11, no. 10, 1957, pp. 258–259.

1958
'Colegio y convento Santa María Goretti en La Victoria', *El Arquitecto Peruano*, no. 246–247–248, 1958, pp. 25–28.
'Edificio para Inversiones Inmobiliarias SA', *El Arquitecto Peruano*, no. 249–250–251, 1958.
'Edificio San Reynaldo', *El Arquitecto Peruano*, no. 249–250–251, 1958.
'Galerías Comerciales Mogollón', *El Arquitecto Peruano*, no. 246–247–248, 1958.
'Premio de Arquitectura Chavín: Espíritu y Realidad', *Dimensión Arquitectónica*, no. 1, 1958.
'Residencia del Señor Jean Schaer', *El Arquitecto Peruano*, no. 246–247–248, 1958.
Linder, Paul, 'Imposible Vivir En La Roma Clásica', *El Arquitecto Peruano*, no. 249–250–251, 1958.
Peters, Paulhans, *Wohnhochhäuser: Punkthäuser* (Munich: Georg D. W. Callwey, 1958), p. 38.

1959
'Edificio de Renta En Miraflores', *El Arquitecto Peruano*, no. 258–259–260, 1959.
'El Banco Continental inaugura su nuevo local en

Miraflores, *El Arquitecto Peruano,* no. 264–265–266, 1959, pp. 26–28.
'La nueva cervecería Piura', *El Arquitecto Peruano,* no. 264–265–266, 1959, pp. 34–35.
'Nuevo Edificio "El Sol"', *El Arquitecto Peruano,* no. 264–265–266, 1959, pp. 23–25.
Linder, Paul, *Examen Vocacional para estudiantes de arquitectura. Experiencias adquiridas* (Lima, 1959).

1960
'Colegio A. von Humboldt', *El Arquitecto Peruano,* 1960, no. 276–277–278, pp. 23–29.
'Wohn-und Geschäftsgebäude in Lima', *Bauen + Wohnen / Construction + habitation / Building + home: internationale Zeitschrift,* 1960.

1962
Pedrazzini, Augusto, *L'emigrazione ticinese nell'America del sud. 2 vols* ([s.l: s.no.], 1962).

1963
'Appunti sulle idee al Concorso di Torino', *Domus,* no. 408, 1963, pp. 4–10.
'Hoffman-La Roche, Lima', *El Arquitecto Peruano,* no. 315–316–317, 1963, pp. 40–47.
Brandi, Cesare, *Teoria del restauro* (Rome: Edizioni di Storia e Letteratura, 1963).
Rogers, Ernesto Nathan, 'Il Concorso per Il Centro Direzionale di Torino', *Casabella Continuità: Rivista Internazionale di Architettura e Urbanistica,* no. 278, 1963, p. 9.
Tönnies, Ferdinand, *Comunita e societa* (Milan: Edizioni di Comunità, 1963).
Velarde, Héctor. '25 Años de El Arquitecto Peruano', *El Arquitecto Peruano,* no. 306–307–308, 1963, pp. 5–6.

1964
'Nuevo Edificio El Pacífico', *El Arquitecto Peruano,* 1964.

1965
'El Banco Comercial', *El Arquitecto Peruano,* no. 332–333, 1965, pp. 33–40.
Le Corbusier, and Giraudoux, Jean, *La carta d'Atene* (Milan: Edizioni di Comunità, 1965).

1966
'El Centro Cívico Concurso de Época', *El Arquitecto Peruano,* no. 342, 1966, pp. 20–21.
Pevsner, Nikolaus, Fleming, John and Honour, Hugh, *A Dictionary of Architecture* (Harmondsworth: Penguin Books, 1966).

1968
Basadre, Jorge, *Historia de la República del Perú* (Lima: Editorial Peruamérica, 1968)
Jimeno, Oswaldo, 'Recuerdo de Paul Linder'. *El Comercio,* 1 December 1968.

1974
Argan, Giulio Carlo, *Walter Gropius e la Bauhaus* (Turin: Einaudi, 1974).
Romero Ramirez, Hugo. 'Teodoro Cron: Su Obra' (Lima: Universidad Nacional de Ingeniería, 1974).

1977
'Arquitectura de un Suizo para un Arequipeño', *El Arquitecto Peruano,* no. 356, 1977.

1978
Wallerstein, Immanuel Maurice, *Il sistema mondiale dell'economia moderna* (Bologna: Il Mulino, 1978).

1979
Le Corbusier (Charles-Édouard Jeanneret-Gris), *Verso un'architettura* (Milan: Longanesi, 1979).

1980
García Bryce, José, *La arquitectura en el Virreinato y la República* (Lima: J. Mejia Baca, 1980).
Linder, Alfredo, 'Las Iglesias de Paul Linder', *Habitar. Revista del Colegio de Arquitectos del Perú,* no. 1, 1980, pp. 3–10.

1982
Dal Co, Francesco, *Teorie del moderno: architettura, Germania, 1880–1920* (Rome / Bari: Laterza, 1982), pp. 3–5.
Heller, Ágnes, *Teoria della storia* (Rome: Editori Riuniti, 1982), p. 289.

1983
Günther, Juan, *Planos de Lima, 1613-1983* (Lima: Editorial Copé, 1983).

1984
Anderson, Perry, 'Modernity and Revolution', *New Left Review* 1, no. 144, 1984.
Ludowieg Telge, Cecilia, *Paul Linder: su obra* (Lima: Universidad Nacional de Ingeniería, 1984).
Giedion, Sigfried, *Spazio, Tempo Ed Architettura Lo Sviluppo Di Una Nuova Tradizione.* 2. ed. riv. ed aumentata. (Milan: Hoepli, 1984).

1985
Dal Co, Francesco, *Abitare nel moderno* (Rome / Bari: Laterza, 1985).
Luchsinger, Christoph, *Hans Hofmann: vom neuen Bauen zur neuen Baukunst* (Zurich: ETH-Hönggerberg, 1985), pp. 141–154.

1986
Bonfiglio, Giovanni, 'Introducción al estudio de la inmigración europea en el Perú', *Boletín de Lima,* no. 18, 1986, pp. 93–127
Tafuri, Manfredo, *Storia dell'architettura italiana: 1944–1985* (Turin: Einaudi, 1986).

1987
De la Torre, Marco, 'Teodoro Cron, la poética del lugar', *Documentos de arquitectura y urbanismo,* a. II, v. 1, no. 2–3, 1987, pp. 48–54.
Graziani, Pietro, *Patrimonio architettonico: aspetti di tutela e organizzazione,* Strumenti / Scuola di specializzazione per lo studio el il restauro dei monumenti (Rome: Multigrafica, 1987).
Miró Quesada, Luis, 'Testimonios y Reflexiones: Inicios de la Arquitectura Moderna en Lima', *Documentos de arquitectura y urbanismo,* vol. 1, a. II, no. 2–3, 1987, pp. 41–47.

1988
Nerdinger, Winfried, *Walter Gropius: complete works* (Milan: Electa, 1988), p. 244.

1990
Droste, Magdalena, *Bauhaus: 1919–1933* (Cologne: Taschen, 1990), p. 12.

1991
Baechler, Joseph, Cámera de comercio suiza en el Perú, and Asociación Winkelried (Peru), *Presencia suiza en el Peru* (Lima: Pacific Press, 1991), p. 61.

1994
Universidad Nacional de Ingeniería, *Inventario del patrimonio monumental inmueble – Lima* (Lima: Universidad Nacional de Ingeniería, 1994).

1995
Zapata, Antonio, *El joven Belaunde: historia de la revista El arquitecto peruano: 1937–1963* (Lima: Minerva, 1995), p. 132.

1996
Dieste, Eladio, Ramón Gutiérrez, Laura Majocchi, and Graciela María Viñuales. *Architettura e società: l'America Latina nel XX secolo* (Milan: Jaca Book, 1996).

1997
Carbonara, Giovanni, *Avvicinamento al restauro teoria, storia, monumenti* (Naples: Liguori, 1997).
Dorich, Luis, *Al rescate de Lima: la evolución de Lima y sus planes de desarrollo urbano* (Lima: Colegio de Arquitectos del Perú-Instituto de Urbanismo y Planificación del Perú, 1997).

1998
'Inmigración europea', *Boletín de Lima,* a. XX, 1998, no. 114.
Bonfiglio, Giovanni, *Dizionario storico-biografico degli Italiani in Peru* (Bologna: Il Mulino, 1998), pp. 133–134.

1999
Rodríguez, Katya, *Historia de la Universidad Nacional de Ingeniería: La apertura a espacios nuevos (1930–1955), vol. III* (Lima: Proyecto Historia UNI – Universidad Nacional de Ingeniería, 1999), pp. 85–86.

2000
Martuccelli, Elio, *Arquitectura para una ciudad fragmentada: ideas, proyectos y edificios en la Lima del siglo XX* (Lima: Universidad Ricardo Palma, 2000).
Rovira, Josep María, *José Luis Sert (1901–1983)* (Milan: Electa, 2000).

2002
Liernur, Jorge Francisco, *Escritos de arquitectura del siglo XX en América Latina* (Madrid / Seville: Tanais, 2002).

2004
Ludeña, Wiley, *Tres buenos tigres. Piqueras – Belaúnde – La Agrupación Espacio. Vanguardia y urbanismo en el Perú en el siglo XX* (Huancayo: Colegio de Arquitectos del Perú, Regional Junín-Urbes, 2004).
Medina Warmburg, Joaquín, 'Paul Linder, arquitecto, crítico, educador: del Bauhaus a la Escuela Nacional de Ingenieros de Perú', *RA: revista de arquitectura,* no. 6, 2004.
Medina Warmburg, Joaquín, *Irredentos y conversos. Presencias e influencias alemanas: de la neutralidad a la postguerra española (1914–1943),* in Pozo, José Manuel and López, Ignasi (coords.), *Modelos alemanes e italianos para España en los años de la postguerra* (Pamplona: Universidad de Navarra, 2004).

2005
'Che cos'è il restauro?' In *Che cos'è il restauro? Nove studiosi a confronto,* edited by Paolo B. Torsello (Venice: Marsilio, 2005).
Jiménez, Luis, and Santiváñez, Miguel, *Rafael Marquina, arquitecto* (Lima: Universidad Nacional de Ingeniería, Facultad de Arquitectura, Urbanismo y Artes, Instituto de Investigaciones, 2005).

2006
Alvarez Ortega, Syra, *La formación en arquitectura en el Perú: antecedentes, inicios y desarrollo hasta 1955* (Lima: Universidad Nacional de Ingeniería, 2006), pp. 131–148.

2007

Beingolea, José Luis, 'Mario Bianco. Clasicismo y modernidad entre Italia y Perú', *Universidad Nacional de Ingeniería* (Lima, 2007).

Riviale, Pascal, 'Los franceses en el Perú del siglo XIX: retrato de una emigración discreta', *Bulletin de L'Institut Francais d'Etudes Andines*, a. 36, no. 01, 2007, p. 112.

Vicente Garrido, Henry, *Arquitecturas desplazadas: arquitecturas del exilio español* (Madrid: Ministerio de la Vivienda, 2007), pp. 200–201.

Villiger, Fernando, 'Emigración europea y suiza al Perú', *Boletín de Lima*, a. XXIX, no. 149–150, 2007, pp. 55–63.

2009

Bonilla, Enrique, and Fuentes, María del Carmen (eds.), *Lima y el Callao: guía de arquitectura y paisaje – an architectural and landscape guide* (Lima / Seville: Universidad Ricardo Palma-Junta de Andalucía, Consejería de Vivienda y Ordenación del Territorio, 2009), p. 210.

Heinich, Nathalie, *La fabrique du patrimoine: de la cathédrale à la petite cuillère* (Paris: Éditions de la maison des sciences de l'homme, 2009).

Mumford, Eric Paul, *Defining Urban Design: CIAM Architects and the Formation of a Discipline, 1937–69* (New Haven: Yale University Press, 2009).

2010

Hayakawa Casas, José Carlos, *Restauración en Lima: pasos y contrapasos* (Lima: Fondo Editorial de la Universidad de San Martin de Porres, 2010).

Pazos, Víctor, 'Theodor Cron: Ipséité et architecture', École d›Architecture de Paris-La-Villette/Université Paris VIII (Paris, 2010).

2011

Belaúnde, Pedro, 'Editorial', *DOCOMOMO Perú: Boletín Informativo*, 2011, p. 1.

Galerie Mera (ed.), *Adolfo Bührer: 1918–2003 – Stetten – Südamerika – Bargen: ein malerisches Leben* (Schaffhausen: Galerie Mera, 2011), p. 56.

Lu, Duanfang (ed.), *Third World Modernism: Architecture, Development and Identity* (London / New York: Routledge, 2011).

2012

Berman, Marshall, *Tutto ciò che è solido svanisce nell'aria: l'esperienza della modernità* (Bologna: Il Mulino, 2012), p. 133.

Carughi, Ugo, *Maledetti vincoli: la tutela dell'architettura contemporanea* (Turin: Umberto Allemandi & C., 2012), p. 14.

Martuccelli, Elio, *Conversaciones con Adolfo Córdova* (Lima: Universidad Nacional de Ingeniería, Facultad de Arquitectura, Urbanismo y Artes, Instituto de Investigación-INIFAUA, 2012), p. 67.

Palmerio, Giancarlo, Montuori, Patrizia and Lombardi, Angela. *Lima: Centro storico. Conoscenza e restauro* (Rome: Gangemi, 2012).

2013

Abugattas, Sebastián, Aramburú, Iosu and Llona, Michelle (eds.), *Guía Arquitectura Moderna en el Centro Histórico* (Lima, 2013).

Moraña, Mabel, *Aguerdas/Vargas Llosa: dilemas y ensamblajes* (Madrid / Frankfurt am Main / Lima: Iberoamericana-Vervuert-Librería Sur, 2013).

Riverso Ortelli, Angela (ed.), *Paolo Mariotta: architetto 1905–1972: AAT, Fondazione Archivi Architetti Ticinesi, Documenti del fondo Paolo Mariotta* (Bellinzona: Casagrande, 2013).

Scaletti, Adriana, *La casa cajamarquina: arquitectura, minería y morada* (Lima: Pontificia Universidad Católica del Perú, Fondo Editorial, 2013).

2014

Bentín Diez Canseco, José. *Enrique Seoane Ros: una búsqueda de raíces peruanas* (Lima: Universidad Nacional de Ingeniería, 2014).

Huapaya, José Carlos, *Fernando Belaúnde Terry y el ideario moderno: arquitectura y urbanismo en el Perú entre 1936 y 1968* (Lima: Universidad Nacional de Ingeniería-Universidade Federal da Bahia, 2014), p. 185.

Mostra Internazionale di Architettura, *Fundamentals: 14. Mostra Internazionale di Architettura* (Venice: Marsilio-Fondazione La Biennale di Venezia, 2014).

Quijano, Aníbal, *Cuestiones y horizontes: de la dependencia histórico-estructural a la colonialidad/ descolonialidad del poder* (Buenos Aires: CLACSO, 2014), p. 790.

2015

Baca García, Manuel. 'Les Enjeux Du Patrimoine Architectural Moderne Du Centre Historique de Lima-Pérou' (MFE-ENS d'Architecture de Nancy, 2015).

Bergdoll, Barry, Carlos Eduardo Comas, Jorge Francisco Liernur, and Patricio del Real, *Latin America in Construction: Architecture 1955–1980* (New York: Museum of Modern Art, 2015).

Ferlenga, Alberto, and Biraghi, Marco, *Comunità Italia: architettura, città, paesaggio. Exhibition catalogue, Milan, Triennale* (Cinisello Balsamo: Silvana Editoriale, 2015).

Frampton, Kenneth, Ferrara, Maddalena, and Molo, Ludovica, *L'altro movimento moderno*, 2015.

Kahatt, Sharif, *Utopías construidas: las unidades vecinales de Lima* (Lima: Fondo Editorial de la Pontificia Universidad Católica del Perú, 2015), pp. 66–67.

Malachowski, Ricardo Jaxa, *Lecciones de elementos y teoría de la arquitectura*, in Ludeña, Wiley (ed.) (Lima: Universidad Nacional de Ingeniería, 2015), pp. 26–27.

Marino, Fabio, 'Enrico Tedeschi, "Un Italiano sulle Ande"' (Santarcangelo di Romagna: Maggioli Editore, 2015).

Pimentel Gurmendi, Víctor, *Víctor Pimentel Gurmendi y el patrimonio monumental: textos escogidos*, in Beingolea, José Luis (ed.) (Lima: Universidad Nacional de Ingenieria, 2015), p. 43.

Purtschert, Patricia and Fischer-Tiné, Harald, *Colonial Switzerland: Rethinking Colonialism from the Margins* (Houndmills, Basingstoke: Palgrave-Macmillan, 2015).

Tamma, Michele, *Cultural Rights, Heritage, Sustainability, Citizens of Europe – culture and rights* (Venice, 2015), p. 485.

2016

Atoche Intili, Javier, *La revista El Arquitecto Peruano y el rol de la fotografía en la conformación del discurso contemporáneo latinoamericano*, in Alcolea, Rubén, Tárrago, Jorge (eds.), *inter photo arch – Congreso internacional* (Pamplona: Universidad de Navarra, 2016), p. 11.

2017

Botti, Giaime. 'Piattaforma Colombia. Scenari Dell'architettura Tra Europa e Americhe Alle Radici Del Discorso Storiografico Nazionale (1936–1963)' (Politecnico di Torino, 2017).

Carughi, Ugo, and Visone, Massimo (eds.), *Time Frames: Conservation Policies for Twentieth-Century Architectural Heritage* (London / New York: Routledge, 2017).

López Soria, José Ignacio, *Filosofía, arquitectura y ciudad* (Lima: Universidad Nacional de Ingeniería, 2017)

Montestruque-Bisso, Octavio, and Martín Fabbri García (eds.), *Mario Bianco: el espacio moderno en el Perú* (Lima: Fondo Editorial de la Universidad de Lima, 2017).

2018

Acevedo, Alejandra and Llona, Michelle (eds.), *Catálogo Arquitectura Movimiento Moderno Perú* (Lima: Fondo editorial Universidad de Lima, 2018).

Gómez Taipe, Wilder Alfredo. 'Las ideas detrás de la obra escrita del arquitecto Luis Miró Quesada Garland y el diseño de la obra denominada Casa Huiracocha. Aportes para una Historia de La Arquitectura Moderna en el Perú' (Universidad Nacional de Ingeniería, 2018).

Hernández Asensio, Raúl, *Señores del pasado: Arqueólogos, museos y huaqueros en el Perú* (Lima: Instituto de Estudios Peruanos, 2018).

Medina Warmburg, Joaquín, *Walter Gropius – proclamas de modernidad: escritos y conferencias, 1908–1934* (Barcelona: Editorial Reverté, 2018).

Ministerio de Cultura (ed.), *Marco legal de protección del patrimonio cultural* (Lima: Representaciones Generales 2000, 2018), pp. 5–29.

Moretti, Silvia, and Morelli, Annalisa, *Il cantiere di restauro dell'architettura moderna: tesoria e prassi* (Florence: Nardini editore, 2018).

Rebaza Soraluz, Luis. *De ultramodernidades y sus contemporáneos* (Mexico City: FCE – Fondo de Cultura Económica, 2018).

2019

Atoche Intili, Javier, 'Tres cartas desde Lima. Paul Linder y los arquitectos europeos', in Medina Warmburg, Joaquín (ed.), *Paul Linder, 1897–1968: de Weimar a Lima – antología de arquitectura y crítica* (Madrid: Ricardo Sánchez Lampreave, 2019), pp. 80–91.

Llona, Michelle and Mejía, Víctor, *Paul Linder, Arquitecto – modernidad universal / sincretismo local* (Lima: Pontificia Universidad Católica del Perú, 2019).

Medina Warmburg, Joaquín (ed.), *Paul Linder, 1897–1968: de Weimar a Lima: antología de arquitectura y crítica* (Madrid: Editorial Lampreave, 2019), p. 422.

2021

Atoche Intili, Javier, 'Gli apporti europei nella costruzione del Progetto Moderno in America Latina. Mario Bianco e il Perù', in Esposito, Daniela, and Montanari, Valeria (eds.), *Realtà dell'architettura fra materia e immagine. Per Giovanni Carbonara: studi e ricerche* (Rome, 2021), p. 500.

2022

Atoche Intili, Javier, 'Lima la moderna (1937–1969): Expansion of modern culture and multi-storey buildings in Peru', in Jordá Such, Carmen et al. (eds.), *Modern Design: Social Commitment & Quality of Life / 17th International Docomomo Conference* (Valencia: Universitat Politècnica de València, 2022).

Acknowledgements

It is with great pride that the cultural association RO.SA.M. presents this book. We are truly grateful to DOM publishers for believing in the literary award La Calcina-John Ruskin. Writing on Architecture from the beginning.

We also extend our special thanks to the director and the owners of the historic hotel restaurant La Calcina and to Hausbrandt Trieste 1892, without whose support this publication would not have been possible.

Finally, many thanks to the president of the jury, to the members of the scientific technical committee for their time and dedication, and to all the friends of the award for coming with us on this journey.

President, RO.SA.M.
Roberta Semeraro

This publication has been made possible thanks to the collaboration of so many people who dedicated their time to reading this text, providing information or materials and telling me their stories. First, I would like to thank my lecturers: Professor Marzia Marandola, for having believed in this project from the very beginning, and Professor Roberta Grignolo, for having patiently guided me through this complex research. I would like to express my heartfelt thanks to Professor Giovanni Carbonara, who recently passed away and to whom I dedicate this monograph, for his valuable contribution to my intellectual and personal education, through moments of discussion, while attending the former Scuola di specializzazione in restauro dei monumenti, and during meetings in the Dipartimento di storia, disegno e restauro dell'architettura in Rome.

I would like to express my gratitude to Mara Micaela Colletta, who advised and supported me in my moments of greatest uncertainty and helped me to look at the city of Lima from a new perspective. My sincere thanks go to scholars Irene Arce, Manuel Baca, José Beingolea, Pedro Belaúnde, Rodrigo Córdova, Wilder Gómez, Luis Jiménez, Cecilia Ludowieg, Elio Martuccelli, Joaquín Medina Warmburg, Octavio Montestruque, Marina Montuori and Adriana Scaletti, with whom I shared my research and from whom I received both valid suggestions, evaluations and valuable study documents. In Milan, my conversation with José Francisco Liernur was of great use to me, as it was fundamental in widening the scope of my research in the Latin American sphere.

I would also like to thank all those who helped me in consulting the documents held at the ETH-Bibliothek, the Fondazione Archivi Architetti Ticinesi, the gta Archiv, the Politecnico di Torino, the Pontificia Universidad Católica del Perú, the Universidad Nacional de Ingeniería, the Università IUAV di Venezia and the Biblioteca Queriniana di Brescia.

I would like to warmly thank the architects Víctor Pimentel, Juan Reiser, the late Adolfo Cordova and José García Bryce, all Peruvian figures of the highest profile as well as protagonists in the history I have tried to reconstruct through my investigations. Special thanks go to my dear professors at the Universidad Peruana de Ciencias Aplicadas, the Dean of the Faculty of Architecture, Miguel Cruchaga, Germán Costa and Franco Vella, who generously shared their experience and knowledge on the subject.

I would like to thank all the organisers, supporters and sponsors of the 'La Calcina – John Ruskin' Scrivere di Architettura Prize, without whose support this book would not have been possible. All my gratitude goes to my parents, Ana María and Feliciano Timoteo, who supported me unconditionally. Finally, I must thank and apologise to Eduardo and Mara because this issue has kept me very busy in recent years – busier than I imagined.

Javier Atoche Intili

The Deutsche Bibliothek lists this publication in the Deutsche Nationalbibliografie; detailed bibliographic data is available on the internet at http://dnb.d-nb.de

ISBN 978-3-86922-595-1

Proofreading
Reuben Ross

Design
Nicole Wolf

Printing
Master Print Super Offset, Bucharest
www.masterprint.ro

DOM
publishers